OCR HISTORY

Churchill 1920–45

AS

Mike Wells | Series Editors: Nick Fellows and Mike Wells

www.heinemann.co.uk

✓ Free online support
✓ Useful weblinks
✓ 24 hour online ordering

0845 630 33 33

Heinemann

Part of Pearson

Heinemann is an imprint of Pearson Education Limited, a company incorporated in England and Wales, having its registered office at Edinburgh Gate, Harlow, Essex, CM20 2JE. Registered company number: 872828

www.pearsonschoolsandfecolleges.co.uk

Heinemann is a registered trademark of Pearson Education Limited

Text © Pearson Education Limited 2009

First published 2009

12 11 10 09

10 9 8 7 6 5 4 3 2 1

British Library Cataloguing in Publication Data

A catalogue record for this book is available from the British Library

ISBN 978 0 435 31258 9

Edited by Grace Publishing Services
Typeset by Saxon Graphics Ltd, Derby
Original illustrations © Saxon Graphics Ltd, Derby
Cover photo/illustration © Corbis/David Pollack
Printed in Spain by Graficas Estella

Cover copyright: © Corbis / David Pollack

Picture credits
The publisher would like to thank the following for their kind permission to reproduce their photographs:

(Key: b-bottom; c-centre; l-left; r=right; t-top)

Alamy images: Photos 12 105b, 117, ClassicStock 139, Mary Evans Picture Library 76, 128, Trinity Mirror/Mirrorpix 141, Interfoto Pressebildagentur
British Carton Archive, University of Kent www.cartoons.ac.uk: Solo Syndication/Associated Newspapers Ltd 44, Solo Syndication/Associated Newspapers Ltd 94
Corbis: Bettman 53, 65,66, 144, Hulton-Deutsch 30
Getty Images: Hulton Archive 112, 152, Time and Life Pictures 68, Popperfoto 105t
Library of Congress: 21
http://www.nationalarchives.gov.uk/imagelibrary/: 148
Press Association Images: viiit, AP 129, PA Archive 116, John Stillwell viiib
Punch Cartoon Library: 10
TopFoto: 132, the Granger Collection 67, Keystone Archives/HIP 95, Jon Mitchell 134, PA 60, Topham PicturePoint 107

All other images © Pearson Education

Every effort has been made to trace the copyright holders and we apologise in advance for any unintentional omissions. We would be pleased to insert the appropriate achknowledgement in any subsequent edition of this publication.

Websites
There are links to relevant websites in this book. In order to ensure that the links are up to date, that the links work, and that the sites are not inadvertently linked to sites that could be considered offensive, we have made the links available on the Heinemann website at www.heinemann.co.uk/hotlinks. When you access the site, the express code is 2589S

Acknowledgements

The author and publisher would like to thank the following individuals and organisations for permissions to reproduce text:

p10 Extract from *Lloyd George: A Diary* by Frances Stevenson, 1971. Used by permission of David Higham Associates; A Diary extract from *A Man and an Institution, Sir Maurice Hanky, The Cabinet Secretariat and the Custody of Cabinet Secrecy* by John F. Naylor (1984). Reproduced by permission of Cambridge University Press; *Churchill: A Study in Greatness* by Geoffrey Best, 2001. Reproduced by kind permission of Continuum International Publishing Group; *Churchill's War: My Life*, published in the Chicago Tribune, 1935. Reproduced with permission of Curtis Brown Ltd, London on behalf of the Estate of Sir Winston Churchill. Text Copyright © The Estate of Sir Winston Churchill; **p11** Churchill in conversation with Kay Hale. Reproduced with permission of Curtis Brown Ltd, London on behalf of the Estate of Sir Winston Churchill. Text Copyright © The Estate of Sir Winston Churchill; **p22** *The Life and Times of Winston Churchill* by Malcolm Thompson. Used with Permission; Extract from *Churchill: A Study in Failure 1900-1939* by Robert Rhodes James. © 1970 Robert Rhodes James. Reproduced by permission of Sheila Land Associates Ltd; **p30** Letter to Lady Churchill, 1918. Reproduced with permission of Curtis Brown Ltd, London on behalf of the Estate of Sir Winston Churchill. Text Copyright © The Estate of Sir Winston Churchill; **p35** Memo 11 Dec. 1920. Reproduced with permission of Curtis Brown Ltd, London on behalf of the Estate of Sir Winston Churchill. Text Copyright © The Estate of Sir Winston Churchill; **p35** Memo 11 Dec. 1920. Reproduced with permission of Curtis Brown Ltd, London on behalf of the Estate of Sir Winston Churchill. Text Copyright © The Estate of Sir Winston Churchill; **p40** *The Collected Writings of John Maynard Keynes* by John Maynard Keynes, published by CUP, 1989. Reproduced with permission of Palgrave Macmillan; Article from *The Times*, May 1925. Reproduced with permission; Extract from *My Political Life* by Leo Amery, 1955. Reproduced by permission of David Higham Associates; **p43** The Chancellor of the Exchequer to the House of Commons, 2 May, 1926. Reproduced with permission of Curtis Brown Ltd, London on behalf of the Estate of Sir Winston Churchill. Text Copyright © The Estate of Sir Winston Churchill; Article from The British Gazette, 4 May 1926. Reproduced with permission of Curtis Brown Ltd, London on behalf of the Estate of Sir Winston Churchill. Text Copyright © The Estate of Sir Winston Churchill; **p44** Extracts from article by Churchill for the *West Essex Constitutionalist*, December 1926. Reproduced with permission of Curtis Brown Ltd, London on behalf of the Estate of Sir Winston Churchill. Text Copyright © The Estate of Sir Winston Churchill; **p46** From an article in *The British Worker*. Reproduced with permission of the Trades Union Congress; **p47** From a letter to the Attorney General, Sir Douglas Hogg, 26 May. Reproduced with permission of Curtis Brown Ltd, London on behalf of the Estate of Sir Winston Churchill. Text Copyright © The Estate of Sir Winston Churchill; **p47** Churchill Speech 31 August, 1926. Reproduced with permission of Curtis Brown Ltd, London on behalf of the Estate of Sir Winston Churchill. Text Copyright © The Estate of Sir Winston Churchill; **p48** Extract from an article in *The Times*, 1925. Reproduced by permission; **p56-7** *My Political Life* by Leo Amery, 1955. Reproduced by permission of David Higham Associates; **p57** *Gandhi and Churchill: The Rivalry that Destroyed an Empire and Forged Our Age* by Arthur Herman, published by Hutchinson. Reprinted by permission of The Random House Group Ltd; **p59** *Churchill Speaks*, by Robert Rhodes James, 1980. Reproduced with permission of Curtis Brown Ltd, London on behalf of the Estate of Sir Winston Churchill. Text Copyright © The Estate of Sir Winston Churchill; **p61** Churchill's public statement on the royal crisis, 5 December, 1936. Reproduced with permission of Curtis Brown Ltd, London on behalf of the Estate of Sir Winston Churchill. Text Copyright © The Estate of Sir Winston Churchill; *Diaries and Letters 1939-45 - Harold Nicolson*, 1967. Reproduced by permission of Juliet Nicolson for the Estate of Harold Nicolson; *Churchill* by Henry Pelling, quoted from Wordsworth Edition 1999. Reproduced by permission of Macmillan Publishing; **p69** Churchill, Broadcast in 1934. Reproduced with permission of Curtis Brown Ltd, London on behalf of the Estate of Sir Winston Churchill. Text Copyright © The Estate of Sir Winston Churchill; Extract from *Churchill: A Study in Failure 1900-1939* by Robert Rhodes James. © 1970 Robert Rhodes James. Reproduced by permission of Sheil Land Associates Ltd; *The Gathering Storm* by Winston Churchill, 1948. Reproduced with permission of Curtis Brown Ltd, London on behalf of the Estate of Sir Winston Churchill. Text Copyright © The Estate of Sir Winston Churchill; *In Command Of History* by David Reynolds. Reprinted by permission of Penguin Books; **p77** Churchill speech in the House of Commons, March 14. Reproduced with permission of Curtis Brown Ltd, London on behalf of the Estate of Sir Winston Churchill. Text Copyright © The Estate of Sir Winston Churchill; *The Neville Chamberlain Diary Letters, Vol. 4: The Downing Street Years* by Robert Self, 2005,Ashgate. Reprinted by permission of Ashgate Publishing; *Churchill and Appeasement* by R.A.C. Parker, published by Pan Macmillan (May 2000). Reprinted by permission of Pan Macmillan, London; **p81** *The Gathering Storm*, 1948 by Winston Churchill. Reproduced with permission of Curtis Brown Ltd, London on behalf of the Estate of Sir Winston Churchill. Text Copyright © The Estate of Sir Winston Churchill; *Winston Churchill and his Legend Since 1945*, 2003, by John Ramsden. Copyright © HarperCollins Publishers 2002. Reproduced by permission of Harper Collins Publishers Ltd; **p83** *Churchill and Appeasement* by R.A.C. Parker, published by Pan Macmillan (May 2000). Reprinted by permission of Pan Macmillan, London; **p86** From a speech to the Reichstag in Berlin, May 1941 by Adolph Hitler. Reproduced with permission of Bolchazy Carducci Publishers; **p86** *Churchill: A Biography* by Roy Jenkins, Published by Pan Macmillan (October 2001). Reprinted by permission of Pan Macmillan, London; **p89** *The Gathering Storm*, 1948 by Winston Churchill. Reproduced with permission of Curtis Brown Ltd, London on behalf of the Estate of Sir Winston Churchill. Text Copyright © The Estate of Sir Winston Churchill; **p90** *Fringes of Power* by John Colville. Reproduced by permission of Hodder and Stoughton Limited; From the diary of Leo Kennedy, diplomatic editor of The Times, 4 May,1940. Reproduced with permission of Curtis Brown Ltd, London on behalf of the Estate of Sir Winston Churchill. Text Copyright © The Estate of Sir Winston Churchill; Churchill extract. Reproduced with permission of Curtis Brown Ltd, London on behalf of the Estate of Sir Winston Churchill. Text Copyright © The Estate of Sir Winston Churchill; **p90-1** Extracts from the memoir by Quintin Hogg, later Lord Hailsham. Reproduced with permission of the Master and Fellows of Churchill College,

Cambridge; **p92** Churchill speech. Reproduced with permission of Curtis Brown Ltd, London on behalf of the Estate of Sir Winston Churchill. Text Copyright © The Estate of Sir Winston Churchill; **p93** Churchill speech. Reproduced with permission of Curtis Brown Ltd, London on behalf of the Estate of Sir Winston Churchill. Text Copyright © The Estate of Sir Winston Churchill; *Diaries and Letters 1939-45 - Harold Nicolson*, 1967. Reproduced by permission of Juliet Nicolson for the Estate of Harold Nicolson; **p94** *Winston Churchill* by Clive Ponting, published by Sinclair-Stevenson. Reprinted by permission of The Random House Group Ltd; **p96** A telegram on 24 May 1940 to the British ambassador in Paris. Reproduced with permission of Curtis Brown Ltd, London on behalf of the Estate of Sir Winston Churchill. Text Copyright © The Estate of Sir Winston Churchill; *Winston Churchill* by Clive Ponting, published by Sinclair-Stevenson. Reprinted by permission of The Random House Group Ltd; **p97** *The Later Churchills* by A.L. Rowse, published by Pan Macmillan (January 1958). Reprinted by permission of Pan Macmillan, London; **p102** *War Diaries 1939-1945, Field Marshall Lord Alan Brooke* by Alex Danchev. Reproduced by permission of David Higham Associates; **p102-3**'Churchill and his Generals: The Tasks of Supreme Command' *Proceedings of the International Churchill Society 1992-3*. Reproduced with permission of Curtis Brown Ltd, London on behalf of the Estate of Sir Winston Churchill. Text Copyright © The Estate of Sir Winston Churchill; **p109-10** *Churchill's Generals* by John Keegan, published by George Weidenfeld and Nicholson, Ltd., 2005. Reproduced by permission of The Orion Publishing Group, London; **p111** *Churchill's Generals* by John Keegan, published by George Weidenfeld and Nicholson, Ltd., 2005. Reproduced by permission of The Orion Publishing Group, London; **p112** *War Diaries 1939-1945, Field Marshall Lord Alan Brooke* by Alex Danchev. Reproduced by permission of David Higham Associates; Churchill telegram to General Wavell, 15 January 1942. Reproduced with permission of Curtis Brown Ltd, London on behalf of the Estate of Sir Winston Churchill. Text Copyright © The Estate of Sir Winston Churchill; **p113** *Churchill: The Greatest Briton Unmasked* by Nigel Knight 2008. Reproduced with permission of Curtis Brown Ltd, London on behalf of the Estate of Sir Winston Churchill. Text Copyright © The Estate of Sir Winston Churchill; **p113** *War Diaries 1939-1945, Field Marshall Lord Alan Brooke* by Alex Danchev. Reproduced by permission of David Higham Associates; **p114-5** Churchill's speech at Guild hall in London. Reproduced with permission of Curtis Brown Ltd, London on behalf of the Estate of Sir Winston Churchill. Text Copyright © The Estate of Sir Winston Churchill; **p115** From article by Kate Connolly in the *Daily Telegraph*. Reprinted by permission of the Telegraph Media Group Limited; **p116** Churchill's memo to RAF Commanders. Reproduced with permission of Curtis Brown Ltd, London on behalf of the Estate of Sir Winston Churchill. Text Copyright © The Estate of Sir Winston Churchill; **p120** Extract from a Churchill broadcast. Reproduced with permission of Curtis Brown Ltd, London on behalf of the Estate of Sir Winston Churchill. Text Copyright © The Estate of Sir Winston Churchill; 'Triumph and Tragedy', final volume of *The Second World War* by Winston Churchill, 1954. Reproduced with permission of Curtis Brown Ltd, London on behalf of the Estate of Sir Winston Churchill. Text Copyright © The Estate of Sir Winston Churchill; Churchill letter. Reproduced with permission of Curtis Brown Ltd, London on behalf of the Estate of Sir Winston Churchill. Text Copyright © The Estate of Sir Winston Churchill; **p131** Churchill recalls the making of the Atlantic Charter, 1950. Reproduced with permission of Curtis Brown Ltd, London on behalf of the Estate of Sir Winston Churchill. Text Copyright © The Estate of Sir Winston Churchill; *Alliance*, by Jonathan Fenby copyright © 2007. Published by Simon & Schuster UK Ltd; **p135** Michael Howard 'Grand Strategy' HMSO 1972 Quoted C. Barnett in *The Rise and Fall of the Grand Alliance*, edited by Lane and Temperly, 1995. Reproduced by permission of Pan Macmillan, London; Churchill's view in 1942. Reproduced with permission of Curtis Brown Ltd, London on behalf of the Estate of Sir Winston Churchill. Text Copyright © The Estate of Sir Winston Churchill; *War Diaries 1939-1945, Field Marshall Lord Alan Brooke* by Alex Danchev. Reproduced by permission of David Higham Associates; **p136** *The Rise and Fall of the Grand Alliance*, by Corelli Barnett, 1995. Reprinted by permission of Pan Macmillan, London; *Churchill: The Struggle for Survival* by Lord Moran, 1966. Reproduced with permission of Constable & Robinson Ltd; **p137** *Closing the Ring*, by Winston Churchill 1952. Reproduced with permission of Curtis Brown Ltd, London on behalf of the Estate of Sir Winston Churchill. Text Copyright © The Estate of Sir Winston Churchill; *In Command Of History* by David Reynolds. Reprinted by permission of Penguin Books; **p138** *In Command Of History* by David Reynolds. Reprinted by permission of Penguin Books; **p142** Churchill in an address to Parliament following Roosevelt's death on 12 April. Reproduced with permission of Curtis Brown Ltd, London on behalf of the Estate of Sir Winston Churchill. Text Copyright © The Estate of Sir Winston Churchill; **p142** *Winston Churchill* by Clive Ponting, published by Sinclair-Stevenson. Reprinted by permission of The Random House Group Ltd; *Churchill: A Study in Greatness* by Geoffrey Best, 2001. Reproduced by kind permission of Continuum International Publishing Group; **p149** *World War II Behind Closed Doors: Stalin, The Nazis and the West* by Laurence Rees, published by BBC Books. Reprinted by permission of The Random House Group Ltd; **p149** 'Triumph and Tragedy', final volume of *The Second World War* by Winston Churchill, 1954. Reproduced with permission of Curtis Brown Ltd, London on behalf of the Estate of Sir Winston Churchill. Text Copyright © The Estate of Sir Winston Churchill; **p151** 'Triumph and Tragedy', final volume of *The Second World War* by Winston Churchill, 1954. Reproduced with permission of Curtis Brown Ltd, London on behalf of the Estate of Sir Winston Churchill. Text Copyright © The Estate of Sir Winston Churchill; Churchill's note to Stalin. Reproduced with permission of Curtis Brown Ltd, London on behalf of the Estate of Sir Winston Churchill. Text Copyright © The Estate of Sir Winston Churchill; *World War II Behind Closed Doors: Stalin, The Nazis and the West* by Laurence Rees, published by BBC Books. Reprinted by permission of The Random House Group Ltd; **p153** Churchill, The Struggle for Survival by Lord Moran, 1996. Reproduced by permission of Constable & Robinson Ltd; *Allies at War*, by Simon Berthon. Reproduced by permission of Harper Collins Publishers Ltd

Contents

How to use this book

Notes for teachers

This book, *OCR History A, Churchill 1920–45*, is designed to support OCR's History A F963 Option B Topic 4 Enquiries specification. After an introductory chapter, which provides the factual context of Churchill's career to 1945, there are four chapters related to the four key issues of the OCR specification. These chapters are intended to cover the main elements of the indicative content set out by OCR.

Enquiries

In the OCR examination, candidates are required to compare sources as evidence, and there are opportunities to practice this skill throughout the book.

Candidates also have to use a set of sources to evaluate an interpretation. In order to help them develop the skills of interpreting sources, applying their own knowledge to assess the sources, and reaching a conclusion about the issue to which the sources relate, there are exercises which are stepped in difficulty. As a result, not all of the activities are in the format of the OCR papers, but they all aim to lead students towards the critical consideration of a set of four or five sources.

Help is given with identifying issues that candidates are likely to have to discuss. Churchill became a national hero during and after the Second World War. His spirit was invoked by politicians for years and there were many biographies and popular histories which used the image created by Churchill in his own history of the Second World War to offer the view of an indomitable national saviour. The iconography – the pictures, statuettes, Toby jugs, commemorative plates and, of course, the statue in Parliament –speak even more of brave defiance. More recent historians take a variety of more critical views, looking at Churchill from a greater distance. The traditional views have been challenged and modified in a way that is a natural and inevitable development in history, but disturbing to many people. Many iconic figures from the past – Napoleon, Bismarck, Lenin, Mao Zedong, for example – have faced reappraisal. The greater the personality, the more intense the historical controversy is likely to be. Though historians' views have been included, the AS paper is not focused on historiography or the different interpretations of historians, but on issues in which evidence may conflict. For example, contemporary sources gave different interpretations of Churchill's handling of the General Strike, 1926. To some he aimed at statesman-like conciliation, to others he made the situation worse by ill-judged polemics. The viewpoints are likely to be different depending on the nature, origin and the date of the source.

Advice is given about using sources as evidence and activities are focused on areas of possible discussion. Because Churchill was a larger-than-life and often controversial figure, there is plenty of conflicting evidence given here. In the examination there may be four or five sources; only one at most will be from a historian, and it is possible that all will be primary sources. Thus it is very important that students have the opportunity to evaluate a range of sources and to test the evidence they provide by using a variety of criteria, including contextual knowledge.

This book cannot be a comprehensive account of Churchill's life in this period, but teachers should remember that candidates are expected to use contextual knowledge in relation to source evaluation. Candidates are not expected to have a very detailed knowledge of every aspect of Churchill's life and times, but rather to develop the skills of source evaluation and an understanding of the key issues.

Source exercises

The activities are based on two different types of exercise:

- Comparison of two sources as evidence for a specific issue – type (a) questions in the exam, with marks out of 30. Students should assess content and provenance and be able to compare the two with a sense of judgment.

- Evaluation and interpretation of a number of sources as evidence for an issue – type (b) questions in the exam, with marks out of 70. Candidates are encouraged to group sources rather than deal with them sequentially and to apply a range of critical criteria and knowledge gained by reading the text. The sources used are cited and there are bibliographies for further reading. There is, of course, a huge literature on Churchill, so some teacher guidance will be necessary. There is such a lot of good historical writing that it is hoped that students will be stimulated to read further.

Please note: the sources in this book, for the most part, are longer than those used in the examination.

Exam support

Each chapter also has detailed exam preparation and support in the Exam Café.

Exam Café focuses on the type of questions assessed in the exam. It is divided into three areas: Relax, Refresh, Result!

- Relax is an area for haring revision tips.
- Refresh your memory is an area for revising content.
- Result is the examiner's area: it includes exam questions, student answers with examiner comments, and tips on how to achieve a higher level answer.

OCR History A, Churchill 1920–45 has been written specifically to provide teachers and students with a taught course that reflects the key issues and skills in the specification topics. Each chapter begins with key questions on a key issue from the specification, which are then discussed in the chapter, with supporting activities.

Additionally, selected chapters include a timeline which gives an overview of the period's chronology. In conclusion, each chapter has a final review of what has been learnt, together with some review questions to help student's self assessment of their knowledge.

Methods of assessment

This book supports British history Enquiries Unit F963, Option B. This is a document study paper of 1.5 hours and is worth 50% of the total AS marks. Four or five unseen sources are set. There are two questions for each study topic. Question (a) is worth 30 marks and question (b) is worth 70 marks. The Churchill study topic must be taken with an AS Period Studies paper on European and World History.

Thanks

The author would like to thank Allen Packwood and Katharine Thomson of the Churchill Archive in Churchill College Cambridge and also Nigel Knight

Notes for students

How to use this book

This book has been specifically written to support you through the OCR A GCE History course. *OCR History A, Churchill 1920–45* will help you to understand the facts and concepts that underlie the topics you are studying. It can be used as a reference throughout your course.

You should refer back to this book during your revision. The Exam Café sections at the end of each unit will be particularly helpful as you prepare for your exam.

Each chapter in the book makes use of the following features:

Activities

The activities have been designed to help you understand the specification content and develop your historical skills.

> **ACTIVITY**
>
> *'A major issue which caused controversy at the time and still divides writers about Churchill was his attitude to communism.'*
>
> Look at the three views in Sources A–C. Summarise briefly what they say.
>
> 1 Which is the most sympathetic to Churchill and which is the least?
>
> 2 At the end of the section on communism, re-read these passages and think about which one you most agree with. Discuss your view in class.

Analysis

Analysis looks more closely at the key events, arguments and controversies under discussion.

> **ANALYSIS**
>
> Churchill had persuaded the Cabinet to send substantial amounts of financial and military aid to the Whites to maintain a military presence in Russia. He had even gained consent for a major attack before the defeat of the Whites had made this too dangerous. He had not persuaded them to commit themselves fully to overthrowing the regime or to negotiating an international grand alliance against communism. When dock workers refused to load a munitions ship bound for Poland, then engaged in war against the Bolshevik regime, the Cabinet had had enough and by November 1920 the British intervention came to an end.

Biography

Short biographies of the key people from the time period you are studying.

> **BIOGRAPHY**
>
> **Michael John Collins (1890–1922)**
>
> He was an Irish revolutionary, elected to the breakaway Irish parliament in 1918. He rose to lead the Irish Republican Army and was a leader in the campaign against the British and a major figure in the illegal government set up by Sinn Féin. 'The Big Fellow', as he was called, did support negotiations with Churchill and Lloyd George to end the fighting and was prepared to accept an Irish free state within the Empire. He then faced armed opposition from those who rejected the treaty and he was killed in an ambush by his enemies.

Case studies

Case studies are used to further illustrate the main questions. Most of the examples can be applied in some way to the topic you are studying for your AS exam.

> **Case Study: Eden, the hero**
>
> Churchill's passionate support of Eden's supposed stand against appeasement and his sleepless night when **Eden** resigned in 1938 over Chamberlain's increasingly personal handling of foreign policy is not supported by Churchill's other views at the time. He had thought Eden was wrong to resign over the issue of Chamberlain's interference and should have waited for a better issue. He and Eden did not collaborate closely afterwards against government policy. Eden was not a passionate opponent of appeasement on moral grounds. The moral argument is still, however a matter of debate.

Definitions

Definitions of new words can be found in the margin next to where the word appears in the text to help put the word in context. All definitions can also be found in the Glossary (p. 000).

> **Autocracy**
> The rule of one person.

Examiner's advice

Advice from the experts on how to avoid common mistakes and achieve the best possible mark in your exam.

EXAMINATION ADVICE

1 When comparing what the sources say about an issue, make your similarities and differences in point by point form rather than describing each source in turn.

2 Consider the sources as evidence, not merely as information.

3 Use a range of questions when looking at the sources as evidence.

Throughout the comparison, there is a **judgement** expected. You are not expected to import knowledge for its own sake; but think what you are bringing to the comparison that someone

Information

You should be thinking like an historian throughout your history course. These highlight content to provide extra detail to the historical narrative in the chapter.

The Napoleonic Wars, 1793–1815

The long series of Wars against France from 1793–1815 had resulted in British victory, but there were severe social and political divisions by 1815. The government of Lord Liverpool faced radical demands for greater democracy, economic protests about new machines, unrest in the manufacturing districts, a bloody suppression of a protest meeting in Manchester and even a plot to kill the Cabinet. Similarly, the end of the First World War led to social unrest. Furthermore, the end of the Second World War brought about a Labour election victory, demands for radical change, and the creation of a welfare state with more interventionist economic and social policies.

Key questions

Each chapter will start by asking some Key Questions. The content of the chapter will help you to find answers to these Key Questions.

Key Questions

Areas of study include:

1 How did Churchill's views on India (and Empire) clash with those of his own party and the government?

2 What was Churchill's attitude towards rearmament and what were his reasons for opposing appeasement?

3 What was Churchill's position between 1933 and 1938?

4 How justified were Churchill's views?

Sources

We have included lots of sources throughout the book to allow you to practise your historical skills. *Note*: the sources tend to be longer than they would be in the exam.

Sources

Ⓐ On 17 March 1919 Churchill told his colleagues,

The War Cabinet must face the fact that the North of Russia would be over-run by the Bolsheviks and many people would be murdered…It was idle to think that we should escape by sitting still and doing nothing. Bolshevism was not sitting still and unless the tide were resisted it would roll over Siberia until it reached the Japanese. …the Baltic States would be attacked and submerged. No doubt that when all the resources friendly to us had been scattered, and when India was threatened, the Western powers would bestir themselves.

Exam support

In our unique Exam Café you'll find lots of ideas to help prepare for your exams. You'll see the Exam Café at the end of each the book.

You can **Relax** because there's handy revision advice from fellow students;

Refresh your Memory with summaries and checklists of the key ideas you need to revise, and

Get that Result! through practising exam-style questions, accompanied by hints and tips on getting the very best grades.

A controversial figure?

Churchill is such an important figure in British history that any book that deals with controversies and debates about him is bound to be, itself, controversial. The AS students who engage with the different contemporary views of this very great personality have to look at contrasting evidence and opinions and make up their own minds. They will learn that sources have to be interpreted and evaluated and that there is no such thing as true objectivity in evidence. This book attempts to present a variety of evidence and to offer a guide to the issues raised by the OCR specification. Students must realise that it is also a source and has to be read critically. It is not a biography and in the space available cannot deal exhaustively with all aspects of Churchill's life and times. The selection of material in itself is a matter of the author's judgement and how the controversies are presented may reveal the author's own judgements. The author's father, who served in the Second World War would have been shocked at the contemporary criticisms given here of a figure whom he regarded as a national saviour. Older generations of the author's family who remembered aspects of Churchill's early career would, perhaps, see too favourable a picture in the evidence here. As with all aspects of history, A level students have to judge for themselves and should not hesitate to reject any aspects of the commentary offered by the author if they feel that evidence or other reading contradict it.

Winston Churchill's funeral cortege passes through Trafalgar Square on 30 January 1965, watched by some of the many thousands that lined the route to pay their respects.

The statue of Churchill in Parliament Square was defaced during anti-capitalist riots in 2000.

Churchill's life and times, his character and the influence he had continues to fascinate both historians and the general public to this day. The gap between the views of many modern historians and the image held by the public has grown. The mass of evidence about Churchill has yielded material which has not always shown in him in a good light as well as confirming his stature. Some historians have not accepted certain premises which an earlier generation took for granted. Some have questioned whether Britain should have fought the Second World War. Some have questioned the wisdom and even the integrity of some of Churchill's pre-war policies and some have questioned aspects of his war-time leadership. In a free society, that is the prerogative of historians; they in turn must accept that their views can be scrutinised and criticised. However, despite academic criticism, Churchill's hold on the imagination and affection of millions of people remains undiminished. Places associated with him, such as his home, Chartwell, the Cabinet War Rooms and the Churchill museum, attract large numbers of visitors. He was a man of enormous energy, sometimes wise, sometimes belligerent, sometimes stubborn, sometimes irrational. During his lifetime he was deeply loved and also profoundly hated. His is often viewed as a remarkable and larger than life character in a period of unique importance for Britain.

This book offers both an opportunity to look closely at the evidence of Churchill's life, and to form your own judgements on the main questions surrounding his decisions during the period. It looks at sources of the period in depth and provides practical activities. These will develop the historical skills of source interpretation and evaluation necessary to achieve success in your history examination.

In this introductory chapter, there is background information to describe:

- Churchill's early life before 1918; this sets the scene for his later development and character.
- How Churchill left a relatively commonplace army career to become a leading political figure.
- Churchill's political career and the effect it had on the people and events around him, as a precursor to the remaining chapters in the book.

Churchill's early life

By far the most entertaining source for Churchill's youth is his own account, *My Early Life 1874–1904*, the basis of the feature film *Young Winston*.

Winston Churchill was born at Blenheim Palace, near Oxford. The Palace was the reward for the military successes of John Churchill, Duke of Marlborough, who had defeated the French in the reign of Queen Anne (1702–14). Blenheim was named after his most famous victory. Winston's father, Lord Randolph Churchill, was an eminent Victorian politician. When Winston was born in November 1874 his father was a Conservative MP. He went on to become Secretary of State for India and Chancellor of the Exchequer. He was well known in parliament as a Tory Democrat producing ideas for social reform to modernise the Conservatives. He taunted and provoked the veteran Liberal Prime Minister Gladstone but was seen as unreliable by mainstream Conservatives. In this respect father and son were remarkably similar. Lord Randolph stirred up extreme Protestant feeling in Ulster against

proposed Liberal Home Rule measures and clashed with the Conservative leader Lord Salisbury. Thinking he was indispensible, Lord Randolph resigned as Chancellor in 1886 but found he was not. His later years were spent in embittered isolation from power and increasing ill health until his death in January 1895, aged just 46.

Lord Randolph has a reputation for being an uncaring father. Winston's mother, Jeanette Jerome, an American from a wealthy family, was warmer. However, upper class parenting left a lot to be desired in the period when Winston was growing up. Children were largely in the care of a nanny in a separate nursery, away from their parents. They were carefully groomed for formal meetings with parents by the nanny to be either admired or admonished. Their entry into adulthood was through a series of steps – Prep School and Public School for boys, then University (Oxford or Cambridge) or Military Academy. For girls, education by a governess and a formal coming out into society was the conventional path. Excessive parental contact was thought bad for a child. Winston was dispatched to St George's school in Ascot and to a private school in Hove where beating was the order of the day. He then went to Harrow for a classical education in which he did not shine. The army beckoned and he was trained at Sandhurst from 1893–94 before becoming a lieutenant in a suitably aristocratic regiment, the Fourth Hussars.

Churchill's army career

Whether his adult life was shaped by a desperate attempt to persuade a remote father to admire him, or a reflection of an active, confident and enterprising personality, is debatable. However, Churchill's early life reads more like a novel. He volunteered as an observer in a civil war in Cuba in 1895. He was in India in 1896 and took part in a military expedition on the North West Frontier in which he was nearly killed. He was sent to the Sudan in 1898, where he took part in a cavalry charge at the battle of Omdurman. The British had been eager to subdue the Sudan, which had broken away from the control of the British-dominated Egyptian government. Britain had taken over Egypt to protect the Suez Canal and the route to India. The expedition to subdue the tribesmen of the Sudan was one of the last great imperial campaigns in which superior British firepower and organisation ensured easy victories over native peoples with inferior weapons. Churchill relished the experience of war, but untypically for a young officer, wrote two books about his experiences (*The Story of the Malakand Field Force*, 1898 and *The River War*, 1899).

In 1899 he stood for parliament as a Conservative candidate for Oldham, a Lancashire industrial town with strong Liberal sympathies. He was defeated, but he now had a taste for politics.

He was then given permission to go to South Africa as a war correspondent to report the **Boer War, 1899–1902**. This time the British were not fighting native peoples with inferior weapons, if superior numbers, but well-trained fighters of Dutch descent who were expert shots and horsemen. Churchill found himself captured but made a daring escape. He turned this incident to good account politically when stories of his escape brought him fame at home. There was a wave of support for the government and the British troops in Africa, and, in the so-called 'Khaki' election of 1900, Churchill's enthusiasm for empire and his adventures won him votes. He was elected MP for Oldham.

It was doubtful whether he had sacrificed a great military career. There was a fine line in the Victorian army between initiative, enthusiasm and bravery, and 'showing off'. Churchill did not always see where that line was. His political and literary interests were also unlikely to make senior officers warm to him.

The Boer War (October 1899–May 1902)

The first white settlers in South Africa were Dutch emigrants who became known as Boers (farmers). They settled initially in Cape Colony but were forced northwards by British annexation of their land until in 1843 they set up two independent Boer republics: the Orange Free State and the Transvaal. Britain initially recognised the two Republics but then annexed the Transvaal in 1877, leading to conflict between the British and the Boers in the First Boer War (1880–81). Following defeat by the Boers the British restored Transvaal independence.

Relations between the two powers remained relatively calm until major gold deposits were discovered in the Transvaal in 1886. This led to a huge influx of 'uitlanders' (foreigners) mainly from Britain, who came in search of their fortune. Their numbers were so great that they eventually exceeded the Boers and this led to confrontation over the uitlanders' political and economic rights. The British government saw this as an opportunity to step in, with the goal of gaining control of the gold mining industry and incorporating the two Boer Republics into a federation under British rule. The British Colonial Secretary, Joseph Chamberlain, sent an ultimatum to the president of the Transvaal, Paul Kruger, demanding equal rights for uitlanders. Kruger replied with his own ultimatum, requiring the withdrawal of British troops from the border of the Transvaal. Neither side gave in, and war was declared in 1899.

At first the Boers effectively fought back the British, but when a new leader was put in charge of the British troops (Lord Kitchener) and Boer families were forced into prison camps, the British eventually overcame the Boers and victory was declared in 1902. The Boers, however, gained self-government in 1910 with the setting up of the Union of South Africa.

A restless politician

Churchill was a restless politician and was moved more by great causes than by party discipline. One of those causes was **Free Trade**. He believed that this was the basis of English prosperity and rejected calls that Britain needed customs duties on imported goods. The Conservatives and Liberals had both accepted this view; but there was a movement within the Conservative **political party** led by Joseph Chamberlain to bring in a new systemof imperial preference, in which goods from the Empire would be admitted to Britain on low duties while other overseas imports would be taxed. This would protect British industry and provide money for social reforms, as well as linking Britain more closely with the Empire. Churchill was critical of this and also of Prime Minister Balfour's failure to take a decisive stand on the issue. Free Trade was the great cause of the Liberals and in May 1904 Churchill changed sides. He literally moved from the government side of the House of Commons to the Liberal side, under Henry Campbell-Bannerman.

Free Trade

Free Trade is the belief that prosperity and peace follow from nations trading without customs barriers. It was the main idea of 19th century politicians from the 1840s onwards and was not seriously challenged as it coincided with a long period of prosperity. By the early 20th century, rival trading nations had turned to protectionism using customs duties to help their industries grow. Free Trade was seen as essential in Britain as it provided cheap food for the workers, but the election of 1906 was the last time that it was a major issue. Gradually, during and after the First World War, Britain retreated into a reliance on her Empire and imposed customs duties on foreign goods. The issue of Free Trade became important again as the USA was eager to end such restrictive arrangements after the Second World War.

Political parties

The established parties were:

- **The Liberals**, the party of Free Trade, reform and international peace. Founded in 1859, its greatest leader was Gladstone (Prime Minister 1868–74; 1880–85, 1886 and 1893–95). The party split on the issue of whether to give Ireland **Home Rule**, but reunited to win a powerful election victory in 1906. It passed important social reforms (1906–14) but was not an effective war party under its leader Asquith. The party split in 1916 and was never again in government on its own.

- **The Conservatives** joined with Liberal MPs who opposed Home Rule in Ireland, forming the Conservative and Unionist Party from 1886. The party opposed radical change and supported the Empire. It too split after 1903 over the issue of Free Trade which some wanted to abandon. It joined the Liberals in a coalition in 1915 and supported the overthrow of Asquith in 1916, allying with Lloyd George from 1916–22 when it became an independent party once more and was in government as such (1924–29).

- **The Labour party** developed out of a desire by working people, various socialist societies and trade unionists to have a party that represented their interests. It grew from an association called the Labour Representation Committee which was created in 1900 to help men from the working class become MPs. It became a full political party only from 1903. It allied with the Liberals and its 59 MPs made relatively little impact until the First World War when Labour ministers joined the Coalition. It rapidly increased its support after 1914 and was able to oust the Liberals as the radical party, taking office for the first time in 1924 and again in 1929–31.

Changing party allegiance is a very drastic step. For most politicians it is political suicide. However there were notable examples in the past where such changes enhanced careers. Gladstone, the Liberal Prime Minister, had started off as a Tory. Joseph Chamberlain had started as a Liberal and ended as a Tory Cabinet minister. Churchill acted at a favourable time. In 1905 the Conservative government resigned and he was made a junior minister in the new Liberal government. This government won an overwhelming victory in the election of 1906. Churchill had backed the winning side.

Home Rule

This refers to a demand that part of a state be given self-government within the greater administrative reach of the central government. In the British Isles, it has traditionally referred to self-government, or devolution. Ireland, had come under increasing English control from the 17th century and was joined with Great Britain by the Act of Union in 1801. Throughout the 19th century there were increasing calls by mainly Catholic Irish in Central and Southern Ireland for Home Rule. After the Easter Rebellion (1916) and a war of independence (1919–1921) Ireland was split into the independent Irish Free State (now Ireland) and Northern Ireland, which is still part of Great Britain.

Churchill in government

Churchill very quickly rose to being an important person in the government and held a large number of ministerial posts which are summarised in the timeline below.

Churchill's ministerial offices

December 1905 –April 1908 — Parliamentary Under-Secretary, Colonial office. Liberal government under Prime Minister Sir Henry Campbell Bannerman

April 1908–February 1910 — President of the Board of Trade; member of the Cabinet. Liberal government under H. H. Asquith

February 1910–September 1911 — Home Secretary; member of the Cabinet. Liberal government under H. H. Asquith

October 1911–May 1915 — First Lord of the Admiralty; member of the Cabinet. Liberal government under H. H. Asquith

May 1915–November 1915 — Chancellor of the Duchy of Lancaster (a name given to a member of the government without specific responsibilities). Coalition government under H. H. Asquith

June 1917–December 1918 — Minister of Munitions. Coalition government under David Lloyd George

January 1919–February 1921 — Secretary of State for War and Air with Cabinet seat. Coalition government under David Lloyd George

February 1921–October 1922 — Secretary of State for the Colonies; Cabinet seat. Coalition government under David Lloyd George

November 1924–June 1929 — Chancellor of the Exchequer, member of the Cabinet. Conservative government under Stanley Baldwin

3 September 1939–May 1940 — First Lord of the Admiralty. National government under Neville Chamberlain

May 1940–May 1945 — Prime Minister

Social reform, 1906–10

Churchill took up an element from his father's career: a belief in the Tory Democracy ideas of social reform (see page 1). He joined one of the younger groups of reformers, which included David Lloyd George. This group left their mark by a series of welfare reforms that were the beginnings of the **welfare state**. Churchill was part of a government intent on dramatic changes that led to conflict with the House of Lords.

The government was also intent on massive naval expansion with the construction of the new **Dreadnought battleships** built in a naval race with Germany. Churchill approved of both the reforms and the naval expansion and was a vigorous speaker and campaigner. His entry to the Cabinet in 1908 was a remarkable step up for a man who only entered politics eight years before.

Dreadnought battleships

Dreadnoughts took their name from the British ship HMS *Dreadnought* launched in 1906. The ships had a revolutionary design of much heavier armour, much larger guns and a more rapid rate of fire power. This heavier but faster and more destructive ship began a naval race as every navy sought to keep pace with Britain.

The Ton-y-Pandy and East End incidents, 1910–11

In 1910 he was in one of the key government posts as **Home Secretary**. It was whilst in this post that two incidents occurred, which it could be argued showed errors of judgement. Firstly, during a Welsh miner's strike at Ton-y-Pandy in 1910, Churchill ordered troops to be sent to the area after a request for military aid from the chief constable of Glamorgan. Although not used against the miners the presence of troops was resented by many who blamed Churchill for sending them. Secondly, when anarchists occupied a house in London's East End in 1911, Churchill himself attended the scene with an air of command and was photographed with troops and police. This would be considered fairly outrageous now but even in 1911 it provoked a lot of criticism. Both incidents, and the reactions to them, reflected the changing mood of the times. The British ruling elite, which included Churchill, felt under pressure from international socialism and anarchism, comparable to the pressure felt today from international terrorism.

These incidents reflected the changing times in Britain, and together with a number of other factors, represented the pressure felt by the British ruling elites:

- the growth in international socialism and anarchism, which was perceived as a threat to the status quo
- the rise of the Labour party, which introduced an element of class politics into Britain – a new and, to some, unwelcome development in the political landscape
- the increasing number of industrial disputes, seeming to some to indicate a threat of revolution
- the violent protests of the **Suffragettes**, who demanded votes for women and were prepared to commit illegal acts to gain publicity
- the danger from Germany. (Germany was rearming itself with a fleet of warships – a possible sign of war with Britain.)

Welfare state

A social system, in which the state assumes primary responsibility for health care, education, employment, and social security.

Home Secretary

The Secretary of State for the Home Department, commonly known as the Home Secretary, is responsible for internal affairs in England and Wales. The post's remit included policing, national security, and a general remit to oversee the beginnings of various social issues.

Suffragettes

The name given to the members of the movement who campaigned for the parliamentary vote for women (women's suffrage). They regarded militancy as justified in view of the failure to achieve the vote after 40 years of campaigning. This militancy evolved from interrupting political meetings to hunger strikes.

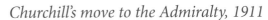

Churchill's move to the Admiralty, 1911

When Churchill was moved from the post of Home Secretary to be **First Lord of the Admiralty** in 1911 he was again at the heart of current events. The British navy was central to British power. The British army was small, but as a naval power it dominated the world. The navy kept links with Britain's huge overseas empire, protected its vital merchant fleets and was able to defend Britain against nearly any invasion. Churchill was immensely excited to be the political head of an institution so central to British imperial greatness.

He already had experience of running major departments and, as with the incidents of 1910 and 1911, he continued to favour a hands-on approach. He poured out his ideas on all aspects of naval policy to senior commanders with a lifetime's experience of naval matters.

The First World War, 28 June 1914–11 November 1918

Churchill was enthusiastic for war in August 1914 and with his military background made no secret that he thought of himself as a strategic expert. He put his weight behind an expedition to hold the port of Antwerp against the German advance in 1914 which failed. He then pursued a plan to end the war quickly by defeating the **Ottoman Empire** and advancing through the Balkans to attack Germany and Austria from the south. This resulted in the *Gallipoli* expedition of 1915 in which units of the British, French, Australian and New Zealand forces made landings on the Gallipoli Peninsular with a view to taking Constantinople (Istanbul, Turkey).

The landings failed and Churchill was blamed:

- for the loss of life;
- the distraction from the main war in the western Europe; and
- for pursuing unrealistic schemes that were more about his own egoism than any realistic strategy.

Gallipoli haunted Churchill throughout his career. His opponents referred to it constantly, both in public and in private, and it may well have influenced his reluctance, when wartime Prime Minister, to attempt an invasion of German-occupied France until the last possible moment.

> **First Lord of the Admiralty**
>
> The office of Lord High Admiral was created around 1400 to take charge of the Royal Navy. It was one of the Great Offices of State and, until 1964 when the office ceased to exist, was managed by a Board of Admiralty known individually as Lord Commissioners. The president of the Board was known as the First Lord of the Admiralty and was always a civilian, while the professional head of the navy was known as the First Sea Lord.

The Ottoman Empire

The Ottoman Empire consisted not only of modern day Turkey but much of the Middle East. It was a vast Turkish sultanate extending into three continents: south-west Asia, north-east Africa, and south-east Europe, founded in the 13th century by Osman I. It was traditionally dominated by Britain, but by 1914 the Empire had joined Germany. British occupation of its capital, Constantinople (Istanbul), would have made an advance into the Balkans possible. However an expedition to achieve this failed in 1915 (the **Gallipoli Campaign**). British forces were quick to occupy the oil fields of the Middle East but were bogged down in unsuccessful advances into modern day Iraq. Britain allied with Arab tribes who rose in revolt against the Turks, and Baghdad fell to Britain in 1917. After the First World War, the Ottoman Empire was broken up into many smaller countries and Britain gained control of Iraq, Transjordan and Palestine, and Churchill continued to think of the Eastern Mediterranean as an area vital to British interests throughout the Second World War.

The Gallipoli Campaign

In November 1914, the Ottoman Empire had joined with Germany and Austria. By 1915 there was a deadlock in the trenches on the Western Front in France. Churchill thought that he might be able to end the war quickly by a rapid naval action. He wanted a front opened against Germany and Austria in the south-east. If successful it would knock the Ottomans out of the war and force the Germans and Austrians to direct resources to counter this new threat.

First he persuaded a sceptical Cabinet to try a naval action to take Constantinople in February 1915, which failed. Then he urged landings at the Gallipoli Peninsula using troops mainly from Australia and New Zealand (the Anzacs). The plan lacked secrecy, was initially short of troops and was executed so slowly that the Turks had plenty of time to prepare. Hamstrung from the outset by these logistical and organisational problems the campaign was a costly failure and was a major political blow for Churchill.

Minister of Munitions

This was a British government position created during the First World War to oversee and co-ordinate the production and distribution of munitions for the war effort. The position was created in response to the Shell Crisis of 1915 when there was much public criticism of the shortage of shells available.

War Cabinet

During World War 1, Prime Minister David Lloyd George formed a small War Cabinet to expedite decisions. Initial members of the War Cabinet were David Lloyd George, Lord Curzon of Kedleston (Lord President of the Council) and Andrew Bonar Law (Chancellor of the Exchequer). Others took their turn in the War Cabinet, including members from the Dominions, but its purpose remained the same.

The Gallipoli venture was a severe setback for Churchill. The Conservatives already bitterly disliked him for leaving the party and for his attacks on them during the debates about the reform of the House of Lords and the social reforms of the Edwardian era. After the troops had been evacuated from Gallipoli, Churchill was demoted from First Lord of the Admiralty and went off to serve as an officer on the Western Front. He returned after his ally **David Lloyd George** became head of the Coalition government in December 1916. This followed a concerted campaign from the Conservatives and Liberals hostile to Prime Minister Asquith. Then in 1917, despite opposition from many Conservatives, Churchill was made **Minister of Munitions**. This was a post that Lloyd George had held and which needed a vigorous personality. Churchill was not a member of the **War Cabinet** though.

BIOGRAPHY

David Lloyd George (1863–1945)

British; Chancellor of the Exchequer 1908–4, Prime Minister 1916–22; Earl 1945.

David Lloyd George made his way from relatively humble origins to become a solicitor and then a Liberal MP. His fiery speeches and obvious energy enabled him to rise quickly alongside Churchill after 1905. He was a radical and innovative Chancellor of the Exchequer, introducing national insurance in 1911 and he organised arms production in the First World War before turning against his Liberal colleagues and joining with the Conservatives to overthrow the Prime Minister, Asquith. He was the leader of a Coalition Government from 1916–22. His pre-war friendship with Churchill was a major factor in Churchill's return to office and Cabinet rank. After 1922 Lloyd George lacked Churchill's ability to 'come back' and never held office again.

The post-war Coalition government

Lloyd George's Coalition government easily won the 1918 election on the back of the First World War victory and by January 1919 Churchill was again in favour: he was in the Cabinet once more as Secretary of State for War. This Cabinet had a number of larger-than-life personalities. The Prime Minister himself, Lloyd George, was an outstanding orator and a colourful figure. Lord Curzon, the foreign minister, was one of the last of the aristocratic figures of the Victorian age. F. E. Smith, (Lord Birkenhead) was, like Churchill, an energetic and witty political figure who made the greatest possible impact whenever he appeared.

Churchill was now where he wanted to be: back at the heart of government and in charge of the army and air force. These were key posts and allowed him to influence post-war policy at the highest level.

Churchill's position at the end of the First World War

By 1918 many of the elements in Churchill's character and views, which were to be of crucial importance later on, were firmly established. When the war ended in November 1918, he was 43 and not of an age when he was likely to be influenced in new directions, though he was open to ideas and read widely. He had already had a very busy political career, but had won some very bitter enemies:

- the Trade Unions had not forgotten his mobilisation of troops during the strikes of 1911;
- many Conservatives had not forgiven him for changing sides to become a Liberal in 1904;
- the failure of the Gallipoli Campaign in 1915 had caused a lot of unpopularity, not only in military circles but in Britain; and
- the Liberals, who had supported Prime Minister Asquith, were bitter at Lloyd George and Churchill for deserting him in December 1916 and joining the Conservatives in the Coalition government.

Notwithstanding his colourful personality and huge skills as a speaker and writer, Churchill was lucky to be in office at all by 1918, and even luckier to be back in the Cabinet in the following year. He owed a lot to his personal links with Lloyd George and his Cabinet, and perhaps to the view that it was safer to have him in the government than criticising on the back benches.

ACTIVITY

Sources A to E (see page 10) are about Churchill in the early 1920s. One important skill is to be able to interpret what the sources are saying.

1. What is being implied by the cartoon in Source A?
2. What does Source B show about Churchill's position in politics by 1920?
3. Describe the tone of Sources C and D?
4. a What knowledge would you use from Churchill's early life to confirm what Source E says in the first line?
   b Is Churchill stating facts or offering an opinion in Source E as a whole?

Source

A　When Churchill died in 1965 the American magazine *Time* produced a colour booklet about his life. This included an engaging series of pictures of Churchill wearing different hats. What is interesting is the tone of the cartoon which accompanied it.

HATS THAT HAVE HELPED ME.

Mr. Winston Churchill (*trying on Colonial headgear*). "VERY BECOMING—BUT ON THE SMALL SIDE, AS USUAL."

B　Frances Stevenson was Lloyd George's secretary, his mistress of many years and later his second wife. The entry in her diary on 24 January 1920 reveals this barbed exchange between Churchill and the Prime Minister and is used in a generally unsympathetic biography of Churchill.

"Winston is the only remaining specimen of a real Tory", *Lloyd George declared, to which Churchill replied that if the* Prime Minister was to include all Parties in his Coalition *"you will have to have me in your new National Party." "Oh no",* *Lloyd George retorted. "To be a party you must have at least one follower."*

Charmley, *Churchill, The End of Glory*, p. 161.

C　The Cabinet Secretary Sir Maurice Hankey met Churchill just after he had been made Minister of Munitions in 1917.

On the whole he was in a chastened mood. He admitted to me that he had been 'a bit above himself' when he had been First lord of the Admiralty, and surprised me by saying that he had no idea of the depth of public opinion against his return to public life, until the appointment (to be Minister of Munitions' was made.

Diary, 22 July 1917; quoted in: Ponting, *Churchill*, p. 208.

D　From a modern historian.

The return of peace in 1918 marked for Churchill the beginning of ten years of considerable celebrity and achievement. He was as prominent in public office as anyone can be who is not actually Prime Minister. He did good work in a variety of really important national and imperial issues. He was at the top of his oratorical form and was one of the most effective parliamentarians. His political performance through the 1920s was first class. Perhaps it was the very turbulence and novelty of the post-war climate that drew the best out of him.'

Best, *Churchill, a Study in Greatness*, p. 92.

E　From an account Churchill wrote of his life for an American newspaper.

They say with truth that I have been a Tory, Liberal, Coalitionist, and finally Tory. My own feeling is that I have been more truly consistent than any well-known public man. I have seen political parties change their positions on the greatest questions. But I have always been a Tory Democrat [Independent] *and Free Trader* [like his father] *as I was when I first stood for Oldham nearly thirty years ago.'*

Chicago Tribune, 1935.

ACTIVITY

Look at Source A on the Churchill family motto.

1   a   From what you have read so far find evidence that Churchill had been '**daring**' and that
        he had showed '**enterprise**' and that he had been '**Faithless**' and that he had been
        '**Fortunate**'.

    b   What more information would you like to know about the origin of the source?

Source

(A) **Churchill in conversation to Kay Halle, girlfriend of his son Randolph,
quoted in interview 1978.**

*The family motto of the House of Marlborough is Faithful but Unfortunate, I, by my daring
and enterprise, have changed the motto to Faithless, but Fortunate.*

Changes in Britain at the end of the First World War

Churchill had already had a varied and colourful career at the end of the First World War.
Britain, too, had undergone some remarkable changes in the period between 1876 and
1918. It had seen the rise of a new political party, Labour, and the emergence of mass trade
unionism. There had been welfare reform, which Churchill had helped to create. There had
been war on a scale unknown in British history before in terms of losses and intensity.
Britain's industrial greatness was on the wane as its staple industries, coal, iron, steel and
engineering, were faced with declining markets principally through foreign competititon.
Though the Empire was at its peak in terms of territory, Britain faced challenges to its
domination, and its colonies came to be seen as more of a burden to be defended than an
asset. However, the main change was the decline of the traditional aristocratic ruling class.

A number of factors contributed to this decline:

- A greater number of men and, since 1918, women were voting than ever before, which
  was changing the political landscape.
- There was a larger and more confident middle class.
- Revenues from land (the traditional source of wealth for the aristocracy) were in
  decline.
- Many aristocratic heirs had been killed leading their troops in the war.

Significantly, the aristocratic Lord Curzon was not chosen as Prime Minister in 1923 over
the middle-class Stanley Baldwin, who came from a manufacturing family in
Worcestershire. After 1918, Churchill also found that his aristocratic background was more
of a political disadvantage than a stepping stone to power. However, his principal problems
were the Gallipoli disaster and the decline of the Liberals, which meant that he had to
consider rejoining the Conservatives.

Changes in the world

Not only was Britain changing, but so was the world. The old empires had collapsed. By 1918 the Russian tsar and his family had been murdered and there was a communist government struggling to maintain power. The Austro-Hungarian Empire was dead and had been replaced by smaller states in eastern Europe. The German emperor was in exile and Germany was going through struggles to establish a new democratic republic. Italy was in the grip of strikes and was thought likely to experience revolution. The USA had emerged as a major force in both economic and military terms: its intervention was seen to have thrown the balance of the First World War in the Allies' favour. Japan had come out of the war much stronger and its ambition to control Asia was starting to make itself felt. China too had been trying, with its Republic established after the fall of the ancient Empire in 1911, to throw off foreign domination. The pre-war world of European domination was giving way to a new and much more uncertain future. There were hopes that the First World War would never be repeated; that a new international order based on a **League of Nations** would ensure a lasting peace; that progress would be made to social justice and democracy. However, conservatives, like Churchill, also saw much that was threatening.

The rise of communism and social unrest

During the early part of the 20th century there had been a considerable movement to the left in many countries. Lenin ruled over a new communist Russia and his opponents had been unable to defeat him in the civil war of 1918–20. In Italy there was a wave of strikes and rural revolts which seemed to threaten the established order, until a right-wing dictatorship was established by Mussolini. There were failed revolutions in Hungary and Germany. Britain encountered colonial disturbances in Ireland, India, Egypt and the Middle East. It also faced the doubling of the trade union movement from 4 to 8 million members and the re-emergence of large-scale strikes. Even the police went on strike in 1919. Miners, transport workers and engineers combined to form a potentially powerful union alliance. Labour replaced the Liberals as the main party of opposition. To many it seemed that old traditions were under threat. In Germany and Italy the old ruling class looked more and more to extreme paramilitary movements to destroy the threat of communism. While these fascist movements were not significant in Britain, many sympathised with anti-communist feelings, and class antagonism was a strong feature of the post-First World War period.

Initially, it was hoped that the continuation of the wartime Coalition government would introduce reform and reward the British people for its wartime efforts. There was talk of 'Homes fit for Heroes', of more help for the poor, of councils to bring together workers and employers, and of a new international order based on the League of Nations. A brief post-war boom encouraged optimism, as did the reassuring figure of Prime Minister David Lloyd George. As a pre-war reformer and as an energetic war leader he seemed to be the ideal man for the job.

The Coalition government, 1918–22

In the end the **Coalition government** turned out to be unable to deal with the mass of problems it faced:

- it could not stop strikes;

League of Nations

An association of countries established in 1919 by the Treaty of Versailles to promote international cooperation and achieve international peace and security. It was not joined by the USA and was unable to stop Italian, German, and Japanese expansionism leading to the Second World War. It was replaced by the United Nations in 1946.

The Coalition government

During the war all three parties joined together to form a Coalition government. The term 'Coalition' continued after 1918, but in fact it was predominantly made up of the Conservatives and those Liberals who supported Lloyd George. The official Liberal party remained loyal to the former PM, Asquith.

- it could not ensure prosperity as a down turn swiftly followed the initial period of prosperity;
- it was forced to divide Ireland into a Protestant north, which remained part of the United Kingdom, and a largely Catholic southern free state;
- it could not defend the peace, as Turkey rejected peace terms and through armed force forced a renegotiation of the **Treaty of Sèvres**;
- it could not prevent ugly violence against opposition in Ireland, Egypt, Iraq and India;
- it could not prevent nationalist movements like Gandhi's Congress party in India gaining support.

Churchill was one of a number of very able Cabinet ministers, but the judgement of the government seemed faulty. Churchill encouraged British military intervention in the Russian Civil War (1918–1920) despite the fact that it was unsuccessful and unpopular at home. An attempt to deal with an Irish separatist movement led only to a cycle of violence between British forces and the Irish Republican Army, which ended in the negotiations that divided Ireland. Britain reduced her armed forces and agreed to limit naval building in the Far East to the advantage of the USA. Relations with France worsened. The USA withdrew from European affairs and would not ratify either the **Treaty of Versailles** or the League of Nations. Without the USA the League was of limited importance.

> ### Congress party
> The Indian Congress party, founded in 1885, was a nationalist movement for Indian independence. In the 1920s and 1930s, under Mohandas K. Gandhi, it promoted noncooperation with the British to protest the feebleness of the constitutional reforms of 1919. During the Second World War, the party announced that India would not support the war until granted complete independence.
>
> ### Treaty of Versailles
> The treaty was signed by Germany and the Allies on 28 June 1919 in the Palace of Versailles. It assigned 'war guilt' to Germany, and imposed huge reparations payments on them, as well as territorial and colonial losses, and restrictions on military power. The treaty also comprised the Covenant of the League of Nations.

> ### Treaty of Sèvres
> The treaty was signed on 10 August 1920 at Sèvres, France, by the Allied Powers and the government of Ottoman Turkey. It abolished the Ottoman Empire, obliged Turkey to renounce rights over Arab Asia and North Africa, and provided for an independent Armenia, an autonomous Kurdistan, and Greek control over the Aegean islands commanding the Dardanelles.

Lloyd George was beset with accusations of what today would be called 'sleaze' – he openly sold peerages and honours – and lost the support of the Conservatives. For instance, when Lloyd George and Churchill wished to resist Turkish opposition to the demilitarisation of the area around Constantinople by force, there was little support. A backbench revolt threw Lloyd George out in October 1922 and he never held office again.

The Conservatives had decided, correctly, that they could form their own government without Lloyd George, Churchill or any other pre-war Liberal opponents. A new Conservative leadership under Andrew Bonar Law and then, after his illness and death, Stanley Baldwin, rejected coalition politics. The Liberals were divided, so the main opposition party became the Labour party. Churchill remained at the forefront of politics because Baldwin preferred to have him in office rather than being a 'loose cannon' on the back benches.

Between 1922 and 1924 there were three elections. The Conservatives won the election in November 1922 with a small majority. In the election that took place in December 1923, Labour did not have an overall majority but formed a government under Ramsay

MacDonald. Dependent on Liberal support, it lasted only from January to October 1924. Churchill bitterly opposed it as 'socialist', though it was noted for its moderation. It was, in any case, unable to act freely because it could have been brought down at any time by Liberal votes.

The Liberals appeared to fear that Labour would bring about a revolution. When a left-wing journalist who urged troops not to fire on protesting workers was not prosecuted, they turned the government out. The following election campaign was marked by claims that the Russian communists were supporting Labour. There was even a forged letter to that effect published in the *Daily Mail* a few days before the election purporting to be from the Russian communist Zinoviev. The losers were the Liberals, as their traditional voters turned instead to the Conservatives. From that point on, the Liberal party that had once been so great, ceased to be a main player in British politics. The wartime split between Lloyd George and Herbert Asquith in 1916 had proved fatal by 1924. The Conservatives won the election and Baldwin appointed Churchill, who was an 'independent' MP at this time, to the general surprise of all, including the great man himself, to be Chancellor of the Exchequer (see pages 37–41, Chapter 2).

The economic downturn of the 1920s

The years between 1924 and 1929 saw a continuing economic downturn and rising unemployment. The great 19th century industries, such as textiles, mining, metallurgy and engineering, were failing. Britain needed to cut costs to keep a declining share of markets. Export industries were hit by Churchill's decision to return to the **Gold Standard**, making the pound over valued and increasing the price of exports. With falling sales, mine owners wanted longer hours and less pay for the miners. The other unions felt obliged to back the mining unions' resistance to this. However, with fewer jobs, it was more difficult to make strikes effective. The government made concessions in 1925 and prepared for a showdown with the miners and the Trade Union movement generally. This came in 1926 with Britain's only major general strike (see pages 41–48, Chapter 2).

The long predicted clash between workers and state seemed at last to be here. Churchill saw it as an issue of who should rule – the elected representatives in parliament or the organised workers. The union leaders saw themselves as duty bound to support the miners – the heroes of the working class – because of their dangerous yet essential work. The miners saw themselves resisting selfish coal owners and defending their living standards. Moderate opinion hoped for a quick end to the dispute before real social violence occured. The myth that there was traditional British good humour and good natured mutual understanding is dispelled by local studies of class hatred and incidents of violence. Churchill had tried to avert the strike and afterwards worked hard to reach a settlement. But during the strike he was at his most belligerent: his newspaper '*The British Gazette*' took an extreme line. However, the TUC did not want the strike and negotiated after 9 days.

Gold Standard

The Gold Standard was a system which underpinned the value of money in a country. Although the currency in daily use would be paper notes and coins, these could be freely converted into fixed quantities of gold, thereby stabilising and ensuring the worth of the country's money supply.

In 1925, Winston Churchill reintroduced the Gold Standard at the pre-war gold price (it had been suspended during the war) which made the British pound too strong for exports to be competitively priced, resulting in lost earnings abroad. It also had the effect of raising interest rates which damaged all areas of business in the British economy.

The British Gazette

The British Gazette was published by the government during the General Strike. Its aim was to promote the government's view of the situation and condemn the striking workers. Only eight editions of the newspaper were published before the strike collapsed but, during this short time, its circulation rose to two million copies. Churchill, with his journalistic and writing experience, guided the editorial policy of the paper and contributed articles.

The miners were forced back to work for longer hours and less money. Trade union activity was much reduced and not until the 1970s did trade union power re-emerge on a similar level. The government passed a law forbidding sympathetic strikes and unemployment gave employers the chance to increase their power. After the onset of a major depression from 1929 after the Wall St Crash, there was little organised workers could do and the inter-war years were not favourable to trade unions.

Churchill's resistance to social change appeared to pay dividends, though he did work for reconciliation. For most of the 1920s he concentrated on reducing spending to cope with the loss of revenue brought by falling employment and trade. In line with the general public feelings towards war, he renewed the Ten Year Rule in 1928 under which the armed services assumed that there would be no major war for 10 years. Public spending was reduced not just on defence, but in other areas. His budgets were often ingenious. Though he has been criticised for doing little to promote the economy, he nevertheless mastered his financial role and delivered his budgets with style. He was seen as a competent Chancellor, open to new ideas and matching financial policies to the realities of the economic situation of Britain in the late 1920s.

British foreign policy and political history, 1925–31

Foreign policy, 1925–26

In terms of foreign policy, the British emphasis was on reconciliation of European hatreds. Churchill himself used the term 'appeasement' of disputes. Britain welcomed Germany back into international affairs.

In 1925 the Locarno Pact guaranteed Germany's western frontiers, while not mentioning the far more controversial eastern frontiers; in particular the lands lost to Poland in the Treaty of Versailles. Germany joined the League of Nations in 1926 and in 1928 Britain welcomed the **Kellogg–Briand Pact** outlawing war. Britain was keen to spend less on defence when imperial problems were proving expensive. In addition, Britain had no wish to involve itself with French concerns, rather a wish to get back to its traditional links with Germany; especially as both countries disliked communism. Britain also established cordial relations with Italian dictator Mussolini and supported an end to conflict in India by talks with Gandhi and the Congress opposition, promising greater self-government (see pages 52–59, Chapter 3).

Labour's partial success, 1929

In 1929, Labour won the election, largely because it seemed to promise more solutions to unemployment and poor trade. Baldwin offered only the slogan 'Safety First'. Once in office, Labour was constrained by being, as in 1924, a minority government dependent on Liberal support. It also faced a huge economic crisis that began with the collapse of the US stock market in October 1929. Unemployment rose and there were bankruptcies and job losses. Financial opinion insisted on the need for Labour to cut spending, but the Cabinet and the party were unhappy about this.

A national government?

Prime Minister Ramsay MacDonald came to think that only a national government could pass the necessary financial measures. As a result he abandoned his party and joined with the Conservatives and Liberals in a **National Government**. Some Labour MPs supported it. The rest went into opposition, amazed at what they saw as a betrayal. The spending cuts were made but the pound was not saved and Britain went off the Gold Standard in September 1931.

Kellogg–Briand Pact
(27 August 1928)

This was the creation of French Foreign Minister Aristide Briand and US Secretary of State Frank B. Kellogg and signed by France, the United States, and 13 other powers. They pledged themselves to 'renounce' war as an instrument of national policy and to resolve all international disputes by 'peaceful means alone'. The treaty contained no enforcement mechanism and was, therefore, unable to prevent war.

The National Government

A government formed from all political parties to resolve a crisis. In 1929, MacDonald left to tender the government's resignation to the monarch; when he returned he shocked colleagues by revealing that he had been persuaded to stay on and lead a national all-party government which would deal with the financial crisis.

The Indian question, 1931

In 1931 Churchill had put some distance between himself and the chance of holding office in any government mainly because of his opposition to concessions in India. He strongly resisted the arguments for Indian independence, believing that British rule in India should be protected, and was a founding member of the India Defence League whose aim was to preserve British power. He rejected any moves to give India any measure of self-government, and was opposed to the conferences held in London with Gandhi and leaders of the Indian National Congress. He aligned himself with reactionary elements in the Conservative party, using language to express his views that was considered extreme and not reflective of public opinion. It was unfortunate that his vivid account of his younger days was published at this time. *My Early Life* described his experiences as a soldier in India and promulgated the opinion that Churchill's views were old-fashioned and out-of-date.

By 1931 Churchill had upset all three main political parties:

- The Conservatives under Baldwin resented his criticisms of his support for reform in India.
- Labour under MacDonald resented Churchill's attitude to the workers and his class politics.
- The Liberals saw him as a renegade who had left his old party and joined the Conservatives.

In times of economic hardship, his political style may have seemed to have been too flamboyant. Also his connections with past governments that seemed from a different social and political era seemed to jar with the requirements of the day. His politics and personality, his pride in the Imperial past and his rhetorical language may have seemed out of place in a modern Britain in which parties worked together to try and offer modern political management.

The rest of the 1930s

The National Government presided over elements of recovery. Interest rates were low. There were tariffs on foreign goods, but cheap imports of food from the Empire. Prices fell and some sections of the economy, like services and consumer goods, did well. The older manufacturing areas went into sad decline. Spending was controlled by the Chancellor of the Exchequer, Neville Chamberlain, who had little in common with Churchill. In foreign affairs, the trend towards appeasing conflicts continued. Despite the *Kellogg–Briand Pact*, little was done to stop Japan taking over a large area of the Chinese province of Manchuria in 1931. The Italian dictator, Mussolini, was allowed to invade and conquer Abyssinia in 1935. The new Nazi dictator Hitler, who had come into power in 1933, was allowed to rearm Germany and remilitarise the Rhineland in 1936.

Churchill was not interested in Italy and Japan, but began to be worried about the threat from Germany. He now began to urge rearmament, especially of the air force, which he saw as the crucial weapon of the future. Few responded. His figures for German rearmament were dismissed as faulty and public opinion, tired of war, was unsympathetic to another arms race. Arms build-ups were widely held to have been a major cause of the First World War.

Public opinon was against war and Churchill was careful to link calls for rearmament with greater suport for the League of Nations. He pressed for greater arms, but when Germany remilitarised the Rhineland in 1936, breaking the *Treaty of Versailles*, he did not advocate armed action and praised Chamberlain's response as 'constructive'. Again, when Germany invaded Austria in 1938, Churchill did not appeal for an armed response. He did not press for opposition to fascist Italy or for intervention in the Spanish Civil War (1936–39). Indeed, in this conflict between right-wing militarists and nationalists and left-wing republicans, he was firmly on the side of the Right. He had in fact stated in 1937 that 'I will not pretend that, if I had to choose between communism and nazism, I would choose communism.'

In 1935, MacDonald was forced to exchange posts with Baldwin who became Prime Minister of the National government. Baldwin showed little interest in bringing Churchill back into government. He did, however, begin rearmament and offered some encouragement to the League of Nations. Like many in Britain he saw pictures and film footage of bombing by Japan in China, by Franco in Spain and by Mussolini in Abyssinia and feared that another war would destroy Britain. In any case British military chiefs told the government that Britain could not defend its Empire if it took on Germany, Italy and Japan. It was likely that any war would bring about the fall of the Empire at enormous cost to life and resources.

The policy of appeasement

When Baldwin retired and Neville Chamberlain became Prime Minister in 1937, Chamberlain was determined to pursue appeasement as a clear and positive policy. Britain needed to rearm but, above all, it needed to reduce its commitments by doing its utmost to reduce conflicts in Europe. Most of these were about the *Treaty of Versailles* and the German-speaking lands lost by Germany in 1919. Germany argued that these native speakers deserved to be in Germany. After the German invasion of Austria in March 1938, it was clear that Hitler would demand that the German-speaking areas in Czechoslovakia should be given self-determination and even a chance to join Germany.

Chamberlain hoped that negotiations would end German grievances, and there is no evidence that this view was not widely held. However, when negotiations led Chamberlain to force the Czechs to meet all of Hitler's demands and give up their German speaking areas to Germany and also land to Poland and Hungary, opinion in Britain began to divide. Trying to settle disputes was one thing, but the dismemberment of a democratic state was another. The Munich conference in which this was agreed came to be seen as a shameful surrender (see pages 78–81, Chapter 3). Churchill himself was publically critical of the Munich conference.

There was another shift of opinion in Britain when anti-Semitic riots broke out in Germany in November 1938. Then Hitler occupied the rest of the Czech lands in March 1939 and Czechoslovakia ceased to exist. This was unpopular in Britain. Chamberlain responded by guaranteeing Poland its independence, if not territory, as it was thought that Hitler would go on to demand the return of Poland's German-speaking territory lost to Germany in 1919.

The Second World War, 1939–45

Churchill urged a Grand Alliance of countries ready to oppose Hitler. However, Chamberlain did not think this was a realistic option. He began negotiations with the USSR, which failed. To resist Germany, Chamberlain worked hard to build up air defences and to increase links with France. Churchill hoped to be appointed to office and his criticisms of government policy after his blistering attack on the Munich conference were now more muted. When Hitler invaded Poland on 1 September 1939 war became inevitable because of opinion in parliament, the Cabinet and the country. Chamberlain declared war

on Germany on 3 September 1939. Churchill then returned to government as First Lord of the Admiralty, a post he had held 25 years previously.

The early years, 1939–41

Germany had signed a neutrality pact with Russia and could attack and conquer Poland with ease. Britain and France did little except build up their forces in northern France. Churchill ensured that the British fleet was active and persuaded the Cabinet to mine Norwegian waters and prepare for an expedition to Norway. The Germans got in first and there was an unsuccessful British attempt to resist them which ended in a humiliating evacuation. The Germans then invaded France and the Low Countries.

Chamberlain took the blame for the failures in Norway (see pages 87–88). He was forced to resign by a virtual backbench revolt. The expectation was that Edward Wood, Lord Halifax the foreign secretary, would become Prime Minister. However, in the event, he was reluctant and Churchill was chosen. As he took office, German forces were defeating France and the British army had to be withdrawn. The evacuation of Dunkirk (1940) was one of Britain's worst military reverses. However, Churchill rallied the nation with defiant speeches. He also believed that the USA would intervene to save Britain and he actively lobbied for their aid.

Hitler did not invade Britain. The British rallied in North Africa where they defeated the Italian forces after Mussolini had joined the war (1940). The British army was rebuilt and the British navy and air force ensured that Britain was defended. The so-called *Battle of Britain* maintained British air superiority over Britain and any German invasion would have been very vulnerable to British naval power.

The *Battle of Britain*

On 18 June 1940, Churchill declared 'the Battle of France is over; I expect that the Battle of Britain is about to begin'. On 2 July Hitler ordered the invasion of Britain to commence. Hitler understood that the invasion was impossible without German air superiority so the battle was a German attempt to destroy RAF Fighter Command and win control of the air.

The single-seat aircraft were evenly matched: the Messerschmit 109E was as fast as the British Spitfire and faster than the Hurricane but the British types were more manoeuvrable. German bombers began by attacking shipping from mid-July to mid-August. The plan was to force the RAF to attack German fighter escorts.

On 13 August, the Germans began the main battle, attacking airfields and aircraft factories. British losses in aircraft and pilots began to exceed replacements. On 7 and 9 September, whilst heavy attacks hit London, the Germans lost 84 aircraft and Hitler postponed the decision to invade. On 15 September Germany renewed its attack on London during which 60 German aircraft and only 26 British were lost. On 17 September Hitler again postponed the invasion and on 12 October it was abandoned. In total the British lost fewer than 800 aircraft; the Germans nearly 1,400. Fewer than 3,000 British aircrew took part, of whom 507 were killed. Churchill's view was that 'Never in the field of human conflict was so much owed by so many to so few'.

Blitz

Heavy bombing of British cities and industrial targets by Germany between 1940 and 1941, in particular London.

From 1940–41 Britain took on Germany and Italy alone. British cities were bombed on a hitherto unknown scale in the *Blitz*, though casualties were nowhere near as high as the authorities expected. Churchill put immense hope in the USA and was delighted when US supplies were extended and the USA provided some old destroyers in return for British bases. The arrival of German forces in North Africa ended the British victories there. When the Germans invaded the Balkans a British force was sent to Greece which was defeated. After conquering Yugoslavia and Greece, Hitler invaded Russia in June 1941. Britain was now no longer alone, but it seemed likely that Russia would be defeated. Churchill went to see President Roosevelt in August 1941 (see pages 126–132, Chapter 4).

Strategy and campaigns, 1941–45

From August 1941 to summer 1945 Churchill spent many dangerous and exhausting hours travelling to see his allies and maintaining the Grand Alliance with the USA and USSR. British strategy was:

1. to retain control of the seas and defeat German U-boats, with the aim of maintaining the vital flow of supplies to Britain and communication;

2. to bomb Germany; and

3. to support its main fighting effort in the Mediterranean.

In October 1942 the Germans were defeated in Egypt and Britain went on to control North Africa. British forces linked up with an American invasion of Tunisia. From there, in 1943, there was an Allied invasion of Sicily and then Italy. Rome fell to the Allies in 1944.

The Second Front, 1944

Ultimately, it was not clear how the victories in Africa and the Mediterranean would contribute to Germany's defeat. Stalin and some of the US military leaders urged a cross-Channel invasion to France to set up a second front (see page 147, Chapter 5). Churchill and his generals resisted this until June 1944. By that time the German army had been severely weakened in Russia at the cost of very heavy Soviet casualties. However, Germany was far from defeated and heavy fighting in Normandy and subsequently in eastern France and Germany was needed to end the war.

The Far East

Britain also had to fight in the Far East. Japan had attacked British colonies in South-East Asia and Hong Kong in December 1941, leading to a humiliating British defeat by numerically inferior forces in Malaya and Singapore. The Japanese also took Burma and theatened India. The USA bore the brunt of the attacks in the Pacific and eventually regained the lost lands and threatened an invasion of the Japanese homeland. US power had virtually destroyed the Japanese navy and air force and US bombing of Japan was severe. British forces reconquered Burma but only the surrender of Japan after the deployment of two atomic bombs by the USA (1945) allowed Britain to recoccupy its lost colonies.

A severely weakened Britain, 1945

By 1945, Britain had suffered considerable physical damage in the Blitz and also by a series of German V1 and V2 rocket attacks in 1944 and 1945. Its trade, investments and economy were severely weakened. It had to accept Soviet control of Poland – the country it had gone to war to defend. Churchill also had had to contend with uneven relations with both Roosevelt and Stalin. There was little American sympathy for Britain with regard to restoring its Empire and every sign the USA would insist on Free Trade policies after the war (see the *Atlantic Charter*, page 130, Chapter 5). Churchill had failed to prevent the spread of the USSR despite his negotiations with Stalin. He had also lost control of the war to the USA who had put their own commander, Eisenhower, in charge of the **D-Day** landings and subsequent campaign against Germany (see page 108).

Churchill's reputation was immense, both at home and world-wide. So it was a huge shock when the Conservatives lost the election of 1945. However, the British electorate wanted real gains from the war in terms of social security, an end to poverty and the chance for a

D-Day, 6 June 1944

When 150,000 US, Canadian and British troops landed on beaches in Normany, France. In one day the troops and supporting airborne bombardment secured 55 miles of coastline.

new society with greater opportunities. They did not want to go back to the 1930s with the old ruling class in charge. Labour offered the possibility of taking the spirit of national unity forward into the post-war world and the British people voted for them. For the first time Labour took office with a majority over the other parties. They faced a Cold War with Russia, huge financial and economic problems, the need to give India greater independence and had to deal with a host of problems and expectations. Churchill faced the loss of power.

Churchill's declining power, 1945–55

He remained a major world figure, urging on the Cold War with his famous 'Iron Curtain' speech in 1946. He continued to write – especially his war memoirs, which were presented as a history of the Second World War rather than the justification for his own actions that they really were. Churchill returned to office in 1951 but few regard this period as his finest hour. He gave way, very reluctantly, to his protégé, Eden, in 1955.

Conclusion

Any summary of this incredibly important period of British history must be inadequate. The period came to be dominated by Churchill in a way that few would have predicted. By his death, Churchill had become a legend: the man of the century, Britain's greatest leader. He was a controversial figure throughout his career and it is not surprising that there has been controversy about his achievements and his place in British history. This book is concerned with examining key elements and issues about which there can be different opinions and uses a variety of sources to show different aspects of his career and character. The nature and extent of his greatness should be considered and assessed in the light of their evidence, but whatever the final judgements, his importance and the sheer power of his personality and influence cannot be denied. He will remain a fascinating and compelling historical figure as long as the 20th century is studied.

Bibliography

Best, G. (2002) *Churchill: A Study in Greatness,* pp. 91, 92. Penguin.

Charmley, J. (1993) *Churchill: The End of Glory*, pp. 161, 227. Sceptre.

Ponting, C. (1994) *Churchill*, pp. 208, 230, 245, 258. Sinclair-Stevenson.

Figure 2.1   Churchill is seen returning from his first visit to Roosevelt in August 1941.

In this chapter, the main issue relates to Churchill's reactions to the problems of post-war Britain. There are several passages for comparison and comment: the main skill concerns interpreting and comparing sources.

Key Questions

Areas of study include:

1   Why was Churchill afraid of communism and social unrest?

2   What was Churchill's work as Chancellor of the Exchequer from 1924–29 and what was its impact on the economy?

3   What was his attitude to the General Strike and what were his attempts to end conflict?

4   What were the reasons for his being out of office after 1929? (The issue of the Abdication will be considered in Chapter 3.)

By the end of the chapter you should be aware of different explanations for Churchill's reaction to post-war problems, and issues about how well his policies met post-war needs. You should also be able to interpret a range of sources and make a comparison between sources. You should be able to deal with what they say about a given issue, and also their nature and value as historical evidence.

Why was Churchill afraid of communism and social unrest?

ACTIVITY

'A major issue which caused controversy at the time and still divides writers about Churchill was his attitude to communism.'

Look at the three views in Sources A–C. Summarise briefly what they say.

1   Which is the most sympathetic to Churchill and which is the least?

2   At the end of the section on communism, re-read these passages and think about which one you most agree with. Discuss your view in class.

Note: This is a 'starter' activity. You will not be expected to consider different historians opions in the AS examination.

Sources

Three historians from different decades give their view on Churchill's policy towards Russia.

 A

Winston's attitude to Russian affairs, and his eagerness to carry on the war there, did much damage to his reputation, still smirched in the public view by the legends of Antwerp and the Dardanelles. Left wing Labour which looked on the Bolsheviks, despite their barbarities to the aristocracy, the Church and the bourgeoisie as champions of the workers and the under-dog denounced Churchill as a reactionary enemy of the working class. Even those on the Right, who shared his views about Bolshevism, were angry with him for trying to involve the country in another war, just when it was settling down to peace. Winston could argue a powerful case for his attitude; but the instinct and common-sense of the nation were opposed to him. Today, in retrospect, one can see more surely that they were right and he was wrong in his attitude.

Thompson, M. (1965) *The Life and Times of Winston Churchill,* Odhams.

 B

The [Russian] episode demonstrated that the features of Churchill's policy that his critics had found disagreeable in the past had not really changed. He had rushed into a highly complex situation with only a general and superficial understanding of its difficulties. The episode brought him very little credit either inside or outside the government.

Rhodes James, R. (1970) *Churchill, A Study in Failure,* p. 158. Penguin.

 C

Eighty years later, with the horrific story of Communist Russia behind us, the reader may conclude that Churchill was not so silly after all. The fate of the Russian royal family really distressed him. All through his life he showed a principled respect for the institution of monarchy. He felt with regard to the Tsarist officers, a chivalrous obligation not to let them down. Much of what he said was sensible. He correctly understood the miseries that Bolshevism would bring upon the Russian people. There are limits to what a nation can do for even the most attractive of foreign causes, and it is a measure of Churchill's passion that he could not see them.

Best, G. (2002) *Churchill: A Study in Greatness.* Penguin.

The pre-1914 world had been an uncertain one. The rise of organised labour, the danger of a civil war between republicans and loyalists in Ireland, the growing revolutionary movements in Europe that had resulted in violent unrest in Russia, Spain and Italy, and the very large socialist parties in France and Germany, all threatened the ruling classes in Europe. The way that the ordinary people of Europe rallied to their nation's call when war came was a relief, but the problems did not go away. In Britain, membership of trade unions doubled during the war. Even at the height of the great battles on the Western Front, there were threats of strikes. Days lost to strikes rose from 2.3 million in 1916 to nearly 6 million in 1918. There were major engineering stoppages in 1917, with radical factory committees being formed. The unions became more radical in their demands, and in the face of unrest, for example in Sheffield in 1916, the government had to concede higher wages. Labour joined the government when the coalitions began in 1915. Then there was a nationalist rising in Dublin in 1916, the so-called Easter Rebellion, which required a substantial armed force to crush. However, for many conservatives the greatest threat came from the Russian Revolution in 1917.

Churchill's attitude to the Russian revolution and civil war

Many in Western Europe had great reservations about the regime in Russia before 1914. Tsar Nicholas II relied heavily on armed force to control his people, despite giving them a parliament after the revolution of 1905. In practice, this had little power and his **autocracy** was not really threatened. However, when war came with Germany in 1914, both Britain and France were glad of Russia's alliance. The strains of war proved too much for the Russian Tsarist regime and mass demonstrations in the capital, Petrograd, in February 1917 got out of control. The tsar could no longer rely on his generals, his army or his people and he abdicated. The establishment of the Russian Provisional government was a relief and certainly helped the US decision to go to war in April 1917. However, the new government proved just as incapable of waging war effectively and was overthrown in October 1917 by a Marxist group, the Bolsheviks, under the leadership of Vladimir Lenin. Lenin had advocated peace and, to the horror of the Allies, made a separate peace with Germany in March. Lenin expected Europe to experience a communist uprising and was unconcerned about signing away huge areas of Russia, breaking all treaty obligations to former allies and having the royal family murdered. Churchill was genuinely horrified. Despite his nominal membership of the Liberals, a progressive reforming party, he saw communism as an evil force and wrote about it in extreme terms. He also urged Lloyd George and his colleagues to take active steps to remove the new regime in Russia.

Autocracy
The rule of one person.

Opposition grew against the Bolsheviks, whose supporters were relatively limited in number. Tsarist military chiefs raised forces and there was a coalition of anti-Bolshevik groups from former liberals to committed Tsarists (the Whites). There was considerable uncertainty as civil war began in Russia in 1918 (Figure 2.2). The British government had a number of options:

1. They could send troops in to safeguard the supplies they had sent to Russia to prevent them falling into communist hands.
2. They could launch a full-scale intervention to keep Russia in the war and overthrow the revolution.
3. They could do nothing and regard the Russian Civil War as a matter over which they could and should have no influence.

Figure 2.2   Map of the European theatre of the Russian Civil War, 1918–21

Faced with a massive German attack on the Western Front in March 1918 and then a very large-scale counter offensive, which in fact won the war in the West, there was little in practice that the British could do except to protect supplies in key ports in Russia. When the First World War ended in November 1918, there was no need to keep Russia as an ally, so any intervention would be to prevent the establishment of a Communist state.

The Cabinet did not come up with a very clear policy, but Churchill was sure of what to do. He was convinced that Britain had a moral obligation to the Tsarist officers who had supported the war effort and that here was a struggle between good and evil. When Churchill entered the Cabinet in 1919 he was insistent on a high level of intervention (see Sources A and B, page 25).

Sources

A On 17 March 1919 Churchill told his colleagues,

The War Cabinet must face the fact that the North of Russia would be over-run by the Bolsheviks and many people would be murdered…It was idle to think that we should escape by sitting still and doing nothing. Bolshevism was not sitting still and unless the tide were resisted it would roll over Siberia until it reached the Japanese. …the Baltic States would be attacked and submerged. No doubt that when all the resources friendly to us had been scattered, and when India was threatened, the Western powers would bestir themselves.

B In July 1919 Churchill told them that he:

… hoped the Cabinet would realise that practically the whole strength of the Bolsheviks was directed against Denikin and Kolchak [the White military leaders] *and if the forces of these two men were put out of action the Bolsheviks would assemble some 60,000 men with which to spread their doctrines and ravages against smaller States, such as the Baltic provinces, Czechoslovakia and Rumania, with whose interests we were identified.'*

Sources A and B: R. Rhodes James, (1970) *Churchill, A Study in Failure* Penguin.

ACTIVITY

Look at Sources A and B.

1   In what ways are these remarks similar in *tone* and content and in what ways are they different?

2   What was Churchill hoping to achieve by these comments?

The Cabinet's policy was so unclear that the British officers in Russia were not sure whether they were at war with the Bolsheviks or not. Lloyd George was not willing to commit large forces and, without a huge expeditionary force, the Whites were not strong enough to resist Lenin who had gained the support of the peasants and controlled key industrial areas.

Churchill's insistence on waging war brought some harsh criticism. The Labour leader, Ramsay Macdonald, wrote in October 1920:

'Churchill pursues his mad adventure as though he were Emperor of these Isles, delighting his militarists and capitalists with a campaign. We have been told one day that we are withdrawing our troops from Russia, and the next we read of new offensives, new bogus governments, new military chiefs as allies.' (Socialist Review, quoted R. Rhodes James, p. 156.)

Lloyd George was becoming equally tired of Churchill's lectures and lack of realism. He was critical of his failure to be a team player and accept Cabinet responsibility, and later wrote:

'The most formidable and irresponsible protagonist of an anti-Bolshevik war was Mr Winston Churchill. He had no doubt a genuine distaste for Communism…. his Ducal blood revolted against the wholesale elimination of Grand Dukes in Russia.'
(Lloyd George, *The Truth about the Peace Treaties*, Vol. 1, p. 324–25.)

ANALYSIS

Churchill had persuaded the Cabinet to send substantial amounts of financial and military aid to the Whites to maintain a military presence in Russia. He had even gained consent for a major attack before the defeat of the Whites had made this too dangerous. He had not persuaded them to commit themselves fully to overthrowing the regime or to negotiating an international grand alliance against communism. When dock workers refused to load a munitions ship bound for Poland, then engaged in war against the Bolshevik regime, the Cabinet had had enough and by November 1920 the British intervention came to an end.

There are a number of criticisms of Churchill's attitude that can be made. It is important to consider whether these criticisms are valid or whether Churchill was pursuing crucial and even far-sighted aims.

1. He took an unrealistic view of Russia. He argued that Tsar Nicholas II was popular and that Russia was doing well in the war. His view was that the revolutions were unrepresentative of the Russian people.

2. He thought that the White armies were noble and popular and likely to win.

3. He thought that after the huge losses of the First World War the British people would accept another major war against a former ally.

4. He did not take into account the sympathy of the British workers and Labour party for Russian social democracy.

5. He did not take into account the unwillingness of Britain's allies in the First World War and the Dominion governments to do any more large-scale fighting.

6. He ignored the practical difficulties of a campaign in a vast country like Russia with frozen Northern ports.

7. He ignored the traditional British policy of non-intervention in the affairs of other countries.

8. The language he used about Russia verged on the hysterical.

ACTIVITY

In connection with the last point in the analysis, study Sources A and B on page 27. One is from Churchill's addition to his study of the First World War, *The Aftermath*, published in 1929. The other is from Hitler's *Mein Kampf (My Struggle)* – an English edition published in 1933.

1. Which do you think is by Hitler and which by Churchill? (The answer is on page 50.)

2. Which do you think has the more extreme tone? Compare the content of the sources. Try reading both sources out loud.

3. What evidence can you find in the two sources for the author's opposition to the communists in Russia? Does this help identify who authored each extract?

Sources

We must not forget that Bolsheviks are blood-stained, that favoured by circumstances in a tragic hour, they overran a great state, and in a fury of massacre wiped out millions of their most intelligent fellow-countrymen, and now for ten years, they have been conducting the most tyrannous regime of all time. We must not forget that many of them belong to a race which combines a rare mixture of bestial cruelty and vast skill in lies and considers itself called to gather the whole world under its bloody oppression.

The revolution has produced a poisoned Russia, an infected Russia; a Russia of armed hordes not only smiting with bayonet and cannon, but accompanied and preceded by swarms of typhus-bearing vermin which slew the bodies of men and political doctrines which destroyed the health and even the soul of nations.

By the end of 1920 the Sanitary Cordon [of independent nations which stood between Russia and the West] which protected Europe from the Bolshevik infection was formed by living organisms vigorous in themselves, hostile to the disease and immune through experience against its ravages.

Note: see page 50 for source details.

Churchill and social unrest

Churchill did not make a great distinction between threats to stability from the Russian Marxists and threats to stability from internal enemies.

When the Cabinet met in June 1920 he made this clear:

> 'The country would have to face in the near future an organised attempt at seizing the reins of government in some of the large cities, such as Glasgow, London and Liverpool. It was not unlikely that the next strike would commence with sabotage on an extensive scale.' (John Charmley, p. 227.)

There was a considerable amount of strike activity in 1919. The trade union movement had doubled its numbers from four to eight million during the war and was assertive about pay and conditions. The Triple Alliance of Railway Workers, Miners and Transport Workers seemed to offer the threat of a powerful joint union action. Some of the union leaders talked the language of syndicalism – a pre-war idea that modern societies could be seriously threatened by concerted union action. There were radical shop stewards in some areas, particularly Glasgow, and the Russian revolution had excited them. Churchill saw the threat of revolution and as Secretary of State for War did not hesitate to use emergency powers. He told the Chief of the Imperial General Staff, Wilson, that, if necessary, he favoured a speedy return of reliable upper class regiments from France to deploy against the workers.

- In January 1919 troops and tanks appeared in Glasgow during a strike for a 40 hours week and strike leaders were arrested.

- In July 1919 there was a major coal strike and Churchill urged colleagues to use force, though his advice was not taken.

■ A police strike in Liverpool was met by deploying troops.

■ Over 50,000 troops were deployed during a rail strike in September 1919, though Lloyd George settled the strike by negotiation.

■ Churchill was eager to recruit a Citizen Guard of opponents of socialism and trade unionism.

The situation had eased by 1920 and Lloyd George did not favour increasing the problems by the greater use of troops. However, by 1920 Churchill's language was becoming more vociferous. In private he called Russia,

'a tyrannical government of these Jew Commissars' and 'a worldwide communistic state under Jewish domination'. (Ponting, p. 230. Source: Curzon Papers, 24 December 1921.)

This sentiment was not uncommon among the ruling class of the time – but not very typical of Churchill's career as a whole.

Churchill quite clearly, though, viewed the Russian revolutionaries and the British organised workers as class enemies. The potential threat was exacerbated by unrest in the British Empire, which then included Ireland. There were movements against British rule in Eygpt, India and by the Irish republican party Sinn Féin. This party had won 73 seats in the election of 1918 but they had not taken their seats and instead set up an independent Irish parliament, establishing a sort of shadow government in Ireland. For Churchill, Ireland was part of a wider picture. He felt there was,

'a world-wide conspiracy against our country by rascals and rapscallions [villains] of the world who are on the move against us, designed to deprive us of our place in the world and rob us of our victory'. (Speech: 4 November 1920, reported in the Daily Telegraph the following day; quoted in Ponting, p. 245.)

Black and Tans

Named after their uniforms, the Black and Tans were specially recruited forces intended to suppress unrest in Ireland. Often hardened by experiences in the First World War, they behaved with some brutality and were not well controlled by the British authorities. The cycle of violence they helped to create became unpopular at home and helped to poison Anglo-Irish relations for years to come.

ACTIVITY

Compare these three sources. What do they tell you about Churchill's attitude to civil and military opposition?

The diary of the leading British soldier, Sir Henry Wilson, for 23 September records:

*'General Tudor made it very clear that the **Black and Tans** are carrying out reprisal murders. At Bilbriggan, Thurkles and Galway yesterday the police marked down certain Sinn Feiners as in their opinion the actual murderers and then coolly went and shot them without question or trial. Winston saw little harm in this, but it horrifies me.'*

Major-General Sir C. E. Callwell, *Field Marshal Sir Henry Wilson: His Life and Diaries*, 1927.

'I do not understand the squeamishness about the use of gas; I am strongly in favour of using poisoned gasses against uncivilised tribes. The moral effect should be so good that loss of life can be reduced to a minimum.'

Churchill in a War Office memo, quoted Ponting, p. 258, May 1919.

Churchill continued to be interested in gas as a weapon. On 6 June 1944 he wrote to the Chiefs of Staff about using it against the Germans in France:

'I want you to think very seriously over this question of poison gas…It is absurd to consider morality on this topic when everyone used it in the last war without a word of complaint from the moralists or the Church…it is simply a question of fashion changing as she does between long and short skirts on women…I want a cold-blooded calculation made as to how it would pay us to use poison gas.'

Holmes, R. *In the Footsteps of Churchill*, p. 311.

Churchill's response to unrest

Churchill it seems would not shy away from extreme solutions to unrest and revolt. To control Britain's newly acquired League of Nations Mandate in Mesopotamia (Iraq) Churchill approved of the use of gas (although it was never used) and RAF bombing. When severe measures were proposed for Ireland, Churchill was enthusiastic. He supported special units designed to suppress Irish nationalist armed forces.

Meeting post-First World War challenges

It does seem that Churchill was highly concerned about threats to post-war stability from a number of different directions. Britain had won the war, at huge cost, but had not gained the security that victory should have brought. It was under threat from domestic unrest; its empire was challenged by nationalism and Europe as a whole was in danger from communism. As a historian, Churchill may well have been aware of parallels with the end of the Napoleonic Wars in 1815 which also saw considerable social unrest. He knew that wars were often 'the locomotive of change'. Was he right to be so concerned?

One view of Churchill's position after the First World War was that he was clearly misjudging the situation. Communism even in Russia did not have overwhelming support; it was defeated in much of Europe. There was not really a revolutionary situation in Britain and there was little interest in revolutionary ideology among working people. There had been discussion of giving greater freedom to Ireland and India before the First World War, so movements to obtain this were not really very new and might have been contained – if this indeed was seen as the desirable path – by moderate and sensible policies.

Another view is that Churchill did foresee and wish to prevent the emergence of forces which were dangerous to British interests. The end of the British Empire would accompany the loss of much of Britain's world power status after 1945. The loss of India in 1947 would prove crucial and heralded the loss of the rest of the Empire. Communism did eventually emerge as a major threat to the West and Churchill foresaw this. Though Britain did not face a revolution at home, there was a great deal of unrest, along with the rise of the Labour party, the doubling of trade union membership and the belief in the political power of strikes. There was no certainty that Britain would not experience similar political turmoil as Russia, Italy, or Germany, for instance. Because we know that class war or revolution did not happen, we cannot argue that from Churchill's perspective it was necessarily ridiculous or extreme to think that it might.

ACTIVITY

Summarise some of the threats to post-war Britain and its Empire. Using material from the chapter and your own research, copy and complete the table

Threat	Churchill's view and proposed course of action
The Russian Revolution of October 1917	
The growth of trade unionism in Britain and the strikes of 1919–20	
The establishment of a government and parliament in Ireland claiming independence from Britain	
Unrest in other imperial territories	

Another side to Churchill

To see Churchill in a permanent state of agitation about conspiracies and enemies is not fair or reasonable. For one thing, his family life was important to him. He had married Clementine Hozier in 1908. By 1918 they had four children and his letter to her at that time reveals another side to Churchill (see Source A).

Figure 2.3   Lady Churchill.

Sources

A Letter to Lady Churchill, 1918.

Do you think we have been less happy or more happy than the average married couple? I reproach myself very much for not having been more to you. But in any rate in these ten years the sun has never yet gone down on our wrath. My dearest sweet I hope and pray that future years may bring you serene and smiling days, and full and fruitful occupation. I think that you will find real scope in the new world opening out to women, and find interests which will enrich your life. And always at your side in true and tender friendship, as long as he breathes will be your ever devoted, if only partially satisfactory. W

Soames, *Speaking for Themselves*; quoted in Best, p. 91.

B Two reminiscences from Churchill's bodyguard, Walter Thompson.

In June 1920 Churchill's mother was seriously ill. She broke her leg so badly that it had to be amputated. Thompson had not found Churchill an easy person to get on with but he saw that Churchill:

"*was very tired. I immediately said that if I were the same blood group I would willingly give my blood (to help Lady*

Churchill). He turned to me and put his arm round my shoulder and said, 'Thompson, I shall never forget this, even it is too late, as I am afraid it is.' Doctors arrived and although my blood group was the same, it was too late."

In August 1920 Churchill faced another tragedy, when his three year old daughter died on a holiday in Kent. Churchill rushed to his house, when he heard the news, leaving Thompson in the garden.

"*A few minutes later he came out, with tears rolling down his cheeks. We walked up and down the garden for what seemed an hour, never speaking a word. Then he was called back in. He was inside for half an hour and he came out again, calmer now. He invited me to view the little body which he said was 'beautiful, like a piece of marble sculpture.'*"

Churchill then went to stay with friends in Scotland. He wrote to Clementine:

"*Went out and painted a beautiful river in the afternoon light with crimson and golden hills in the background. Alas I keep feeling the hurt of Duckadilly (his daughter Marigold's pet name).*"

Hickman, *Churchill's Bodyguard*.

Defence and disarmament – Churchill the politician

As well as husband and father and visionary advocate of vigorous measures, Churchill was a politician and a minister with responsibilities. Foremost among these was to demobilise the huge number of British men and women in the armed forces – over 3,500,000. There had been disturbances in the forces and protests about being sent overseas. While these might have added to Churchill's concerns about threats to discipline and order, he was quick to respond by a 'First In, First Out' scheme which demobilised longer serving members of the armed services first. This worked well and the mutinies subsided. He also had to deal with reducing the huge costs of military expenditure.

There was a desire to return to normal financial prudence. So however much Churchill advocated sweeping military solutions, he was practical enough to respond to the need to cut spending. He had no hesitation in reducing the RAF. Britain ceased to be the leading air power that it had been in 1918 and by 1921 had only three independent air squadrons to the French forty-seven. Churchill also rejected a proposal for government help to promote civil aviation. Short-term political objectives dominated.

In 1919, Churchill proposed the Ten Year Rule. Both the mood of the nation and political pressure was for reduction of defence capacity and Churchill adopted a radical solution. The spending on defence should be based on the assumption that the British Empire would not be engaged in any great war for the next ten years. This remained the basis of British defence policy under successive governments until 1932.

Ireland – repression and conciliation

Churchill's position as Secretary of State (Minister) for War and Air brought him close to nearly all the major concerns of the post-war Coalition including Ireland.

Since the 1870s there had been a political movement to give Ireland **Home Rule,** or local self-government within the Empire. The problem was that in Ulster in the north-east, the majority (75 per cent) were Protestant whereas in Ireland as a whole Catholics predominated. So there were fears in Ulster that 'Home Rule means Rome Rule'. These fears were exploited by the Conservative opposition in England, eager to prevent any Irish self-government. Churchill's father had played a leading part in defeating Home Rule in 1886 and opposition grew more extreme from 1912 with Conservatives backing a separate Ulster armed force to prevent Home Rule.

Churchill had taken a robust line, favouring the imposition of Home Rule by force if necessary. The hitherto peaceful Home Rule party in Ireland was frustrated at delays to self-government when the House of Lords rejected Home Rule for the third time. Yet it could only force a delay as the measure was due to come into force in 1914. By this time both Ulster Unionists and Irish Nationalists had armed themselves and a civil war was expected. The First World War came along instead and Ireland rallied to the British cause. However, extreme nationalists sought German help and launched a futile armed rebellion in Dublin in April 1916, (the Easter Rebellion). They got little Irish support, but when the British government executed the leaders, sympathy began to flow from those who saw them as Republican martyrs. This was made worse by the extension of conscription to Ireland. The election of 1918 returned 73 Republicans, now known as Sinn Fein ('Ourselves Alone' in Gaelic). The government could have merely introduced the Home Rule (which had actually passed in 1914 but had never been implemented). Instead they decided to resist Irish demands for total independence.

ACTIVITY

What qualities do Source A and Source B reveal of Churchill? Use evidence from the text to support your answer.

Home Rule

From the 1870s a movement had arisen to give Ireland a separate parliament and a degree of self-government within the Empire. Home Rule supporters did not demand complete independence, but their opponents saw this as a likely result and feared that the Catholic majority in Ireland would use their influence to oppress the Protestant minority.

The Irish War of Independence, 1919–21

Sinn Féin was opposed to British rule and wanted total Irish Independence. Lloyd George's government were determined to resist any opposition to maintain British authority and Churchill supported this. The Cabinet agreed to make troops available for 'maintaining order', a move seen by Irish nationalists as military repression. Volunteers were brought in to assist the Irish police called Auxiliaries or 'Black and Tans' (see also page 28). Violence accelerated. In 1920 Ulster (now known as Northern Ireland and Ulster province of Ireland) was given its own parliament within the UK. It was allowed to oppress its Catholic minority for the next 50 years.

The reprisals and violence in Ireland as a whole were ruining Britain's reputation abroad, particularly in the USA, and had become distasteful to the British public and the British establishment, including the King. The British had been unable to defeat the Irish Republican Army (IRA) or win 'hearts and minds', so the only solution was negotiation. By May 1921 Churchill showed his political acumen and was urging a truce, moderating his hard line of 1920. The truce was agreed on 11 July 1921 with Churchill taking a lead role in the negotiations.

The key negotiator on the Irish side was **Michael Collins**. 'The Big Fellow', as he was known, was a prominent member of the IRA and a strong, larger-than-life personality. He, Churchill and F. E. Smith, **Lord Birkenhead** (Churchill's closet ally in politics), managed to put differences behind them and work together. The final settlement was only made possible by Churchill's political skills when he said that failure to sign would mean 'a real war'. Collins believed him, signed the treaty and Southern Ireland became a Free State within the Empire. As a result Churchill became intensely unpopular among the Conservatives and Collins among the more radical Irish. Civil war broke out in Ireland and anti-treaty forces seized the centre of Dublin. Churchill put considerable pressure on the Free State government to crush the rebellion and there was a distinct threat of British intervention. In the end, British forces gave assistance but the Irish government fired on fellow Irishmen, ended the rebellion and executed their opponents. The Lloyd George government had ended the Irish problem for a generation and Churchill had proved an effective negotiator and had shown good judgement in giving the Free State Government the chance to put down the rebellion before Britain sent in large-scale military forces.

BIOGRAPHY

Michael John Collins (1890–1922)

He was an Irish revolutionary, elected to the breakaway Irish parliament in 1918. He rose to lead the Irish Republican Army and was a leader in the campaign against the British and a major figure in the illegal government set up by Sinn Féin. 'The Big Fellow', as he was called, did support negotiations with Churchill and Lloyd George to end the fighting and was prepared to accept an Irish free state within the Empire. He then faced armed opposition from those who rejected the treaty and he was killed in an ambush by his enemies.

Colonial matters, 1921–22

In 1921 Churchill was made **Colonial Secretary**. He was highly interested in the Middle East and set up a separate Middle East department. The newly acquired lands of Iraq and Transjordan were transferred to the control of pro-British rulers, Feisal and Abdullah respectively. British troops were withdrawn once initial control had been established. He was less successful in Palestine. The wartime Balfour Declaration had promised to restore the Jews' Biblical homeland in Palestine. However, the Colonial office had to consider the interests of the Arabs and, while confirming Jewish rights, a white paper of 1922 affirmed that the Arab population of Palestine would not come under Jewish jurisdiction or be members of a Jewish state. Therefore neither Jews nor Arabs were given control but a compromise attempted to give both rights.

Churchill was an able negotiator and in both cases attempted compromises, which were seen as successful by contemporaries despite, as was the case with Ireland, a period of violence followed an inconclusive settlement. In the meantime, Southern Ireland accepted Free State status and Northern Ireland remained part of the UK. In Palestine there was an attempt to reconcile the interests of the Arabs, the former subjects of the Ottoman Empire, with the Jewish immigrants.

Turkey again – the Chanak Crisis

Rather less judgement was shown over the Chanak Crisis, an episode which ended the Coalition as once again Turkey proved a disaster for Churchill.

The original peace treaty with the Ottoman Empire (Turkey), which had sided with Germany in the First World War, was the ***Treaty of Sèvres*** in 1920. Britain and France gained valuable lands in the Middle East (Syria, Lebanon, Iraq and Transjordan). The Dardanelles were made a demilitarised zone under British occupation and the Greeks, who were belated allies to Britain, were given the area round Smyrna (Izmir). The situation was radically altered by a revolutionary movement within Turkey led by a reforming army officer Mustapha Kemal. This movement went through central Turkey, drove the Greek settlers from Smyrna and advanced on the demilitarised zone of the Dardanelles. Churchill opposed the policy of supporting Greece and was concerned about Muslim opinion. His analysis of the situation was accurate. Britain had far more interest, given her Middle East territories, in maintaining good relations with the Muslim world. The Greeks had been somewhat inconsistent allies in the First World War and the settlement in Smyrna was unrealistic and difficult to defend. Churchill did not share the pro-Greek sympathies of Lloyd George when it came to considering Britain's imperial interests.

Colonial Secretary

The Empire after 1919 was at its height with gains from the fall of the Turkish Empire and the acquisition (albeit under mandate of the League of Nations) of German colonies. India came under a separate ministry, but the Colonial Secretary was responsible for a huge amount of territory and a vast array of different colonial people being administered by Britain.

The Dominions

The Dominions were the 'white' parts of the Empire, which enjoyed a measure of self-government under the Crown – Australia, Canada, New Zealand and South Africa. Lloyd George had brought the Dominion leaders into decision-making during the war and they attended the negotiations which led to the Paris Peace treaties.

When the Turks took Smyrna in summer 1922 his view had changed and he joined Lloyd George and Lord Birkenhead in an aggressive policy to force the Turks into a negotiated peace. A large Turkish force faced a small British force at Chanak at the entrance of the Dardanelles opposite the Gallipoli Peninsular, the scene of the 1915 campaign. On 7 September Churchill fully supported Lloyd George's refusal to negotiate but rather to think in terms of a military victory over Kemal. However Churchill ignored the practical problems of fighting a major war. He ignored public opinion and that of the bulk of the backbench MPs, and the reluctance of **the Dominions** to become involved in a war which had no real point:

- Kemal was the dominant force;
- the Greeks had already been driven out; and
- there was little real British interest at stake.

There was every reason to negotiate and to consider the lives of the British troops defending Chanak. There had been little attempt to consult France or Italy, guarantors of the *Treaty of Sèvres*. In the event, slightly ambiguous instructions to the British commander General Harrington left him enough freedom to negotiate with Kemal on his own account and war was avoided.

The *Treaty of Sèvres*, August 1920

The treaty originally divided the Ottoman Empire into zones of influence, demilitarised the area around the Straits and Constantinople (Istanbul) and allocated major areas of the Middle East to France and Britain under mandate of the League of Nations, granting independence to Arab kingdoms. The Greeks were given Eastern Macedonia and Smyrna. After the nationalist rising the treaty was substantially amended in 1923 and the new Turkish state maintained control of Anatolia (central Turkey) and there was no further allied occupation.

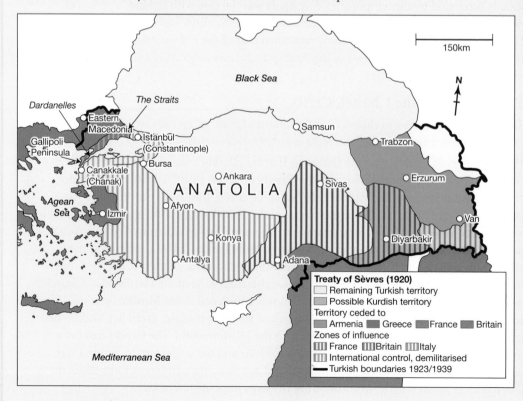

Sources

(A) **Churchill's attitude to Turkish sovereignty in 1920.**

We should make a definite change in our policy in the direction of procuring a real peace with the Moslem world and so relieving ourselves of the disastrous reaction both military and financial to which our anti-Turk policy has exposed us in the Middle East. The restoration of Turkish sovereignty over the Smyrna province is an indispensible step.

Memo, 11 December 1920; quoted in: Rhodes James, R. p. 180.

(B) **By 1922 his attitude had changed as he recalls in *The Aftermath* (1929):**

I found myself ...with a small group of resolute men [Lloyd George, Lord Balfour and Sir Austen Chamberlain] We made common cause. The nation might not support us; they could find others to advise them. The Press might howl, the Allies might bolt. We intended to force the Turk to a negotiated peace before he should set foot in Europe.

From: R.R. James, p. 182.

ACTIVITY

1   How do Sources A and B differ in their attitude to Turkey?

2   What had happened to explain this change? Examine the provenance and the contents to explain this change.

3   What do the sources show about Churchill's personality and his reaction to challenge and crisis?

Conservative MPs had had enough of Lloyd George, and a hostile meeting of Conservative ministers and backbenchers at the Carlton Club brought about his resignation in October 1922. Churchill wrote of the event with engaging good humour, despite his disappointment, saying that he had been in hospital recovering from having his appendix out:

> *'and in the morning when I recovered consciousness I learned that Lloyd George Government had resigned and that I had lost not only my appendix, but my office as Secretary of State for the Dominions and Colonies.'* (R. Rhodes James, 1970, p. 190.)

Churchill changes parties – the situation in 1924

Churchill went on to lose his parliamentary seat at Dundee and failed to gain a seat as a Liberal Free Trader and another seat as a **Conservative 'Constitutionalist'**. He did not return to parliament until 1924 when he stood as a Conservative for Epping.

The years of 1922–24 must have seemed a bleak time for any return to a position of power. The Conservatives, or 'leading beasts' of the Coalition, were not as powerful again. Neither Curzon nor Lloyd George of the Conservative party returned to office.

Conservative 'Constitutionalist'

During the early 1920s, after a collapse in support for the Liberal Party, a number of parliamentary candidates ran for election under a 'constitutionalist' banner. They supported the idea of controlling government authority through existing laws. Many of these candidates who were successful in the 1924 general election went on to join the Conservative Party.

Sources

A In 1924 the writer Philip Guedella published a series of essays on leading figures in the literary and political world. The portrait of Churchill was not flattering.

High up on the short waiting list of England's Mussolinis one finds the name of Winston Spencer Churchill. For those who still remember his father, its presence on that list is a bitter comment on the logical conclusion of Tory Democracy. It is the depressing destiny of almost every Liberal to become a stern unbending Tory. Opening with a fine democratic flourish, Mr Churchill seems to have declined in middle age to becoming a reactionary [someone opposed to change] Mr Churchill is seeing Red. His waking vision is haunted by constant hallucination of sinister little communist figures, lurking in corners with foreign accents and inexhaustible supplies of dangerous pamphlets. That dramatic instinct which is his strength as a historian is a source of weakness as a politician. An anxious public was beginning to worry about economic problems after the war. Mr Churchill answered them with wild-eyed exclamations about Moscow. There was a total loss of contact with reality. One seems to see him, in a wild vision of a distant future, marching black-shirted on Buckingham palace with a victorious army of warlike people.

Guedella, P. (1924) *A Gallery*.

B Churchill visited Italy in 1927. By this time the view of Mussolini had changed. Many people had viewed him as the man who rescued Italy from anarchy during the political turmoil of the 1920's, but by 1927 he had established a virtual dictatorship and had accepted responsibility for the murder of a leading socialist opposition figure in 1924. Churchill was full of praise for the regime, telling journalists in Rome that had he been an Italian he would have been with the fascists in their victorious struggle against Leninism.

For an American newspaper he wrote:

I visited the island of Rhodes, then part of the Turkish Empire. I have just visited it again [Rhodes was under Italian rule after 1920 though it reverted to Greece after the Second World War] under Mussolini's rule. What a change is presented! The dirt, the squalid and bedraggled appearance are gone. Everything is clean and tidy. Every man, however poor, looks proud of himself. Not a beggar is to be seen, and even the cabmen are well shaved. They all seem very happy.

C Mussolini had taken office in October 1922 at the head of a black shirted fascist movement determined to defeat socialism and communism in Italy. That Churchill could be seen, even ironically, as an English Mussolini in waiting was a sad reflection on him. The theme reappeared in 1933 in a cartoon in the *Daily Herald*, the pro-Labour newspaper which saw him as a sort of English Hitler.

> ### ACTIVITY
>
> Look at Sources A, B and C on page 36.
>
> 1 To what extent do these sources suggest that Churchill had become a right-wing extremist?
>
> 2 How similar are they and how far do they support each other?
>
> 3 Compare their origins – why were they written and were they serious and considered judgements?

As it was, there was considerable use of force against Irish nationalists (see pages 31–32), Iraqi tribes (see page 29) and Indian civilians. Yet, for all his advocacy of force, Churchill had reduced Britain's armed forces and set a standard for the continuing reduction (the Ten Year Rule) to a dangerous level. It is not surprising that, when he later advocated massive rearmament, there were some scathing remarks as to whose fault Britain's weak position was.

Consistency was not his strong point:

1. He had gone from a pro-Turk policy to a policy of opposing negotiations with the Turks.

2. He had gone from a hard line in Ireland to negotiating with the Irish nationalists.

3. He had gone from bombing Iraqis to withdrawing troops and giving them *de facto* independence.

4. He had also, of course, gone from being a Liberal to a Conservative (see chapter 1).

What was Churchill's work as the Chancellor of the Exchequer from 1924–29 and what was its impact on the economy?

Churchill was out of politics in the turbulent period between October 1922 and September 1924. He was fortunate that the Conservative leader, Andrew Bonar Law, who replaced Lloyd George as prime minister, fell ill. Law would almost certainly have kept Churchill out of office. Churchill was also fortunate that the Labour government of 1924 was short lived and that the Liberals lost credibility, first by supporting it and then by bringing it down. The swing to the Conservatives helped him and so did the rise of **Stanley Baldwin**. In one of the most extraordinary decisions in modern British political history, Baldwin, castigated as a man of 'the second XI' by Churchill and one of the chief opponents of Lloyd George, invited Churchill to be **Chancellor of the Exchequer** (see also page 14).

Churchill had no economic knowledge or financial experience – his own finances were usually chaotic. When asked whether he wanted to be Chancellor he assumed that Baldwin meant Chancellor of the Duchy of Lancaster, a minor government position. Against all expectations Churchill was once again in the Cabinet and in charge of economic policy in one of the most difficult periods in British economic development.

There seemed to his contemporaries, and to subsequent writers, not one but two Churchills. One was the ideologically-driven extremist; the other was the humorous, wise negotiator and parliamentarian, mindful of political necessity and doing his job as minister in line with government policy. Churchill's work as Chancellor of the Exchequer largely followed the second path. His reaction to the General Strike may well have followed the first, but there is some debate possible here.

Chancellor of the Exchequer

In the inter-war period was more concerned with the Government's finances than the economy as a whole, as is the case in modern times. He oversaw the Treasury and presented annual budgets outlining taxation and expenditure. It was a major office and Churchill, as well as most of his contemporaries, was surprised when in 1924 he was given this appointment as he had little financial experience. His own personal finances remained somewhat chaotic throughout his life.

BIOGRAPHY

Stanley Baldwin (1867–1947)

Baldwin was the son of a successful Worcestershire manufacturer and inherited his father's seat in parliament in 1908 as Conservative member for Bewdley. He served in the government during the First World War and was President of the Board of Trade in 1921. He was a leading figure in bringing down the Lloyd George coalition and became leader of the Conservatives after Bonar Law resigned through ill-health in 1923.

Baldwin was Prime Minister (1924–29) and he joined a coalition government with Labour in 1931 in the National Government, becoming Prime Minister again in 1935–37. He seemed to represent a solid, respectable middle class conservatism and was somewhat removed from Churchill in outlook and personality. The two fell out seriously about India, the King's abdication, and rearmament in the 1930s, but Baldwin supported Churchill in the 1920s. Churchill was particularly critical of Baldwin in his memoirs.

Financial and economic policy – the Gold Standard

Contemporaries debated the wisdom of many aspects of Churchill's budgets. However, the main issue was his 'Return to Gold' in 1925.

One of the key elements of the British pre-war economy was the Gold Standard. It was extremely important for British traders and for financiers that the pound sterling was seen as totally stable. It was one of the great international currencies. Anyone using it had the assurance that it was 'as good as gold' because it had a fixed value in gold. It was one of the foundations of British prestige and economic stability. It had a physical aspect in the use of sovereigns – a real gold coin with 123 grams of 22 carat gold. The coin did not *represent* value, as modern currency does, it had the *actual* value. The Bank of England's notes were based on actual gold reserves.

During the war, international payments and trade were seriously disrupted and Britain was forced to go 'off gold'. Gold coins were replaced by paper money. There had to be less control on money printed. As with all the major currencies, the scarcity of goods and the volume of money in circulation, generated by government spending, all contributed to price rises. The pound lost its pre-war value in terms of what it could buy. The inflation was not as severe as in other countries, but it was marked. Financial wisdom after the war stressed the need to restore the pound to pre-war value. The Bank of England followed generally 'deflationary' policies of restricting money supply, and restricting credit in order that the pound would not continue to lose value. A parliamentary committee appointed by Labour in 1924 reported that every effort should be made to return the pound to the Gold Standard and a fixed value against the US dollar. Gold sovereigns could never return, but it was argued that so much of Britain's wealth came from financial services that a strong and secure pound was a necessity. The problem was that the value would have to be raised against the US dollar. The crucial fact in this complex subject is that, in practice, before 1924 the pound was worth $3.80. After April 1925 it went back to its pre-war value of $4.87. The effect would be to make British exports considerably dearer. The financial banking, and insurance sectors would benefit but export industries would find it more difficult to be competitive.

A major British export was coal and the industry was already suffering from being undercut by German and Polish coal production. A 10 per cent rise in prices would be difficult. It would mean wage cuts as profits fell. However, economists argued that wage cuts could be offset by cheaper imports and that the economy as a whole, apart from the export sector, would benefit from falling inflation and a strong pound.

Britain's most famous economist of the post-war era, **John Maynard Keynes**, was in no doubt that the Return to Gold at such a high exchange rate would be a disaster.

BIOGRAPHY

John Maynard Keynes (1883–1946)

Keynes was one of Cambridge University's most brilliant economic thinkers and his theories have had massive impact on governments. He was critical of the damage the *Treaty of Versailles* had had on the world economy (see his book *Economic Consequences of the Peace 1919*) and was concerned that pinning the pound to gold would reduce exports and restrict spending power in the UK.

He later produced the influential *General Theory of Employment, Interest and Money 1936*, which became a sort of post-war Bible for governments. His reputation suffered from those who favoured monetarism in the 1970s and 1980s and thought that Keynes had encouraged reckless government spending and inflation. The 2009 'Credit Crunch' has revived interest in his recipes for beating depression and unemployment.

Keynes is not such an infallible figure that his criticisms of Churchill's Return to Gold need to be taken as sure and certain proof of the misjudgement of the policy. There were plenty of opinions at the time that supported the measure, especially as sound finance was a major requirement for a British economy that was heavily dependent on 'invisibles' such as insurance, financial services and foreign investment.

ACTIVITY

Interpreting a view

1   Source A is a difficult passage. Using the table below, try to find three consequences of Churchill's policy that Keynes saw as bad for Britain.

Consequence – explain in your own words	Quote briefly from the passage

2   In contrast to Keynes, pick out three advantages which Schuster finds in the policy from Source B.

Advantages – explain in your own words	Quote briefly from the passage

3   Does Source C agree more with Keynes (A) or Schuster (B)? Explain your reasons.

Sources

(A) A leading economist of the times is critical of the 'Return to Gold'.

We know as a fact that the value of sterling money abroad has been raised by 10%. This alteration in the external value of sterling has been the deliberate act of the Chancellor of the Exchequer and the present troubles of our export industries are the inevitable and predictable consequences of it. Thus Mr Churchill's policy of improving the exchange by 10% was sooner or later a policy of reducing everyone's wages by 2s (10p) in the £.

Deflation (a fall in prices) does not reduce wages automatically. It reduces them by causing unemployment. The proper object of dear money (i.e. a rise in interest rates, which accompanied the Return to Gold) is to check an incipient boom. Woe to those whose faith in a strong £ leads them to aggravate a depression.

Keynes, M. *The Economic Consequences of Mr Churchill,* published in 1925; quoted in: Knight.

(B) Churchill's decision has given him a poor reputation as an economist. Yet Keynes was not the only voice. The Churchill archive has an interesting account from May 1925 of another perspective.

At the gathering of the British Bankers Association Sir Felix Schuster, its president, offered on behalf of his fellow bankers warm congratulations to the Chancellor of the Exchequer upon the return to the Gold Standard. It was, he said, a momentous and heroic occasion…an event of the most momentous importance which will affect the welfare of everyone…it would lessen the cost of living and the cost of production, that in the course of time we would again become the principal lenders to foreign countries, greatly to the advantage of our industries. ….The greatest effort on the part of our producers of all classes was needed to overcome the powerful competition which we had to meet owing to changed circumstances all over the world.

The Times, May 1925, Churchill Archive.

(C) Leo Amery, (quoted Rhodes James, p. 226) has this verdict. Amery was a leading Conservative politician of the 1920s and 1930s.

The combination of deflation and free imports which Churchill stubbornly maintained bore its immediate fruit in wage reductions, long drawn industrial conflict and continuous heavy unemployment; its long term results in the conviction of the working class that Socialism alone could provide a remedy for unemployment. The chief author of a great Prime Minister's defeat in 1945 (in which Churchill lost the election, despite having won the war) was the Chancellor of the Exchequer of twenty years before.

My Political Life 1955, Hutchinson (out of print).

Stretch and challenge

Assess the economic reasons for the Return to Gold and assess how justified they were.

1   How would you go about assessing Churchill's policy in returning Britain to the Gold Standard? Note that the pound was based on gold reserves, as was the case before 1914, and not allowed to fluctuate in value.

2   What information would you need to know and what further research would you need to do?

See also the Further reading list on page 51 at the end of this chapter.

Churchill's other work as Chancellor of the Exchequer

Churchill was committed to Free Trade and to reducing expenditure. In this he was in a line of Liberal policy that went back to the previous century. He attempted to help industry by de-rating industrial premises in alliance with his Cabinet colleague Neville Chamberlain, the Minister for Local Government. This involved allowing the owners of factories and workshops freedom from local taxes put on the owners of property – the equivalent to today's council tax. He also found money for Chamberlain's extension of the welfare state in increasing benefits in 1926. The reduction in defence spending, started in 1919, was energetically continued. Churchill came under criticism for the technical quality of his budgets but he delivered them in an energetic and entertaining way, and he remained in the post for the full term of government.

What was his attitude to the General Strike and what were his attempts to end conflict?

Key events of the General Strike

1919	Sankey Commission on Coal recommends 'Nationalisation'
1924	Dawes Plan – German coal mines recover. More competition
1925	Return to Gold. Coal exports dearer
31 July 1925	Red Friday. Other unions back miners' strike and government agrees to 9 months subsidy and a commission of enquiry
March 1926	Samuel Commission reports. Long-term changes but short-term pay cuts. Wages cut. Miners resist and call for TUC help.
1 May 1926	TUC agrees to a General Strike
2 May 1926	Negotiations between TUC and Government break down
3–13 May 1926	General Strike

Churchill's urbane and amusing budget speeches stand in considerable contrast to his impassioned utterances about the General Strike. The origins of the Strike lay in the special position that the coal industry held in Britain. Coal was the basis of the entire industrial revolution and became one of Britain's major export industries. Coal was a vital product that heated homes and powered trains and electricity. The miners were seen by many workers as the heroic element of the industrial working class. Their leaders were among the most militant and they were at the heart of concerted union organisation with the **Triple Alliance**. They had secured special concessions before, and during, the First World War.

Triple Alliance

The Triple Alliance was a grouping of three powerful Trade Unions: The National Union of Mine Workers, The National Union of Railwaymen and the National Transport Workers' Federation, formed in 1914 . They hoped that the solidarity of the workers would give them power. But in 1921 the other unions refused to back the miners. Nevertheless there was more joint action in 1925 when threats from the three unions played a major part in preventing wage cuts for miners. The alliance was not revived after the General Strike.

Sankey Commission (1919)

John Sankey chaired the commission that recommended nationalisation of the coal industry in 1919. Lloyd George rejected its recommendation.

Samuel Commission (1926)

It recognised that the coal industry needed to be reorganised but rejected the suggestion of nationalisation. The report also recommended that the government subsidy should be withdrawn and that the miners' wages should be reduced to save the industry's profitability.

Because of their importance, a special commission (the **Sankey Commission**) reported on the mines in 1919, and the industry, though returned to owners after wartime nationalisation, was given a subsidy to cushion its workers against falling prices and wages because of foreign competition. The railwaymen and transport workers had backed the miners in a show of strength on 'Red Friday' in 1919. Yet the coal industry represented the essential problems that governments faced. Why should the taxpayer subsidise the industry against the realities of the market? The fact was that British coal was overpriced in comparison with Polish and German coal. Its workers were cushioned against wage cuts, which would make the industry more competitive. The government had been intimidated by the miners, but with rising unemployment and the need to cut back spending it would only be a matter of time before there would be a clash. The 'Return to Gold' in 1925 precipitated problems with coal exports. Mine owners wanted to cut wages and make production cheaper. The unions again protested; the miners' union led by A. J. Cook were particularly stubborn and 'Not a minute on the day. Not a penny off the pay'. was a memorable slogan.

However, since 1919 things had changed. In 1926 another commission (the **Samuel Commission**) reported. The subsidy continued, but only for a year. It was a year in which the government was able to make preparations: they drew up plans to stockpile essential supplies and enlist volunteers to run key services. The crisis was predicted to come in 1926 when government aid was withdrawn and employers would impose longer hours and lower wages. With growing unemployment, the other unions were less willing to support the miners and in fact in 1925 had backed down from confrontation. By 1926 there was a sense of guilt and the TUC did support a miners' strike. The Government attempted to negotiate but a decision by the *Daily Mail* printers to refuse to print an anti-union article raised the issue of whether this was a strike over pay and hours or a strike over the power of trade unions. Churchill believed it was the latter. He saw it as a clash between elected government and powerful unions for control of the nation. He believed in the threat from socialism and saw the strike as a showdown for the control of Britain.

Sources

A **The Chancellor of the Exchequer expresses his view about the Strike to the House of Commons.**

The miners of course have a right to strike. But that is an entirely different thing from the concerted, deliberate organized menace of a General Strike in order to compel Parliament to do something which otherwise it would not do. However, when the threat of a national strike is withdrawn, we shall immediately begin, with the utmost care and patience to talk with the unions again and undertake the long and laborious task which has been pursued over these many weeks, of trying to rebuild on solid economic foundations, the prosperity of the coal trade. That is our position.

Churchill, speech, 2 May 1926, Churchill archives.

B **Churchill writing in his official newspaper.**

This is the most destructive industrial disturbance which this country has experienced in generations. The trade unions have become the tool of the Socialist Party and have brought politics into industry in a manner unknown in this country before now. The extremists are able on every occasion to force the moderates into violent action. Moscow influence and Moscow money have droned the voice of reason and good feeling. A General Strike is a challenge to the State, to the Constitution and to the nation. There is no room for compromise.

Churchill, article, *The British Gazette* 4 May 1926.

ACTIVITY

Contrast the tone of Churchill's views in Sources A and B. Consider why these factors might explain any differences:

- Who was Churchill addressing?

- What is the nature of each source (a speech, an article)?

- What had changed between Source A and Source B?

- Compare Churchill's attitude to this crisis with his attitude to the Chanak Crisis.

He became increasingly extreme in Cabinet and was distracted by being given the control of the official government newspaper, *The British Gazette*. Its pages, printed abroad to avoid the Printers' Union refusal to publish it, were full of class hatred and reactionary political rhetoric. Churchill supported the use of emergency powers: deployment of armed forces and the use of volunteers to run essential services. The parallel with the situation in Italy prior to 1922, when strikes led to social unrest and political violence, was plain to see. In that country, large-scale strikes had helped the rise of the dictator Mussolini as he seemed to offer an alternative to socialism. But the heart of neither the Government nor the TUC was in the Strike and it lasted only nine days. Again there were two aspects to Churchill apparent in this episode:

- One was the ideologue committed to rhetoric and extreme solutions.

- The other was the mature politician, ready for compromise and negotiation.

Sources

(A) The following extract is from a newspaper article written by Churchill in 1926.

THE CHALLENGE TO THE CONSTITUTION

...We have been confronted with the most destructive industrial disturbances which this country has experienced for generations. The fact that the Trade Unions have become the tool of the Socialist [Labour] Party has brought politics into industry in a manner hitherto unknown in any country...The extremists are able on nearly every occasion to force the majority into violent courses...the Moscow influence and the Moscow money have been powerful enough to drown the voice of reason and good feeling.

The miners ought not to have allowed themselves to be led by the nose in this shocking manner...There is the greatest difference between an industrial dispute, however lamentable [unfortunate], and a general strike. An industrial dispute about wages, hours, conditions etc., in a particular industry ought to be settled in a spirit of compromise, with give and take on both sides...But a general strike is a challenge to the State, to the Constitution and to the nation. Here is no room for compromise.

Extracts from an article by Churchill for the *West Essex Constitutionalist*, December 1926 (Churchill Press Cuttings, CHPC 7). Reproduced by permission of Curtis Brown Ltd and the University of Southampton. Copyright: Winston S. Churchill 1999.

(B) A gardener, the Prime Minister Baldwin waters a rock garden. Note who flourishes – the flowers 'Goodwills' are Baldwin himself, the Prime Minister (top flower) Churchill (below on the left) and Churchill's Cabinet ally, Lord Birkenhead, then Secretary of State for India. The miners' leader, A.J. Cook, is on a barren leafless plant. The employers' representative and coal owner Sir Evan Williams is shown amid ruins and there are references to ruined industry and starvation wages. The mine owners are shown as cactuses. (Think why – what characteristics do cactuses have?)

'The Political Flower show: Rock garden section' by David Low which appeared in *The Star*, Friday 28 May 1926.

ACTIVITY

1   Summarise the argument in Source A. What does it tell you about Churchill's attitude to the strike?
    a   Read the passage aloud and judge the tone in which was it written.
    b   What statements are factual?
    c   What statements are unfounded opinion?

2   Source B appeared after the Strike and takes a different view. It is a complex cartoon. Try to interpret it and to assess where its sympathies lie.

3   Compare both these sources as evidence for the strike:
    ■ Look first of all at their nature.
    ■ Compare where they appeared.
    ■ Compare when they appeared.
    ■ Compare who wrote them.
    ■ Compare why they were produced.
    ■ Which has the greater value for understanding attitudes to the Strike?
    ■ Compare their reliability – do they give a fair portrayal of the situation?

ANALYSIS

From the complex story of the General Strike, there are certain points which are worth considering:

1. The theory of syndicalism, of the political power of General Strikes, had little appeal for the TUC leadership who were more concerned with practical problems of supporting members in times of unemployment, falling wages and reduced trade. Men like Walter Citrine, the TUC general secretary, were not radical socialists and did not want to challenge the elected government through industrial action.

2. The huge prestige of the miners, and the feeling of guilt by the Triple Alliance in not helping them in 1925 on the so-called **Black Friday**, made it difficult for the TUC to stand back and refuse support in 1926 when the miners went on strike against lower wages and longer hours. However, this was different from using the miners as an excuse to exercise political power.

3. Negotiations between the TUC and the Government had been taking place right up to the outbreak of the Strike. What ruined these talks was the decision by the printers of the *Daily Mail* to refuse to print an anti-strike article. To the government this seemed as if press freedom was being threatened and that there was indeed a constitutional issue.

4. The TUC did not have extensive plans for co-ordinated action and did not initially call out all workers. The preparation had been much greater on the Government side and, during the year in which they had subsidised the mines, there had been preparation for the maintenance of essential supplies.

5. Despite incidents of violence there was no social revolt. It is possible to underplay the disruption. There were 1,389 prosecutions for violence. Had the strike gone on longer then a more serious social crisis could well have followed. But the point is that the TUC did not want this. The very shortness of the strike and the willingness of the TUC to end it to avoid the danger of conflict indicated that this was not the showdown that had been predicted since pre-war industrial unrest had so worried governments. The whole economic situation, with the decline of Britain's staple industries – coal, shipbuilding, and engineering – had made union power much less great. Realistic trade unionists were aware of the changes and few thought that the strike would topple the state. It has been seen as 'the Strike that no one wanted'.

'Black Friday

On 1 April 1921 there was a miners' strike because the miners faced pay cuts. The miners looked to the Triple Alliance to support them, but the National Union of Railwaymen and the Transport and General Workers Union withdrew from the strike on 15 April 1921, leaving the miners to be defeated in July. This date was known as 'Black Friday'.

Churchill's view on the strike

Churchill saw the General Strike as a struggle between the traditional values of democracy and constitutional government on the one hand and the power of labour on the other. The strike threatened Britain's power and he saw it in the context of the threat from communism. A tendency to see complex issues in simple terms characterised many of his public utterances and fuelled his support for a display of military power to overawe the strikers. Baldwin allowed him an outlet by making him editor of the propaganda paper *The British Gazette*. It was widely circulated, reaching a peak of 2,200,000 by 12 May 1926.

The British Gazette is referred often in extract, but the whole issue makes interesting reading. There is some international news, some cricket commentary and Churchill's statements do not dominate as much as might be expected.

An editorial by the former foreign secretary Sir Edward Grey argued that the real issue was not miners' wages but '*whether democracy is to be preserved in Britain or whether the country could fall into Fascism or Communism*' from the 10 May 1926. With hindsight we know that this did not happen, but to people in 1926 this could not be taken for granted. The tone of Gray's article is measured in a way that Churchill's own contributions were not.

The general arguments of *The British Gazette* under Churchill's editorship were:

- that the strike was Bolshevik inspired;
- that resistance to the strike was justified however violent;
- that Labour Party leaders were wild socialists and using the strike for political purposes;
- that strike leaders should be held financially responsible for losses in the strike.

Churchill's critics

The more responsible newspaper owners were in heated conflict with Churchill over the paper. The rival Trade Union newspaper, *The British Worker*, was also bitterly critical. Lloyd George described the *Gazette* as '*an indiscretion, clothed in the tawdry garb of third rate journalism*'. What made it worse was that it was the work of a very senior government minister in his 50s, not a young hothead.

ACTIVITY

1. How useful is this Source for understanding Churchill's role in the General Strike?

2. How could your own knowledge help you assess this Source?

Source

The British Worker, 10 May 1926

The idea of representing a strike which arose entirely out of industrial conditions and had entirely industrial aims as a revolutionary movement was mainly Mr.Churchill's. It is a melodramatic 'stunt' on Sydney Street lines...The nation has kept its head in spite of the alarming tricks played upon it. Mr. Churchill has failed again, and everybody knows it.

From: *The British Worker*, a newspaper produced by the TUC during the Strike.

Conciliation

When the Strike ended, Churchill showed his skill of conciliation. He had considerable sympathies for the hardships of the miners, who remained on Strike until forced back to work by sheer need in the autumn. He attempted to work with the mine owners to get some compromise, but could get nowhere. He supported the *Trade Disputes Act* which made sympathetic strikes illegal but was unhappy about the treatment of the miners. Churchill persuaded the Labour leader Ramsay MacDonald to negotiate on his behalf with the ministers to start negotiations with the owners. The miners agreed to consider wage cuts but wanted to negotiate on a national not a regional basis. Churchill used all his negotiating skills to persuade the mine owners, and their dogged representative Sir Evan Williams, to agree. Churchill prepared to use legislation to get a settlement which would lay down hours and conditions, but Baldwin refused. Churchill pressed for an imposed settlement to help the miners get back to work. His energy and willingness to impose solutions by compulsion were here in the interests of the workers, but again were too forcefully put to be persuasive.

Sources

(A) **From the *New Statesman*, a political magazine sympathetic to the left, 22 May, 1926.**

The Prime Minister proposed to go ahead with negotiations and avert the Strike, he was faced with the immediate resignation of his colleagues – Churchill, Neville Chamberlain, Bridgeman, Amery, Joynson-Hicks and Cunliffe-Lister. So he gave way…Mr Churchill was the villain of the piece. He is reported to have remarked that he thought "a little blood-letting" would be all to the good.

We do not know whether there is anyone left who still honestly believed that the Strike was a "revolutionary" attempt to subvert the British Constitution. It was a strike in furtherance of a trade dispute and nothing more.

Ought we to thank Mr Churchill or ought we to hang him on a lamp-post? It would be best that he should be hanged.

The Churchill Archive.

(B) **Churchill was stung and he wrote to the Attorney General, Sir Douglas Hogg on 26 May:**

My dear Hogg

I wish you would look at the enclosed [New Statesman] article [see Source A above]

It is wholly untrue and unfounded. As you will know, my arguments in Cabinet were all directed to keeping the Military out of the business [of the Strike] and to using, even at great expense, very large numbers of citizens unarmed. I am sure I never used any language not entirely consistent with this. The charge seems to be a gross libel on a minister in the execution of his duty. I would expect a full apology and for them to pay £1000 to some charity.

The Churchill Archive.

(C) **31 August, 1926. Churchill spoke in the House of Commons about the deadlock between the miners and the coal owners.**

Look at the year we have just passed through, an utterly wasted year. The Trade Union masses are lamentably impoverished, Business is all disorganised. All this year has been squandered in what is the most melancholy and at the same time most ignominious breakdown of British common sense.

But it is still not too late if we proceed together in a sincere spirit, if we remember that we all have to dwell together in this small island of which it is our bounden duty, whatever our political opinions, to make the best and not, as we are now doing make the worst.

Quoted in Gilbert, *Winston S. Churchill, Volume 5*, p. 185–86.

(D) **A letter in the Churchill Archive from the MP for Bristol dated 11 November 1926.**

Dear Winston

I must send you a piece of news that has come to me through my agent in Bristol. He attended an open-air Socialist meeting where the coal question was being discussed and the speaker, by no means an irresponsible person, having twice been a Labour Parliamentary candidate, told his audience that if only the matter [of settling the dispute between Miners and Coal owners after the General Strike] had been left in your hands some weeks ago it would have been settled and the men [the miners] would have had a square deal. I think this is good hearing from such a source and is likely to be an indication of a much wider and similar feeling in the country.

The Churchill Archive.

What were the reasons for his being out of office after 1929?

What was Churchill's position by 1929 and what were his prospects? He had taken a huge amount of criticism:

- Financial experts had substantially criticised his budgets.
- Liberals had seen him as a renegade.
- *The British Gazette* had been seen as extreme and had alienated the unions and Labour.
- The armed services were unhappy about the severe cuts in expenditure.
- The continuing unemployment was blamed on the return to the Gold Standard.

On the positive side,

- Churchill's stand for Constitutional government was seen as heroic by some.
- He had supported useful social reforms such as the extension of pensions and National Insurance in 1929 and the reforms in the rating of industry by local government.
- He was a master of parliamentary repartee and often disarmed critics by humour and self-deprecation.

The Times put it well in 1925:

> '*Except in a class war, Mr Churchill could never lead England, but his immense intellectual fertility (inventiveness) and vigour, his ability to think in terms of great issues, the reach, variety and weight of his debating and oratorical gifts make him the ideal complement to the deeper moral power of his leader [Baldwin].*' (Quoted in Pelling, p. 344, 1999.)

In their opinion, Churchill provided the colour and delight in ideas that the duller Baldwin lacked.

However this was probably not a good basis for a lasting relationship. From 1929 Churchill, now in his mid-50s, appeared to be increasingly out of touch with his party and the public on some vital issues. He was out of government for ten years and many would agree with *The Times* in thinking that he 'could never lead England'. Looked at from the perspective of 1929, Churchill's achievements had not been great over the previous twenty years. His wartime judgements had brought about a considerable amount of criticism. His post-war attitudes to communism were seen as unrealistic. His economic and financial policies were not generally admired and the continuing economic problems made the 'Return to Gold' seem more misguided than it did in 1925. He was not made part of the National government that was formed in 1931, as this was a government of moderate 'middle of the road' political figures. His campaign against reform in India marked him out as an opponent to a cross-party consensus policy of moderate change and made him appear out of touch with modern politics. In many ways this was very unfair. Churchill had worked for reconciliation after the General Strike and his views on the relationship between workers and employers were not reactionary. He had an instinctive sympathy with the working class that his earlier record as a social reformer showed. And whilst his outlook towards working people was somewhat romanticised, framed as it was through his upper-class upbringing, it was far removed from the selfish and limited outlook of many mine owners and exploitative employers. He brought both a freshness of vision and a sense of humanity to political life which were valuable assets. Despite all this he was still not popular amongst many sections of society.

Neither was he popular with the party leaders. After 1931 they, together with the influential **Neville Chamberlain** with whom Churchill had clashed on a number of issues, were dominant and kept Churchill away from the centre of power. Both his own misjudgements and the ill feeling he had generated kept him in the 'wilderness' until 1939.

BIOGRAPHY

Neville Chamberlain (1869–1940)

Chamberlain was the son of a famous politician, Joseph Chamberlain, and was educated at Rugby and Mason College, Birmingham. He served as Lord Mayor of Birmingham in 1915–16 and was brought into the wartime effort as director general of National Service at the end of 1916. His tenure was brief, marked by increasing clashes with Lloyd George. In 1918 he was elected Conservative MP for Birmingham Ladywood. He entered government following the collapse of the Lloyd George coalition in 1922, and was Minister of Health in March 1923 and then, in August, Chancellor of the Exchequer, serving until the party went out of office. On the party's return to power in November 1924, he was again Minister of Health, introducing important measures of social reform. He was appointed Chancellor of the Exchequer in November 1931, and Prime Minister in 1937. He mistakenly believed he could negotiate successfully with Hitler, and pursued a policy of appeasement. He also increased British rearmament. He took no action to stop German expansion in Austria and agreed to allow Germany to have German-speaking areas of Czechoslovakia at the Munich Conference in 1938. When Hitler broke the agreement and occupied Czech areas, Chamberlain gave a guarantee to Poland and in September 1939 Britain went to war with Germany when Hitler invaded that country, and Chamberlain became a wartime leader. He invited Churchill into the Cabinet. In 1940, with the failure of the Norwegian campaign, Conservatives voted against the government and the government's majority fell from its normal 200 to 80. Chamberlain submitted his resignation as Prime Minister. He died six months after leaving Downing Street.

The major issues were domestic; the emphasis was on national consensus and on avoiding international and imperial conflicts. This was not a promising time for someone of Churchill's temperament. His attitudes to India and to royal affairs made an existing situation worse.

Conclusion

During this survey of Churchill's career from 1920–29 there have been a number of activities based on comparing the use of source material. When comparing sources it is important to consider what they say, what evidence they bring to answering the question, and to make a judgement.

The key issue for this chapter is: *How and why did Churchill react to the problems of post-war Britain*? During the period of 1918–29 there were a number of apparent inconsistencies in both Churchill's character and his approach to issues. On the other hand, in his way, he was faithful to some central questions. For example, the need to preserve the social order and to defend British interests. Whenever the legitimate authority was threatened, he was quick to turn to tough solutions. So when the pre-war Ulster Unionists threatened to disrupt the Liberals' Home Rule reform, he favoured military action. He also supported the use of force against Irish nationalists in 1918 because they would not wait for reform in Ireland but set up their own government. He favoured a hard-line against Russian Bolsheviks because they threatened the social order. Unrest in the British Empire was to be suppressed for similar reason and union power at home, which seemed to stand against elected constitutional government, was similarly to be overawed by force. Later he was to oppose Indian nationalism and Hitler's expansion for similar reasons – they threatened the existing order. At the heart of Churchill's outlook was the need to preserve a world order in which Britain and its Empire played a leading role. Threats to that order whether from Hitler's Germany, whether from rebellious Irishmen or protesting Indians, whether from Bolshevik Russians or British trade unions had to be met with the utmost energy and determination.

The interesting aspect of the key issue, and the skill of comparing sources, is being able to use that skill to weigh Churchill's character and central beliefs against his apparent inconsistencies. Why did he shift so rapidly from one party to another? Why did he go from one position on the General Strike to another? If you can use this chapter to develop your own theory as to what the essential elements of Churchill's personality were, then you can test this out against his future actions. At this stage you will be making only provisional judgements.

Exam Café *At this point, it would be useful to undertake an audit to see what skills you are comfortable with and what you need more support in developing. Go to pages 164-73 of the Exam Café and complete the activities there.*

ANSWER TO ACTIVITY

See page 27

A is from Hitler's *Mein Kampf* (My Struggle) and B from Churchill's *The Aftermath*.

Bibliography

Keynes, J. M. (1925) *The Economic Consequences of Mr Churchill,* Hogarth.

Amery, Leo (quoted Rhodes James 226 *My Political Life 1955,* Hutchinson.

Best, G. (2002) *Churchill: A Study in Greatness,* pp. 91, 92. Penguin.

Callwell, C. E. Major General (1927) *Field Marshal Sir Henry Wilson: His Life and Diaries,* Cassell.

Charmley, J. (1993) *Churchill: The End of Glory*, pp. 161, 227. Sceptre.

Gilbert, M. (1976) *Winston S. Churchill,* Volume 5, p. 185–56. Heinemann.

Guedalla, P. (1924) *A Gallery*, p. 243. Constable.

Hickman, T. (2008) *Churchill's Bodyguard – The Authorised Biography of Walter H. Thompson.* Headline.

Holmes, R. (2005) *In the Footsteps of Churchill*, p. 311. BBC.

Knight, N. (2008) *Churchill: The Greatest Briton Unmasked*, David and Charles.

Lloyd George, D (1938) *The Truth about the Peace Treaties* Vol 1, p. 324–25. Gollancz.

Pelling, H. (1999) *Winston Churchill*, p. 344. Wordsworth Editions.

Ponting, C. (1994) *Churchill*, pp. 208, 230, 245, 258. Sinclair-Stevenson.

Rhodes James, R. (1970) *Churchill: A Study in Failure*, pp. 156, 158, 180, 190. Penguin.

Thompson, M. (1965) *The Life and Times of Winston Churchill,* p.199. Odhams.

Further reading

Bordo, M.D. (2008) Gold Standard. *The Concise Encyclopedia of Economics.* http://www.econlib.org/library/Enc/GoldStandard.html.

Knight, N. (2008) *Churchill: The Greatest Briton Unmasked*, Ch 2. David and Charles.

Mathias, P., Pollard, S. (eds) (1989) *The Cambridge Economic History of Europe,* Volume. 8: *The Industrial Economies: The Development of Economic and Social Policies.* Cambridge University Press, Cambridge.

Moggridge, D. (1962) *Return to Gold, 1925: The Formation of Economic Policy and Its Critics*, Occasional papers, 19. University of Cambridge, Dept. of Applied Economics. Cambridge University Press.

Pollard, S. (ed) (1970) *The Gold Standard and Employment Policy Between the Wars.* Methuen.

In this chapter, Churchill's views about the Empire and India and the clash this caused with his own party will be explored. The main elements of the specification content dealt with relate to the key issue of 'What were Churchill's views about Imperial and Foreign Policy from 1930 to 1939'. The episode of the abdication of Edward VIII and its importance to Churchill's career will also be discussed. His attitudes to India and the abdication crisis were both very important in terms of how seriously his views were taken regarding foreign policy, for instance, German rearmament. Also discussed will be the stance Churchill took towards British rearmament, the growing power of Germany from 1933 and his opposition to appeasement.

> ### Key Questions
>
> **Areas of study include:**
>
> 1   How did Churchill's views on India (and Empire) clash with those of his own party and the government?
>
> 2   What was Churchill's attitude towards rearmament and what were his reasons for opposing appeasement?
>
> 3   What was Churchill's position between 1933 and 1938?
>
> 4   How justified were Churchill's views?

Building on the skills in Chapter 2, there will be more opportunites for extended critical use of sources. Activities are designed to develop the skills of *interpreting* and *assessing* sources, as well as comparing them, whilst using knowledge of the period as a whole.

How did Churchill's views on India (and Empire) clash with those of his own party and the government?

Round Table Conference

The idea of all parties sitting round a table to gain agreement on major issues. The term implied that there would be the opportunity to share views and that the participants would be equally able to express their ideas as opposed to a more confrontational lay out when participants talked from either side of a table.

Churchill's attitude to proposals to introduce reforms into India led to a serious rift with Baldwin and the Conservative leadership. Churchill disliked a proposal from the Viceroy Lord Irwin (later Lord Halifax), a former Conservative minister. This proposed that there should be a **Round Table Conference** to discuss giving India the status of a Dominion within the Empire, that is allowing it to govern itself along the lines of the self-governing 'white' Dominions of Australia, Canada, South Africa and New Zealand. This followed a parliamentary report of a committee under Sir John Simon and was in line with the constitutional reforms of 1909 and 1919, which had introduced a measure of self-government in India. Since then, there had been an active political movement for greater independence led by the Indian Congress Party and its very special leader **Mahatma Gandhi** and his allies – the Nehru family.

BIOGRAPHY

Mahatma Gandhi (1869–1948)

Gandhi was the leader of the Indian nationalist movement against British rule. He adopted a policy of non-violent protest. He was known as 'Mahatma' (Great Soul). Churchill referred to him as 'a half-naked fakir' and bitterly opposed his nationalist ideas.

Mohandas Gandhi was born in 1869 in Gujarat. After university, he went to London to train as a barrister. He returned to India in 1891 and in 1893 went to work as a lawyer in South Africa. He took up the cause of exploited Indian immigrants and became a political activist. He was arrested and imprisoned and developed the idea of *satyagraha* ('devotion to truth'), a new non-violent way to redress wrongs. Gandhi returned to India in 1914. He led protests against British attempts to repress nationalism. When the British fired on protestors at Amritsar in 1919, his support increased and he led a mass movement. The old Indian National Congress party was transformed and he led mass marches and boycotts of British goods. In 1922, Gandhi himself was sentenced to six years of imprisonment. He was released after two years. In 1930, Gandhi began a new campaign of civil disobedience in protest at a tax on salt, leading thousands on a 'March to the Sea' to avoid the tax. In 1931, Gandhi attended the Round Table Conference in London in 1931, as the sole representative of the Indian National Congress. Gandhi was part of the 'Quit India' campaign during the war. He took part in the negotiations which led to the partition of India into a largely Muslim Pakistan and a largely Hindu India in 1947, but was deeply opposed to the split and had hoped for unity. He was killed by a Hindu fanatic in 1948.

British rule in India began in the 18th century; first by the East India Company and then, after violent disturbances in 1857, by the British Government directly. In 1876 Queen Victoria had been declared the Empress of India. As Empress she ruled over nominally independent princely states, which were in fact ruled by Britain and were areas of direct British rule. India was a country of 350 million people and was seen as 'the jewel in the Crown' of Britain's Empire. However, British rule was challenged by an independence movement who protested peacefully but practised effective disturbance by civil disobedience. Its leader Ghandi was seen as a saint by some but Churchill detested him and the whole idea of making any concessions to India, or having the Round Table Conference at all. From September 1930 Churchill became the figurehead of a very determined opposition to change in India. In December 1930 Churchill spoke at a meeting of **The Indian Empire Society**, a reactionary imperialist organisation set up to oppose reform.

The Indian Empire Society

This was a lobbying organisation set up by Sir Michael O'Dwyer and Lord Sydenham to protect the British Raj or rule in India and oppose change. Its members were mostly administrators and judges who had worked in India. Sir Charles Oman, a distinguished historian was a member. It was highly unrepresentative of opinion within Britain or India by 1930 and Churchill was unwise to associate himself with it by speaking at some of its meetings.

India – consensus politics

Some issues in British politics did not and do not become matters of party debate but political parties try to work together to get the best policy. India was one of these issues and Churchill, by not accepting this middle ground, made himself look out of touch with mainstream politics.

Baldwin, as Conservative leader, the Liberals and the Labour government had taken a joint stand in supporting discussions, so Churchill was taking on the entire British political establishment. The Viceroy, Lord Irwin, negotiated directly with Ghandi, who had been arrested for civil disobedience, and released him to attend the Round Table Conference in 1931. This horrified Churchill. The issue came up again in 1933 when a white paper, which emerged from the discussions of 1931, proposed an elected federal government for India. Churchill had the support of two major newspapers, the *Daily Mail* and *The Morning Post* and founded the India Defence League. However, though it gained the support of 57 Conservative MPs, there was little popular enthusiasm. Churchill tried to persuade the Lancashire public that more Indian independence would lead to India imposing restrictions on Lancashire cotton imports, but this did not convince. In 1935, **Randolph Churchill** stood, against his father's wishes, as an independent Conservative on the India platform in a by-election, but he split the Conservative vote and the Labour candidate was elected. This increased Churchill's unpopularity in the party and he found little mass-following for a campaign which was not very effective and seemed to be an outdated defence of old-fashioned empire.

BIOGRAPHY

Randolph Churchill (1911–68)

Randolph was educated at Eton and Oxford. He worked as a journalist and writer but had stormy relations with his father and had a reputation as a heavy drinker and a self-opinionated and overbearing caricature of Winston. He attempted to enter parliament in 1935 and failed. He did serve as an MP 1940– 45 but was also a serving officer, working with the SAS in Libya. He also went on a military and diplomatic mission to Yugoslavia in 1944 as part of the British support for the Partisans. He began a large-scale biography of his father which was continued by the historian Martin Gilbert.

The problem lay with the alternatives. Either the government had to offer concessions or it had to rely on force with massive repression of a popular and well-organised protest movement in India. In 1935 the *Government of India Act* conceded a federal government where the Congress party was able to manage internal policy, though India remained under British control in all vital aspects.

Government of India Act, 1935

This provided for establishment of an India Federation. It separated Burma from India and set up rival assemblies which were elected on a much wider franchise than previously. Direct elections were introduced for the first time. The right to vote was increased from seven million to thirty-five million. There were more Indian representatives in the governments of the states but the Governors appointed by Britain kept some powers. Britain kept overall control and did not consult the Indians in 1939 when war was declared. A federation of semi-autonomous states and princely states was planned but did not happen because the princes objected. Elections took place in 1937 and Congress did form local governments until the war.

India after 1939

After 1935, India concerned Churchill less than the issue of German rearmament, but it became an issue again when he became Prime Minister in 1940. He was not interested in any plans for change in India, or indeed anywhere else in the Empire. His Colonial Secretaries, Lord Lloyd (to 1942), and Oliver Stanley thereafter, shared his conservatism. The declarations of belief in freedom, such as the *Atlantic Charter*, were seen as essentially white freedom by Churchill. The constitutional experiment in India had not been very extensive. Under the 1935 *Government of India Act* only eight provinces had any form of local self-government, and these were dominated by the Congress party. Indian political leaders were not consulted when the Viceroy declared war on India's behalf in 1939. The Cabinet rejected Congress demands for a **constitution** for India after the war and the congress party resigned from all the provisional governments, effectively ending the power sharing of 1935. Churchill opposed any concessions or any 'running about after Ghandi' to negotiate. Though he agreed to Indian representation on a national defence committee, Churchill thought that self-government would mean the end of Indian troops fighting for the Empire.

Constitution

This is a fixed set of rules by which a country is run. The demand was for Indian self-government as an independent state.

***Atlantic Charter*, 1941 (see Chapter 5 pages 130–131)**

This was drawn up at the first of the Churchill-Roosevelt wartime meetings (9–12 August 1941) during the Second World War.

BIOGRAPHY

Clement Attlee (1883–1967)

Attlee was British Prime Minister 1945–51; then made an Earl in 1955. Clement Attlee's government (1945–51) is widely regarded as Labour's most successful government. The administration decisively shaped post-war Britain, establishing the policies for full employment, the welfare state, mixed economy, and passage from the British Empire to the British Commonwealth.

The Cripps Mission

However, with the collapse of British power in Malaya and with Japan threatening India in 1942, there had to be concessions. **Clement Attlee**, the Labour Party's leader who had become deputy Prime Minister in March 1942, proposed a post-war constitution to stop a revolt in India and to please America.

Churchill reluctantly agreed to a leading Labour figure, Sir Stafford Cripps, going to India in April 1942 to discuss giving control over most of the administration of India to the Indians. Churchill did not support Cripps's views, did not want the Viceroy controlled and got the Cabinet to reject an agreement that Cripps had negotiated about Indian control of defence. The consequent failure of the mission led to Congress taking up a 'Quit India' campaign. In August 1942 the Congress party was made illegal and its leaders, including Gandhi, arrested. There was unrest on a large scale and a return to civil disobedience which required a substantial British military presence. Churchill's view was that there should be:

> 'No apology, no quitting, no idea of weakening or scuttling.'
> (Conversation with Sir A. R. Mundaliar, quoted Ponting: p. 698.)

The Bengal Famine

The most controversial episode was the terrible famine in Bengal in 1942–43 which claimed three million lives. Wavell, the Viceroy and Leo Amery the Secretary of State for India were critical of the Churchill government's failure to send enough relief. There is evidence of racial contempt for Indians on Churchill's part but also a desire to avoid any religious strife between the followers of the two largest faiths in India, Islam and Hinduism. Churchills views on Empire were, at best, old-fashioned and he still believed that it was the 'white man's burden' to help India and its people. He did not believe that the Indians could be trusted to rule themselves without serious problems occurring. (see sources A and B).

Sources

A **Wavell's Diary October 1943. Lord Wavell had been appointed Viceroy of India and recorded his meeting with Churchill and the government.**

October 7

Cabinet at 6 pm...Spinelessness, lack of interest, opportunism. PM waved the bogey of Gandhi at everyone. PM worked himself up to a tirade against Congress and all its works and digressed into the Indian army becoming politically minded and anti-British. The more I see of politicians, the less I respect them; is this a contemptible Cabinet?

October 8

Winston saw me alone. He produced a directive which was utterly meaningless, e.g. it exhorted me to get on with the war, to improve the lot of the Indians, to make peace between Hindu and Muslim. Amery [Leo Amery the Colonial Secretary] *on reading it said 'you are wafted to India on a wave of hot air'. PM was menacing and unpleasant when I saw him and indicated that only over his dead body would any approach to Gandhi take place. He fears a split in the Conservative party and trouble in parliament over any political advance in India.'*

Wavell's Diary, October 1943. p. 22. Oxford University Press.

B **Amery's diary 10 November 1943, Churchill Archive.**

Cabinet, at which I brought up again my earnest demand for more shipping [to take food to India]. *I did not press for India's demand for 50,000 tons a month for twelve months, but concentrated on asking for 150,000 tons over December* [in the light of the demands for shipping for Italy] *January and February. Winston, after a preliminary flourish on Indians breeding like rabbits and being paid a million a day for doing nothing, asked Leathers* [the minister in charge of shipping] *for his view. He said he could manage 50,000 tons in January and February* [1944]. *Winston agreed with this and I had to be content. I raised a point that Canada had telegraphed to say a ship was ready to load on the 12th and they proposed to fill it with wheat* [for India], *Leathers and Winston were vehement against this.*

C A modern historian comments on Churchill and India.

Churchill proved callously indifferent to the famine. Since Gandhi's fast, his mood about India had progressively darkened. Despite what he imagined as Gandhi's crushing defeat, the British were left with the same problems as before. In May Churchill ripped into Amery accusing him of creating a modern Frankenstein by putting modern weapons in the hands of 'sepoys' [a term for Indian soldiers]. *Amery noticed that he was almost quite childish about it.*

He proved just as irrational about the famine issue: he was resolutely opposed to any food shipments. Ships were needed for the landings in Italy. Sending food to India would mean a loss of valuable transport. Besides, Churchill felt it would do no good; famines or no famines, Indians will 'breed like rabbits' Amery remembered. 'Naturally I lost patience and couldn't help telling him that I couldn't see much difference between his outlook and Hitler's which annoyed him not a little.'

Amery prevailed on him to send some relief, but only a quarter of what was needed was sent.

Herman, A. (2008) *Gandhi and Churchill: The Epic Rivalry That Destroyed an Empire and Forged Our Age*, p. 513.

ACTIVITY

1   Compare Sources A and B (page 56) as evidence for Churchill's attitude to India

2   To what extent is the secondary source C above believable in the light of your own knowledge and your study of other sources?

Was Churchill right?

He did understand the problems of division between Hindu and Muslim and pointed to the dangers of conflict if India were given independence. The massacres that took place in 1947 when Indian independence was granted and millions were killed in religious riots show that his fears were justified. Few denied the problems of self-government in such a varied area with extremes of **caste**, poverty and different traditions. Yet India sustained democratic government after 1947; it had a highly-educated middle class capable of rule. On the other hand there was no real justification for ignoring the demands of the nationalists and relying on increasing repression. The fact that the three parties adopted a non-partisan approach was an indication that the consensus of opinion was for moderate reform. Indian forces were loyal in the Second World War and their contribution in the First World War surely deserved recognition. Baldwin thought that Churchill was motivated by nostalgia rather than reason. It could be argued that his speeches were too extreme to meet the mood of the times and his impatience alienated many MPs.

Caste

A position in Indian society inherited from Hindu parents at birth and from which there is no transfer throughout life. There are four major caste groups (Varnas) characterised by social function: Brahmins as educators, Kshatriyas as warriors, Vaishyas as merchants, and Shudras as labourers. Tasks perceived as involving pollution were undertaken by the *Avarna*, or 'Untouchables'.

Source

A An extract from *Time Magazine*, 31 March 1931.

Some interpretation was necessary in London last week when the Conservative Party Committee on India announced that Conservative Party Leader Stanley Baldwin had decided as follows:

"The party cannot participate in any further round table sessions in India."

Strictly interpreted, this sentence is nonsense. The entire British press assumed that by "in India" he meant "on India" which would make sense, and mean that the Conservative Party had resolved to have no more truck with half-naked St. Gandhi and his crew.

This is exactly the course which Winston ("Winnie") Churchill, ambitious rival of Mr. Baldwin for leadership, has been urging upon the Party. Headlines blazed "Baldwin Surrenders to Churchill." A new page of British party history seemed about to turn.

Oddly enough, however, Mr. Baldwin had meant by "in" precisely "in," though that was (strictly) nonsense. Not being strict Mr. Baldwin had meant something perfectly sensible, something about like this:

"The Conservative Party cannot participate in any further negotiations on Indian soil, but will participate if another round table conference be held in London."

That anyone should have misinterpreted his words seemed to Mr. Baldwin wilful, diabolic. Like a large, well-meaning cow stung by a hornet, he charged into the House of Commons, defied Mr. Churchill to wrest the party leadership from him, made a great speech, an English speech, a speech to wring tears from honest eyes.

"If there are those," cried Stanley Baldwin, and looked Winston Churchill in the eye, "if there are those who, if they were in the majority in our party, would approach this question in a niggling, grudging spirit—who would have had forced out of their reluctant hands one concession after another—for God's sake let them choose another man to lead them! But, if they are in a minority, let them refrain from throwing difficulties in the way of those who have undertaken an almost superhuman task on the successful accomplishment of which depends the prosperity of the British Empire."

At this almost the whole House of Commons cheered—Laborites, Liberals and most Conservatives—the basic weakness of Mr. Churchill being apparent.

"I have not surrendered!" cried Mr. Baldwin, turning again upon Mr. Churchill. "I have not surrendered to my Right Honorable Friend!" (i.e. Churchill).

Shrill with emotion came the cry of Lady Astor, "God forbid that you should!" (Tears).

Shadow Cabinet

This is the term given to the opposition members who take on the job of being the 'opposite numbers' of members of their government in order to criticise their policies. For example, shadow foreign secretary watches the policies of the real foreign secretary and leads debates on foreign policy for the opposition.

ACTIVITY

1. What does Source A show about what was thought of Churchill's motives for criticising Baldwin over India?

2. What does it show about Churchill's support in the House of Commons and his wisdom in pursuing the India issue?

3. What does it show about Baldwin's ability to meet Churchill's criticisms?

Churchill had lost heavily in the economic crash after 1929. He had to do a great deal of writing and lecturing to keep up the family estate at Chartwell. He was not a strong team player in the **shadow Cabinet** (or Business Committee as it was known at that time). He was certainly not helped when a National government was formed after Labour was split over measures to deal with the financial and economic crisis in September 1931. The joint ministry formed by Conservatives, Labour and Liberals was not the place for Churchill and he was offered no post and hence no salary. Distracted by having to be extremely busy, his judgement over India may have let him down. By the time of the war, his attitudes had hardened and his lack of sympathy with reform contrasted with the grand statements about a war for freedom. His views on Indians seem unacceptable when Britain was at war with a racist regime and the Bengal Famine was remembered with bitterness for years afterwards in India, and helped to turn opinion against the Raj.

Sources

(A) **Churchill opposes the *Government of India Act* in the House of Commons, 5 June 1935.**

Does this Bill mean a broadening of Indian life, a widening and elevating of Indian thought? Does it mean that the Indian worker when he rises to his daily task will have a better chance of '…life, liberty and the pursuit of happiness'. India is a country, almost a continent, which has responded to the influence of British peace, order and justice and all the applications of modern science. New wealth, new food, new facilities…They have been brought into being in the last 50 years. Such a vast helpless mass of people requires extra British guidance. All you offer them are liberal formulas…and decline.

R. Rhodes James (ed) *Churchill Speaks*.

(B) **Roosevelt: telegram to Churchill, 12 April 1942.**

The feeling is held almost universally that the deadlock [in the talks between Britain and Indian leaders] *has been due to the British government's unwillingness to concede the right of self-government to the Indians…It is impossible for American public opinion to understand why, if there is a willingness on the part of the British government to permit the component parts of India to secede* after the war from the British Empire, it is unwilling to permit them to enjoy during the war what is tantamount to self-government.*

The Churchill Archive.

*Leo Amery, the Secretary of State for India, had put forward a plan that each individual Indian state might have independence after the war within a loose federation of India.

ACTIVITY
What considerations governed Churchill's attitude to Indian independence between 1931 and 1945?

ACTIVITY

Consider the sources:

1. On what grounds does Churchill in Source A oppose more self-government for India?

2. What does Source B see as the British government's attitude to Indian self-government?

3. How useful are these sources as evidence for British attitudes to Indian self-government?

The Abdication Crisis

If India was a lost cause, then Edward VIII was even worse. As Prince of Wales, Prince Edward had shown many lapses of judgement, not least his preference for older women as mistresses. Freda Dudley Ward was the divorced wife of a former Liberal minister and Lady

Furness was a society hostess, but his most notable attachment was Mrs Wallis Simpson whom he met in 1930.

Wallis Simpson was a divorced American woman married to a wealthy banker. The Prince's relations with her grew steadily more passionate. The liaison continued when he became King in 1936 and was the subject of comment on the continent, but the British press was generally careful not to intrude on royal privacy. However, the question of a future queen became a pressing matter, especially after Wallis applied for a divorce from her husband, who obligingly agreed to be 'caught' conducting an affair (the usual method for gaining a divorce on the grounds of infidelity when the real reason was incompatibility). The King was the head of the Church of England and the attitude of the Church to divorce was hostile. In the climate of the time, when so many had made huge sacrifices for 'King and Country' in the First World War and middle-class morality was at its height, it would have been very difficult for the King to put his personal interests before his public duty and marry Mrs Simpson.

Churchill was at odds with Baldwin and the establishment over India. Now he took them on in support of the King. Baldwin had not wanted to be involved in the King's private life but had been forced to express his view that a marriage with Mrs Simpson would not be acceptable. He hoped that the King would reconsider. Alfred Duff Cooper, a friend of the King, was opposed to any pressure being brought and then Churchill intervened. He was all for making a public speech supporting the King and demanding that parliament and the people should be consulted before any decision was made. Beaverbrook, the proprietor of the *Daily Express*, was ready for a campaign. But the King was not prepared to tough it out and was prepared to abdicate rather than not marry Mrs Simpson. When Churchill tried to raise the matter in the Commons he was howled down. Even his friends were critical of making a delicate and private matter into a public debate. It was Churchill's worst time in the 1930s and he had misjudged seriously. There was no question of a public campaign in support of the King and it became clear to Churchill and others who would support them that the King would not resist.

Figure 3.1   After the abdication, the ex-king and Wallis Simpson visit Hitler.

A worthy cause?

Even today, it is somewhat doubtful whether a monarch would be wise to marry someone like Mrs Simpson. In 1936 it would have weakened the monarchy considerably and Baldwin and the Archbishop of Canterbury gave appropriate advice. Churchill and a group of 'King's Friends' saw themselves as loyal knights of old, defending the right of the young monarch to marry for love. As a result, the reputation of Churchill plummeted. The King abdicated in 1937 and he went off to France to marriage with Wallis Simpson and exile. His brother, George VI, turned out to be a wonderfully modest symbol of modern monarchy, and his wife, Lady Elizabeth Bowes Lyon, later the Queen Mother, won hearts. Edward VIII had been unstable both before and after becoming King. He refused to discuss business and made unwise commitments to the German ambassador to persuade Baldwin into talks with Hitler over the Rhineland. His circle of friends was also unwise and it is doubtful whether he would have been a popular or effective monarch. Few missed Edward VIII and Mrs Simpson. The new King and Queen detested Churchill and used all their influence to prevent him returning to government.

Sources

A Churchill issued a public statement on the royal crisis, 5 December 1936.

I plead for time and patience. The nation must realise the character of the constitutional issue. There is no question of any conflict between the King and parliament, parliament has not been consulted in any way, nor allowed to express any opinion. The question is whether the King is to abdicate upon the advice of the ministers of the day. No such advice has ever before been tendered to a Sovereign in parliamentary times.

If an abdication were to be hastily extorted the outrage so committed would cast its shadow forward across many chapters of the History of the British Empire.

The matter is pregnant with calamity and all the evil aspects will be aggravated beyond measure if the utmost chivalry is not shown by ministers and the British nation to a gifted and beloved King.

R. Rhodes James, *Churchill: A study in Failure*, pp. 349–50, Penguin Edition, 1973.

B The diarist and former diplomat Harold Nicolson wrote in his diary, 3 December 1936.

I do not find the people angry with Mrs Simpson, but I do find a deep and enraged fury against the King himself. In eight months he has destroyed the great structure of popularity which he had raised.

Nigel Nicolson (ed) *Harold Nicolson, Diaries and Letters*.

C A modern historian describes one of Churchill's bleakest moments.

When the House of Commons met on Monday 7 December it was apparent that its members had taken the pulse of their constituents, and found that the King had little support. Churchill had not done this. After Baldwin made a statement, Churchill rose and asked for an assurance that no irrevocable step would be taken before the House had had a chance to discuss the matter. To his astonishment he found, as he said later 'that it was physically impossible to make myself heard'. He was shaken by the hostility of the House and on his way out said that his political career was finished.

Pelling *Winston Churchill*, Macmillan 1974, pp. 381–2, quoted from Wordsworth edition.

ACTIVITY

1   How do Sources B and C compare with Source A in their view of support for the King in parliament and country?

2   'Churchill was wrong and misguided to support Edward VIII in the way that he did'. How far do these sources support this interpretation?

EXAMINER'S ADVICE

First of all think how the sources might be used to agree or disagree with the statement. Which parts of Source C show Churchill was misguided? What does Source B say about public opinion that might lead you to think he was misguided? Which sources go together? How could you use Source A to show that Churchill was doing the right thing? Do you need to explain what 'wrong' might mean in this question – morally? Politically? What does 'misguided' mean?

Try first of all explaining why there might be some discussion about these issues. Then group the sources. Then explain their link with the issue in the question. Next use your own knowledge to see if you agree and finally come to a view about whether Churchill was 'wrong' or 'misguided' or both.

So by 1937 Churchill had isolated himself from mainstream politics. Few saw his attitude to India or to the abdication as anything more than eccentric.

- His economic policy of the 1920s seemed misguided when Britain abandoned the Gold Standard in September 1931 and suffered no apparent misfortunes.

- His Free Trade policy was replaced by a policy of Protection.

- Wartime misjudgements continued to be held against him.

When rearmament had to begin again Britain found itself behind its rivals. Churchill's **Ten Year Rule** (see page 31), whilst sensible policy in 1919 as Britain struggled to right itself after the First World War, had been continued by successive governments. When it was overturned as a policy in 1932 it was not replaced by an arms-building programme by the National Government of Ramsey Macdonald, of which Churchill was not a member. When Mussolini's Italy invaded Abyssinia in 1935, Churchill's earlier words of praise for the Italian dictator seemed ill-advised. When tensions arose in Palestine between Arabs and Jews, people remembered Churchill's attempts at compromise and pointed to its failure. He had alienated Baldwin and MacDonald and found little favour with the new leader of the Conservatives, Neville Chamberlain (see pages 16–18, Chapter 1), despite some earlier co-operation. Churchill seemed to be a hangover from an earlier Britain. Cut off from mainstream politics, Churchill surrounded himself with 'experts' and loyal personal followers. Those in Churchill's circle, like Brendan Bracken and 'the Prof', Frederick Lindemann, were seen as untrustworthy by many Conservatives. His judgements and his public utterances came to seem increasingly out of step with the times despite Churchill's many obvious plus points. He had a wealth of experience in government, was well-informed and was open to new ideas in a way that would have done credit to a much younger man. He had studied the history of Europe and intellectually was far from naive or old-fashioned. Rather than Churchill however, it was the government that seemed to be in line with public opinion and taking a modern and realistic view of Britain's role in foreign affairs.

It is in this context that Churchill's struggle to convince the government and public of his views on defence and foreign policy must be seen. His warnings about and criticisms of

Ten Year Rule

First adopted in August 1919, this was a British government guideline that the armed forces should draft their estimates 'on the assumption that the British Empire would not be engaged in any great war during the next ten years'. In 1928 Churchill, as Chancellor of the Exchequer, made the rule an ongoing one so that it remained in force unless specifically countermanded. It was abolished as government policy after four more years in 1932.

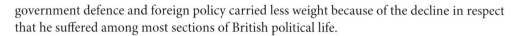

government defence and foreign policy carried less weight because of the decline in respect that he suffered among most sections of British political life.

What was Churchill's attitude towards rearmament and what were his reasons for opposing appeasement?

In January 1933 Hitler was legally chosen by President Hindenburg to be Chancellor of Germany. The Nazi party had a substantial 196 seats in the Reichstag. Hitler used constitutional means to give himself first powers to defend the state in February, using a presidential decree as his predecessors had done. The Enabling Law of 1933 gave him, by the power of a Reichstag law, full dictatorial power for four years. He waited until the President had died before declaring himself Führer (Leader) in 1934. His ambitions to revise the *Treaty of Versailles* had been common to German governments since 1920.

The Treaty of Versailles

The Germans were forced to accept a peace treaty in 1919 called the *Treaty of Versailles* which involved substantial demilitarisation and the loss of colonies and lands on Germany's borders. The humiliation was one of the reasons for Hitler's rise and a major reason for British sympathy for Germany in the 1920s and 1930s until Hitler began to take over land which had never been German in 1936.

Churchill showed a remarkable degree of understanding of Hitler's aims and had from November 1932 warned against German rearmament which he saw as inevitably leading to expansion and war. However, he was not entirely sure about the nature of Hitler's rule. In 1935 he wrote:

'We cannot tell whether Hitler will be the man who will once again let loose upon the world another war in which civilization will irretrievably succumb, or whether he will go down in history as the man who restored peace and honour to the German nation.'

(Quoted: Charmley, p. 271)

Churchill was not against revising the *Treaty of Versailles* but he wanted this to be from a position of strength. He also wanted to keep the superiority of armaments over Germany by rearming Britain (see timeline, page 64).

Throughout the 1930s the post-1918 settlement was challenged by Japan, Italy and Germany. The USA remained firmly isolationist. The USSR was preoccupied with massive internal changes although it did become a member of the **League of Nations** in 1934. British governments had to decide how far to rearm and what attitude to take to expansion by major powers.

The League of Nations

An association of countries established in 1919 by the *Treaty of Versailles* to promote international co-operation, peace and security. Its aims included imposing collective military and economic sanctions against any nation that violated the political independence and territorial integrity of another. However, the USA never joined the League of Nations and it was discredited by its failure to prevent Japanese expansion into China, Italy's conquest of Ethiopia, and Germany's seizure of Austria. The League ceased its activities during the Second World War. It was replaced in 1946 by the United Nations.

A summary of events in international affairs 1933–39

A major problem for Britain was that Germany, Italy and Japan pursued expansionist policies. Britain did not have the resources to stand up to all three potential threats – Germany in Europe, Japan to her Asian empire and Italy to North Africa and the Eastern Mediterranean.

1931	Manchurian crisis. Japan occupies Chinese province of Manchuria
Jan 1933	Hitler comes into office
October 1933	Germany leaves the League of Nations
1933	Further incursions by Japan into China
January 1934	Ten-year peace pact between Germany and Poland
January 1935	The Saar region votes, after 15 years under League of Nations control, to return to Germany
March 1935	Germany re-introduces conscription
June 1935	Baldwin becomes Prime Minister. Defence White Paper
June 1935	Anglo-German naval treaty – Britain agrees to the German battleship fleet being rebuilt to 33% of that of Britain
October 1935	Italy invades Ethiopia. Hoare-Laval pact which would have given Italy two-thirds of Ethiopia
March 1936	Germany remilitarised the Rhineland
July 1936	Spanish Civil War begins
October 1936	Rome-Berlin Axis signed
May 1937	Neville Chamberlain becomes Prime Minister
July 1937	Japan launches major invasion of China
March 1938	Austria annexed by Germany
September 1938	Czech crisis. Munich conference gives Germany the Sudetenland of Czechoslovakia
March 1939	Hitler occupies Moravia and Bohemia. Slovakia allowed to be independent. Poland takes Teschen from Czechoslovakia which ceases to exist as an independent country
1939	Britain guarantees Polish independence, but not its territory
April 1939	Spanish Civil War ends
April 1939	Italy invades Albania
April 1939	Britain re-introduces conscription
1 September 1939	Germany invades Poland
3 September 1939	Britain declares war on Germany

ANALYSIS

Churchill's attitudes to rearmament and to foreign policy are described in his own massive account of the 1930s and 1940s, *The Second World War*, which runs to six volumes, published from 1948. The first, *The Gathering Storm*, presents what is probably still the usual picture of the 1930s.

Broadly, the arguments in Churchill's account are as follows.

Figure 3.2   Spitfire fighters.

1 Air Defences

By 1939 British air power was considerably strengthened by the development of the Spitfire fighters (figure 3.2) but Churchill had warned that Britain was vulnerable from German aircraft development after 1935.

Churchill saw the danger from Hitler and warned of the need to maintain armed superiority. He was horrified at the growth of a German air force and warned Britain to build up its air defences.

He was influenced by his own wide reading and his special advisers like Frederick Lindemann, 'the Prof', and advocated the use of radar and other air defences. He was shocked by the limited responses of the National Government under **MacDonald** (1931–35) and Baldwin (1935–37) and disgusted by Baldwin's admission that he had dared not offer rearmament until after the election of 1935 as he would have lost. Politics had come before the needs of national defence. Churchill's views were vindicated when Britain's air defences became crucial in 1940.

Figure 3.3 Chamberlain and Hitler in 1938.

2 Churchill's call for an alliance

Churchill had seen the menace of Germany early on. Baldwin had been too concerned with a quiet life and Chamberlain by the mistaken belief that he could appease Hitler, and get him to agree to rational discussion and agreement.

Churchill had been in favour of a Grand Alliance against Germany. He was horrified at Chamberlain's lack of response to the American President Roosevelt's call for an international conference in 1938. He called for an alliance with the USSR to recreate the alliance system which had existed in the First World War between Britain, France and Russia. Chamberlain had done nothing until he sent a low-level mission in 1939 by which time it was too late as Germany and the USSR had signed a non-aggression treaty. (*Punch* shows the agreement between Hitler and Stalin August 1939, see figure 3.4.)

WONDER HOW LONG THE HONEYMOON WILL LAST?

Figure 3.4 *Punch* cartoon showing the agreement between Hitler and Stalin, August 1939

3 Standing up to Hitler

Churchill believed that the greatest mistake was to not threaten war in 1938 when Hitler threatened Czechoslovakia. When Czechoslovakia was threatened then it was the time to take action. Hitler's remilitarisation of the Rhineland, his annexation of Austria, his large-scale rearmament and his pacts with Italy and Japan had shown his intentions. Instead, Hitler was strengthened, the German generals were deprived of any chance of opposing Hitler; Britain lost the possible support of the large Czech army and any chance of Russian support. In the end, Chamberlain went to war over Poland in much less favourable circumstances a year later.

4 The moral high ground

The moral weakness shown in appeasing Hitler was a matter for national shame and Baldwin and Chamberlain were to blame. The resignation of **Anthony Eden** in 1938 had been a tragedy which kept Churchill awake, thinking of this brave young man protesting against weak policies. The 1930s had seen lone voices standing out against weak and misguided national leaders.

The issues here are:

■ How accurate a picture does this interpretation give of the period?

■ How justified were Churchill's criticisms both at the time and in his later book?

BIOGRAPHY
Anthony Eden (1897–1977)

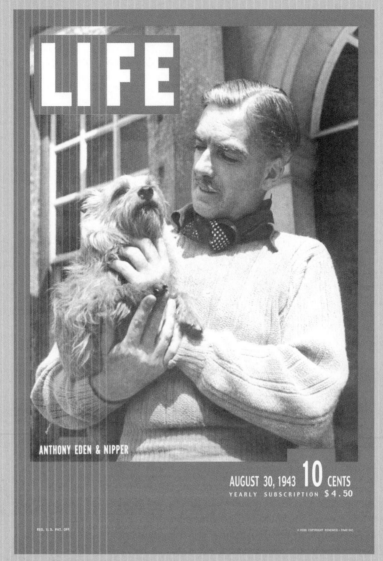

Eden, *LIFE* Magazine, April 1938.

Eden was from a Conservative upper-class background and a brilliant linguist. He served in the First World War and entered Conservative politics in the 1920s. Specialising in foreign affairs he became Minister for the League of Nations in 1934 and Foreign Secretary in 1935 after opposing Sir Samuel Hoare's attempt to do a deal with Mussolini when Italy invaded Ethiopia. He fell out with Chamberlain over the manner of his dealings with Italy rather than over the principle of appeasement and resigned in 1938. He was not close to Churchill at the time. Churchill saw him as an anti-appeaser. Eden was Foreign Secretary again 1940–45 and then deputy leader of the Conservatives. Utterly in Churchill's shadow, he took over as Prime Minister from Churchill in 1955 but had to resign over the invasion of Suez in 1956. He later became Lord Avon and wrote extensive memoirs of his time at the heart of politics.

The issue of air defences

Sources

A Churchill's broadcast to the nation, November 1934.

As we go to and fro in this peaceful country, with its decent ordinary people going about their business under free institutions, and with so much tolerance and fair play, it is startling and fearful to realise that we are no longer safe in our island home…Only a few hours away by air there dwells a nation of nearly 70 million…who are being taught from childhood to think of war and conquest as a great and glorious exercise and death in battle as the noblest fate of man. It is in the grip of a group of ruthless men preaching a doctrine of racial pride, unrestrained by law…I am afraid that if you look intently at what is moving towards Great Britain you will see that the only choice open is the grim choice…Whether we shall submit or whether we shall prepare…We must, without another hour's delay begin to make ourselves at least the strongest air power in the European world.

Broadcast in 1934; quoted in: R. Rhodes James, 1980, p. 313.

B Lord Halifax, (Lord Privy Seal) on rearmament, 1935.

Are we to judge the situation so serious that everything has to give way to military reconditioning of our Defence Forces? Such a conclusion in fact, seems to rest on premises not only of the inevitability but of a certain degree of certainty as to the early imminence of war which I am not prepared to accept.

Lord Halifax, December 1935 (Quoted: R. Rhodes James, p. 298: *Churchill, A Study in Failure,* Weidenfeld and Nicolson, 1970. Penguin, 1973.)

C Churchill looks back in the 1930s on his post-war memoirs.

Looking back, I am astonished at the length of time that was granted to us. It would have been possible in 1933 or even in 1934 for Britain to have created an air-power which would have imposed the necessary restraints upon Hitler's ambitions, or would perhaps have enabled the military leaders of Germany to control his violent acts. More than five whole years had yet to run before we were to be confronted with the supreme ordeal [i.e. war] Had we acted…with reasonable prudence and healthy energy, it might never have come to pass. Based on superior air power

Britain and France could safely have invoked the aid of the League of Nations and all the states of Europe would have gathered behind them.'

Churchill, W.S. (1948) *The Gathering Storm,* pp. 106.

D A modern historian, Charmley, writes on the cost of rearmament.

British rearmament had to be done in a manner that ensured that the economy did not collapse under the strain. This was something which Churchill never really appreciated. The original defence estimates for 1935 were £124 million and by 1938 they were due to rise to £132 million....The amount of money allocated to the air force was increased from the £20 million in the 1935 White paper on Defence to £45 million for the year 1936; for the following year…spending was up to £60 million. Total spending on defence was forecast to rise…to £239 million. Not only had the Air Force been well-treated, but the emphasis was on the development of bombers for a counter-strike against Germany.

Charmley, J. *Churchill,* pp. 304–5

E Another modern historian, Reynolds, discusses the exaggeration of the threat posed by the German air force by Churchill.

What mattered when assessing the Luftwaffe threat was not the crude total of planes, but …the number of combat aircraft for which the Germans had fuel, spare parts and trained pilots… On these criteria, it would seem that Churchill exaggerated German potential, for instance predicting in September 1935 2,000 front line aircraft by October 1936 and possibly 3,000 a year after that. In fact the total was barely 4,000 even in September 1939. Only in 1938 was Britain designated a likely enemy and the Luftwaffe never really developed the capacity or doctrine for strategic bombing, In 1930's Britain discussion of the German air threat was conducted in alarmist rather than analytical terms. Churchill…exaggerated fears about bombing. During the whole war only 147,000 British people were killed or maimed. In July 1936 his estimates were 5,000 dead from a single air-raid. These exaggerations stimulated air rearmament but induced diplomatic paralysis (i.e. a diplomatic failure to try to stop Germany). It seemed suicidal to risk war.

Adapted from: Reynolds, D. *In Command of History,* p. 99.

ACTIVITY

1   Look at the sources on page 69 and say briefly what each is saying about Churchill's attitude to air power.

2   'Churchill was absolutely right to be critical of government defence preparations.' Using the sources and your own knowledge assess this interpretation.

    a   Which sources might show that he was right and which sources might show that he was wrong?

    b   Taking each source in turn, what is there about these sources that make them reliable/ unreliable?

    c   In your evaluation, do you think Churchill was justified in being critical?

Try to use your own knowledge as much as possible and also be sure to offer a firm judgement.

Note: In this activity there are two sources by historians. You should concentrate on the views they contain. Remember that in the examination there will only be, at most, one extract from a secondary source.

The menace of Germany

There is no doubt that Churchill was quick to point out the danger from a rearmed Germany and that he had a clear view of the Hitler regime. What is less clear is whether the growth of the German air force was as dangerous as he thought, and whether the government would have reacted in much the same way without Churchill's views. He may well have hoped to become Defence Minister and was annoyed when the post went to the lawyer Sir Thomas Inskip in 1936.

Churchill was very critical of foreign policy between 1933 and 1939 in his account of the Second World War. The impression given is that Hitler was first allowed to rearm and that there was no effective strategy to deal with Hitler's expansion. The main elements as they appear in Churchill's books are:

- The governments failed to support the League of Nations (see page 63).
- Baldwin permitted German naval expansion and did not dare, in the 1935 General Election, to be honest with the electorate about the need to rearm.
- German troops were allowed to remilitarise the Rhineland in 1936, something expressly *forbidden* by the *Treaty of Versailles*.
- Instead of a grand alliance, Chamberlain sought to placate Hitler by visiting him three times in 1938.
- Hitler's demands for the German-speaking part of Czechoslovakia, the so-called Sudetenland, to be added to the Reich were agreed against the wishes of the Czech government.
- Finally, any desire of France to resist was undermined by Britain.

What are the issues?

Could Britain have offered more resistance?

The armed forces were worried about the possible threat to Britain not just from Germany, but also from Japan, which had been expanding into China and threatened Britain's South-East Asian empire and interests in China. Then Italy, under Mussolini, was a threat to British Egypt and the Suez Canal, and also Malta, Gibraltar and the entire Mediterranean Sea route. The advice from the service chiefs was that Britain was overstretched and had to reduce the areas of possible conflict. It was unlikely that Germany wished to attack Britain or take any of its possessions. This was much less clear in the case of Japan. Also, Britain had fallen out with Italy when Mussolini attacked Abyssinia in 1935 and Britain had supported sanctions against Italy. As Churchill was not in government he did not have to consider this advice or look at the wider position. He made very little reference to the Far East, whether at the time or in *The Gathering Storm*.

Secondly, there was Britain's financial and economic situation. With unemployment remaining high and a need for domestic recovery from the economic crisis of 1929–31, to which his own policies in the 1920s might have contributed, rearmament and a massive build up of military power would have been difficult.

Thirdly, opinion in the Dominions was not sympathetic to another war against Germany. There was no guarantee that the Empire would respond automatically to any attempt to 'stand up to Hitler'. The Dominion leaders were generally behind Chamberlain, as was the bulk of the Conservative Party and the royal family.

The Grand Alliance

Churchill's proposed alternatives were:

1. massive air rearmament,
2. a reliance on the French army,
3. alliance with Russia, and
4. co-operation with America.

These were all questionable.

Air defences might deter but they could not defeat Germany by themselves. Churchill was not advocating the creation of a large British Expeditionary Force.

France was very divided in the inter-war years and relied heavily on massive defences such as the **Maginot Line**, even though the First World War had shown that even the greatest defences could be broken.

Russia was undergoing a period of massive social and economic change under Stalin. Russian power was feared throughout Eastern Europe and it was unlikely that any strong alliance could be made to defend that area because of that. Poland after all had signed a pact with Germany in 1934.

As for the USA, isolationism was deeply ingrained and President Roosevelt would not be able to gain support for a war to help Britain even if he had wanted to. It seemed doubtful whether his proposal for an international conference on Europe in 1938 would have yielded anything or was even made with any real intention of it being taken up.

The Maginot Line

A very impressive series of heavily fortified positions that ran the length of France's eastern frontier with Germany. Building started in 1930 under minister of war André Maginot. The aim was to hold any German attack until full mobilisation of the French army was complete. It failed because it did not extend to the Belgian frontier and the Germans in 1940 simply went round it.

It encouraged a defensive mentality which prevented France from taking advantage of the German distraction in Poland 1939.

Practical problems

Both Baldwin and Chamberlain were working on the basis of expert military, economic, financial and diplomatic advice. Both believed that a modern war would be devastating and wanted to avoid it. Both were conscious that Britain had responsibilities to defend its vast Empire at a time when resources were low and public opinion seemed to be very opposed to military solutions. Both thought that Britain needed time to rearm and that, however obnoxious or immoral Nazi Germany was as a regime, it was essentially popular with Germans, it could not easily be overthrown and so it had to be negotiated with. Until 1938 German demands had not been unreasonable or involved non-Germans being added to the new state. Since 1918 Britain had negotiated:

- trade treaties with communist Russia;
- an end to violence with Irish groups that had used terrorism; and
- greater self-government for India.

Governments have to negotiate and not always with people or regimes that they find agreeable. Neither Baldwin nor Chamberlain thought it wrong to rearm or had great regard for the German dictator. For instance, neither had written about either Mussolini or Hitler as admiringly as had, on occasion, Churchill.

The need for more decisive action

Against these points, Churchill seemed to have more insight than Baldwin or Chamberlain into the nature of the Nazi state. Attempts to deal with Hitler were unsuccessful and did lead him to despise Chamberlain and to assume that the democracies would not fight Germany.

Little was done to enlist Russian support and little was done to cultivate the Americans. This may have been realistic, but was it wise given Britain's limited resources and the unreliability of France as an ally? Given the extreme danger that Hitler posed, was Churchill really wrong to stress the need for even greater rearmament, despite the difficulties, and to make a greater effort to build up outside support against him?

Much can be made of Churchill's position outside the constraints and responsibilities of government. However, that was his strength. Oppositions have to oppose and, to some extent, Churchill saw himself as an opposition figure. However, there is no doubt that he very much wished to be in government. He never cut off links with his party or its leader and there were limits to his opposition that are not explained in *The Gathering Storm*.

> ### Source
>
> (A) **A modern historian, John Charmley writes of the double game Churchill played in his bid for political power in 1939.**
>
> *Harold Macmillan (the future Prime Minister and in 1939 a critic of the government among Conservative MPs) may have written to* The Times *demanding the creation of a broad-based national government, but Churchill played an altogether cannier game...he did nothing which could have erected a barrier between him and a place in the government.*
>
> *At a meeting of Conservative backbenchers on 21 March 1939, whilst others pressed the case for conscription, he remained silent, 'very much a politician' Amery noted (in his diary) ....As fresh crises arose in April he kept in close touch with Chamberlain and Halifax (the foreign secretary) and let his strong desire to enter the government be known.*
>
> Charmley, J. (1993) *Churchill: The End of Glory*, pp. 360–61.

Should Britain have gone to war in 1938?

This is so much a matter of 'might have been' that any judgement must be guesswork. Britain had a strong moral case, but would that in practice have meant that the USA or even the Dominions would have supported war? Would the French army have helped the Czechs to resist? Given their largely defensive attitude and the poor performance in 1940 it remains doubtful. The British had no forces available for Czechoslovakia as the Chiefs of Staff had made very plain.

Would Russia have supported the Czechs and not joined with Hitler? Given the huge problems of Russia in 1938, in the midst of Stalin's purges, his massive agricultural and industrial programs, and his distrust of the West, there must be some doubt. In any case, how could Russian troops have got to Czechoslovakia short of invading the countries inbetween? If Britain had gone to war in 1938, in advance of the vital radar technology and fighter aeroplanes that were being developed at that time, would it have had the strength to stop an invasion by Hitler? This is doubtful. Would Hitler have given in, or would he have been overthrown by rebellious generals appalled at the thought of a premature war against France, Britain, the Czechs and possibly Russia? There is simply no way of knowing, but there is no evidence that Hitler would have given in either.

> **Case Study: Eden, the hero**
>
> Churchill's passionate support of Eden's supposed stand against appeasement and his sleepless night when **Eden** resigned in 1938 over Chamberlain's increasingly personal handling of foreign policy is not supported by Churchill's other views at the time. He had thought Eden was wrong to resign over the issue of Chamberlain's interference and should have waited for a better issue. He and Eden did not collaborate closely afterwards against government policy. Eden was not a passionate opponent of appeasement on moral grounds. The moral argument is still, however a matter of debate.
>
> Britain had no formal agreement with Czechoslovakia. Churchill had not been against giving German speakers more rights and making changes in Czechoslovakia. Chamberlain argued that the moral point was that the consequences of war were so terrible, every effort must be made to avoid it. Against this, Churchill felt that the Czechs had been betrayed and that Britain had shown moral cowardice. This became widely accepted and made it difficult for Chamberlain to persist with appeasement in 1939.

ACTIVITY

Was Churchill right to be so critical of Chamberlain?

You may change your mind when you come back to this section when revising, but in a paragraph explain your view now.

What was Churchill's position between 1933 and 1938?

Churchill wanted three things with regard to Hitler's Germany:

1. A strong British rearmament, particularly in the air force to meet any threat.
2. A strong understanding with France whose army Britain would have to rely on in the event of any clash with Germany.
3. Support for the League of Nations as it was the only way that public opinion would accept any action against Germany and the only means of gaining international support.

The major international events and his reactions are summarised below

In summary, the major international events of 1933–39, and Churchill's reactions to them, are as follows:

1. **Hitler's coming to power, 1933**. Churchill openly criticised Hitler's anti-Semitism and regarded the regime as a 'grim dictatorship' with dangers for Britain.
2. **German rearmament**. Churchill called for extensive British rearmament, especially of the air force.
3. The *Anglo-German Naval Treaty*, **1935**. Churchill's criticism was that it undermined any Italian resistance to German revisionism by showing that Britain would act independently. However, Churchill did not make it a major issue.
4. **The Italian invasion of Ethiopia, 1935**. Churchill expressed no great criticism of the Hoare-Laval Pact in December 1935 in which Britain agreed that Mussolini should have most of Ethiopia. His concern was whether Italy would become an ally against Germany or not, and do he did not express in public any criticism of the invasion.
5. **The remilitarisation of the Rhineland, 1936**. Churchill was entirely supportive of British policy – to regret the infringement of the Versailles Treaty and Locarno Pact; to express a willingness to support France and the League and do nothing. Chamberlain spoke of the welcome unanimity of the House of Commons on the issue.
6. **The Spanish Civil War, 1936–39**. Churchill was sympathetic to the conservatism of the Nationalists and did not criticise the Chamberlain government's policy of non-intervention and neutrality.

The invasion of Austria in 1938 – the Anschluss

Hitler was an Austrian by birth and resented the ban on Austria and Germany joining imposed by the *Treaty of Versailles*. This seemed to go against the principle of self-determination advocated by President Wilson for other areas of Europe in which nationalities could live together in one country. There was a strong Nazi movement within Austria and, excited by the advent of Nazism in Germany, the Austrian Nazis attempted a coup in 1934 in which the Austrian Prime Minister Dollfuss was shot. However, Italy made it clear that a union between Austria and Germany was unacceptable and threatened military intervention. The coup failed. Between 1934 and 1938 there were closer relations both between Germany and Austria and between Italy and Germany. Union seemed more of a possibility and it was less likely that Britain or France would interfere. Hitler put pressure for closer links but the Austrian leader, Schuschnigg, attempted to prevent German domination by holding a referendum in Austria to ask if the Austrians favoured independence from Germany. Had they voted 'yes' then it would have been difficult for Germany to claim that any union was to fulfil the desire of all German speakers to be together. To prevent the referendum, German troops invaded in March 1938 and the Anschluss or Union was proclaimed. Few called for war over the issue in either France or Britain. Churchill saw it as evidence of the need for preparation for war but did not advocate taking military action. It made Chamberlain more eager to find a general settlement of outstanding problems from the *Treaty of Versailles*.

This produced a very dramatic and effective speech by Churchill in which he called for a Grand Alliance and a military commitment to France. However a number of things must be noted.

Firstly, there was no question of Churchill advocating any military action to reverse Hitler's seizure. The Grand Alliance was a means of deterring future aggression. France and Britain were to be the cornerstone of this. Russia's support was taken for granted. South-eastern Europe was to be encouraged to join and the whole would be within the League of Nations. Chamberlain agreed that nothing could be done to reverse the Anschluss and that measures should be taken to negotiate to prevent more territorial changes to be made by Germany alone. But as he saw the Grand Alliance as impossible, his method was to initiate discussions to bring Hitler to negotiate future changes as part of a general settlement, rather than have a repeat of the Austrian episode in which Hitler acted without consulting the Versailles powers. As there was general agreement that Versailles had been unfair and that Hitler's desire for Germans to be within Germany was not in itself unreasonable, the consensus in the country was to prefer this to threats of war or war itself.

Secondly, there was little sign of how Churchill was going to bring about the Grand Alliance or any indication that he would attempt to form an internal 'alliance' of anti-German elements at home. He seemed unwilling to link up with Liberal and Labour opponents of government policy, or to quit the Conservatives, or to form a new party or movement dedicated to standing up to Hitler. He had been far more active in encouraging anti-government elements over the India issue. Also, his criticisms of defence policy fell more on Baldwin than Chamberlain, to whom he still looked to give him a job.

Thirdly, when Chamberlain rejected the idea and made his own proposals, Churchill graciously called it a 'fine speech'; he welcomed Chamberlain's increase in rearmament and also the beginnings of staff talks with France in April 1938. He did not resign from the Conservative party, or establish a very strong group within it against Chamberlain. Chamberlain made every effort to charm Churchill, explaining his speech to Churchill in private before he made it to the Commons. Behind the rhetoric of Churchill's speeches, there was much less direct opposition than appeared. This was shown when Konrad Henlein visited England in April 1938.

Henlein was the leader of the Nazi party in Sudeten Czechoslovakia who had agitated for self-government. Henlein saw both Churchill and Chamberlain on a visit to England and persuaded both of them of Hitler's peaceful intentions and that a settlement might be reached over the German-speaking areas of Czechoslovakia. Churchill spoke optimistically about this in public, totally misreading the situation and being taken in as much as Chamberlain. He did not immediately press for action to be taken to prevent the Sudetenland from changing its status.

Figure 3.5   Henlein was a PE teacher who became the leader of the Sudeten Nazis. He is seen here with Hitler. He was a persuasive person who made a strong positive impression on British leaders in his visit in 1938.

Sources: Austria produced stirring speeches by Churchill

A Churchill's speech in the House of Commons on the Austrian Anschluss.

The gravity of the event of March 12 cannot be exaggerated. Europe is confronted with a programme of aggression, nicely calculated and timed, unfolding stage by stage, and there is only one choice open, not only to us, but to other countries, either to submit like Austria or else take effective measures while time remains to ward off the danger....If we go on waiting upon events, how much shall we throw away of resources now available for our security and the maintenance of peace? How many of our friends will be alienated, how many potential allies shall we see go one by one down the grisly gulf? How many times will bluff succeed until behind bluff ever gathering forces have accumulated?

Churchill's speech in the House of Commons, 14 March; quoted: *The Gathering Storm* p. 244.

B In the same speech Churchill argued:

If a number of states were assembled round Great Britain and France in a solemn treaty for mutual defence against aggression: if they had their forces marshalled in what you might call a Grand Alliance; if they had their staff arrangements concerted; if all this rested, as it can honourably rest, upon the Covenant of the League of Nations...if this were sustained by the moral sense of the world; and it were done in the year 1938...then I say that you might, even now arrest this approaching war.

Parker, R.A.C. (2000) *Churchill and Appeasement*, pp. 143–44.

C Chamberlain wrote to his sister on 20 March:

The plan of the Grand Alliance, as Winston calls it, had occurred to me long before he mentioned it...I talked about it to Halifax and we submitted it to the Chiefs of Staff and Foreign Office experts. It is a very attractive idea; indeed there is everything to be said for it until you come to examine its practicability. From that moment the attraction vanishes. You only have to look at the map to see that nothing that France or we could do could possibly save Czechoslovakia from being overrun by the Germans if they wanted to do it.

Chamberlain's letters Ashgate edition, 2005, ed: Robert Serf.

D Chamberlain's speech of 24 March was a key one and has been analysed by R.A.C. Parker.

Churchill himself described it as "a very fine speech" Chamberlain defined and defended appeasement. He reminded his hearers that "peace is the greatest interest of the British Empire". But he did not preach surrender. Britain would fight if its vital interests were menaced.....Britain "must be strongly armed for defence and for counter-offence". Then Chamberlain moved to the central issue. Should Britain promise to go to war if France went to war to defend Czechoslovakia, or should Britain promise to defend Czechoslovakia against aggression? This, he felt, would be a sacrifice against sovereignty. The decision to go to war would be made for Britain by foreigners.

If war broke out no one could tell who might be involved. This is especially true of two countries like Britain and France, with long associations of friendship, with interests closely interwoven, devoted to the same ideals of democratic liberty and determined to fight to uphold them...He announced accelerated rearmament. Production "will be substantially increased."

Adapted from: Parker, R.A.C. (2000) *Churchill and Appeasement*, pp. 155–7.

ACTIVITY

How far did Churchill and Chamberlain have different views about the consequences of the takeover of Austria by Hitler in March 1938?

1 Using Sources A–D identify the main points of disagreement between Churchill and Chamberlain by March 1938.

2 Are there any points of agreement?

3 How far do the sources support the view that Churchill's views were unrealistic?

Czechoslovakia and the Munich Crisis

This was the most significant of Chamberlain's attempts to appease Hitler. Churchill certainly opposed government policy, but his reactions to the events do need careful consideration, as a myth has grown up about Churchill's opposition. This section will briefly outline the crisis and put in table form what Churchill's reactions were.

To set the scene: Czechoslovakia was created as an independent state in 1919 from Austro-Hungarian, *not* German, territory. However it had 3 million German- as opposed to Czech-speakers in an area which came to be known as the Sudetenland. The term was not in use in the days of the Austro-Hungarian Empire. After 1933 some Sudeten Germans wanted to join with Germany; not all, especially the Social Democrats or anti-Nazis. The pro-Nazis were led by a former physical education teacher called Heinlein. Czechoslovakia was a democracy with a reasonably large army and it was allied to France. Any attempt by Hitler to invade could have led to a war and this might have involved Britain. After 1937 Chamberlain was anxious not to let this happen. Arguably, Czechoslovakia should have given its different national groups (Slovaks, Ruthenes, Poles, Germans, etc.) a degree of self-government. After the Anschluss with Austria Hitler began to demand more rights for the Germans in Czechoslovakia and in the summer German demands increased. Chamberlain wanted to be proactive and not just wait for a crisis to occur. Hence British attempts to mediate – the Runciman mission in July 1938 (see page 79 Table 3.1). The British military chiefs had told Chamberlain that there was little Britain could do for the Czechs in the event of a war. The table below outlines key elements in the development of the situation which culminated in Chamberlain flying to meet Hitler to negotiate in person. The first meeting in Bavaria saw Chamberlain agree to German demands. When he returned to Germany, meeting Hitler in the Rhineland at Godesberg, Hitler had increased those demands. Chamberlain had been made to look foolish and had seemed to bring war nearer. However, Mussolini intervened and proposed a four-power conference at Munich. Here, without discussing it with the Czechs, Chamberlain agreed with the demands that Hitler had made at Godesberg and the Sudetenland was transferred to Germany, of which it had never been a part. The Czechs had to allow Slovakia independence and lost lands to Hungary and Poland. Russia, to which France and the Czechs were allied, was not consulted.

Chamberlain's actions at this time in negotiating the future of other countries without consulting them and being unable to stand up to a powerful dictator in a strong position was to be echoed by Churchill himself as the Second World War came to a close (see p.147–148).

Table 3.1   Events leading to the Munich Crisis of 1938.

Event	Description	Churchill's reaction
26 July 1938 Runciman Mission	Chamberlain announced that Sir Walter Runciman would lead a mission to Czechoslovakia as a mediator. The mission began in August and ended in deadlock on 7 September	Churchill made no comment in the Commons and later publicly welcomed the mission. In a newspaper article Churchill wrote that 'the Czechs owe it to the western powers that every concession compatible with the...integrity of their state should be made' (Charmley p. 343 *The Daily Telegraph* 26 July article)
August 1938 German military exercises – one million men mobilised **12 September Hitler spoke at Nuremberg** denouncing Czechs. Rioting in the Sudetenland	The very scale of the German military exercises seemed a threat to the Czechs which was made more explicit in Hitler's speech at the Nuremberg Rally. On 11 September Chamberlain warned that: 'Hitler cannot with impunity carry out a rapid and successful military campaign without fear of intervention by France and by Great Britain.'	On 1 Sept Churchill passed a note from Maisky, the Russian ambassador, suggesting that the Council of the League of Nations be asked to discuss the impending war. In private, Churchill accepted that this might mean that 'the civilised world will have to accept the demands of Nazi Germany'. Churchill urged the government that together with France and Russia the use of German forces against the Czechs would raise 'a capital issue'. He was sure the USA would give moral support. On 10 Sept Churchill visited Chamberlain and advised that Hitler should be told that if he invaded 'we' should be at once at war. Churchill urged the government, in blunt and brutal language, in an article in *The Daily Telegraph* to deter Hitler.
15 September Chamberlain announced his intention to meet Hitler	Chamberlain had been planning to fly to see Hitler. This was a dramatic and unusual measure for the time	Churchill had not been consulted and was taken by surprise. He told Oliver Harvey on 15 Sept that it was the stupidest thing that he (Chamberlain) had ever done. (Harvey Diary, quoted Charmley p. 344)
Meeting at Berchtesgaden. Hitler demanded that Czechoslovakia cede its German-speaking areas. Chamberlain persuaded Cabinet and the French government that this was necessary	19 September a joint statement by France and Britain to the Czech government urged the transfer of German speaking areas to Germany. 21 September the Labour leaders met Chamberlain and told him that the plan had betrayed the Czechs	Churchill flew to Paris to encourage Reynaud and Mandel not to resign. They were the French ministers most opposed to appeasing Hitler. He urged them to stay in the French government to resist. On 22 Sept he was bitterly critical, still urging a combination of powers and regarding the deal as a surrender

Event	Description	Churchill's reaction
22 September, Chamberlain was at Godesberg, the Rhineland, where Hitler insisted on immediate transfer to be completed by 1 October, with territorial transfers of some Czech territory to Poland and Hungary	Hitler's unreasonable demands made it seem that Britain would have to go to war. 25 Sept Halifax disagreed with Chamberlain's desire to appease still more, and a majority of the Cabinet refused Hitler's terms. 27 September the French military commander, Gamelin, came to London and agreed action in the case of German invasion	Churchill urged joint action by Britain France and Russia – supported by League of Nations Union. Churchill talked to Halifax and Chamberlain – 'we three all seemed very much together.' Churchill was for joint military action
28 September Chamberlain announced that Hitler had agreed to talks at Munich	Chamberlain had been negotiating with Mussolini to mediate and to have another conference to end the threat of war	Churchill shook Chamberlain's hands in the House of Commons, according to *The Times*. No account has him remaining seated in the general enthusiasm on the Tory benches. Churchill's press statement wished the Prime Minister 'God speed'. But by 29 Sept, Churchill was, according to a close associate, in a 'towering rage and deepening gloom'.
5 October Munich debate in the House of Commons to discuss the Munich agreement.	Chamberlain had agreed to Hitler's terms and had obtained an agreement for future co-operation. On his return from Munich Chamberlain was cheered and he seemed highly popular. By the time of the debate there were more mixed feelings. The Government won the vote of confidence on Munich with ease.	Churchill spoke strongly about the defeat and the moral failure: 'Silent, mournful, abandoned, broken, Czechoslovakia recedes into darkness'. On 6 October 1938 Churchill did not vote against the government, but abstained in protest.

ACTIVITY

1   Using the information in this table, consider whether Source A on page 81 is valid or not. Look especially at the judgements in **bold**.

2   Now look at Source B. To what extent does the table confirm or challenge Churchill's views in Source A?

3   Using the information you have studied do you think the table above confirms either the view of Churchill himself (Source A) or the view of Ramsden (Source B)?

Sources

(A) **Churchill's views on the Second World War.**

*It is my purpose...**to show how easily the tragedy of the Second World War could have been prevented;** how the malice of the wicked was reinforced by the weakness of the virtuous....*

*Neville Chamberlain was alert, business-like and opinionated and self-confident in a very high degree. He conceived himself able to comprehend the whole of Europe and indeed the world. **He was throughout the period the masterful opponent of all emergency measures.** He had formed decided judgements about all the political figures of the day, both at home and abroad, and felt himself capable of dealing with them. His all pervasive hope was to go down in History as the great peace-maker and for this **he was prepared to strive continually in the teeth of facts and face great risks for himself and his country**. I should have found it easier to work with Baldwin, as I knew him, than Chamberlain; but **neither of them had any wish to work with me, except in the last resort.***

Excerpts from: *The Gathering Storm*, 1948, Churchill's first volume in his *History of the Second World War*

(B) **An historian's analysis of these same views.**

It is difficult to match The Gathering Storm's account of a six year lone crusade (by Churchill against the governments) with the fact that Churchill did not cast a single vote against the Government on foreign and domestic policy before the Munich Crisis. He did not quickly denounced the Naval treaty made with Hitler in 1935, he hoped for a deal with Mussolini to split the fascist dictators, he did not at first support effective action against Mussolini over Abyssinia, he was apparently relieved when Britain and France did not act quickly to kick Hitler out of the Rhineland, and he only began to abstain in foreign policy votes in May 1938. It would be hard to grasp from The Gathering Storm *the optimism that Churchill felt when Chamberlain became Prime Minister in 1937, but that is certainly what he told his readers in Colliers magazine at the time. And when Eden resigned in February 1938 Churchill was fourth quickest of four hundred Tory MPs to sign a round robin that expressed undiminished confidence in Neville Chamberlain.*

Ramsden, J. (2003) *The Man of the Century: Winston Churchill and his Legend Since 1945*, p. 208.

What did Churchill do after Munich?

He devoted a lot of energy to writing *A History of the English-Speaking Peoples*. He made sure to visit his constituency in Epping where he had become unpopular for his stand against Chamberlain. He was sure to praise the Prime Minister's quest for peace. He waited for events to prove him right. He was not disappointed: Hitler's forces moved in to take over Prague and split up Czechoslovakia in March 1939, adding Bohemia and Moravia to the Reich. He approved of Chamberlain's action in guaranteeing Poland its independence and was in a lot of contact with Chamberlain and Lord Halifax, giving advice and letting it be known that he wished to return to government.

On 21 August the **Nazi-Soviet Pact** was signed and on 1 September Germany invaded Poland. Churchill was invited to join a small War Cabinet on 1 September. However, most of the Conservative Party probably did not want to see Churchill back. Churchill was restrained when Chamberlain declared war on 3 September, taking care to praise him. On 3 September Churchill was appointed First Lord of the Admiralty. This was much more than Churchill had imagined being given. After 10 years Churchill was back in Cabinet in the same post as he had occupied in 1914.

The Nazi-Soviet Pact

Ribbentrop, the German foreign minister, signed a pact with Molotov, his Russian counterpart, and Stalin that there would be friendship between the two countries. Secretly they agreed to divide Poland between them. It meant that Hitler could invade Poland and subsequently France and the Low Countries without worrying about Russian intervention. Distrustful of millions of innocent Russians, Stalin seems to have trusted Hitler and was surprised when he ignored the pact and invaded Russia in 1941.

EXAMINER'S ADVICE

Remember that historians' interpretations are secondary data sources and not considered in the AS level exam.

Historians have their own agendas or ideas that they seek to prove and disprove. Additionally, historians are looking at *themes* in history, or similarities and differences in people and events, and why these might occur. Keep this in mind whenever you use an historian's view to support your own work. Do you agree with them? Why? Why not?

How justified were Churchill's views?

Some issues which you might consider are:

1. Does Churchill's reliance on an alliance against Germany depend on too many 'ifs': if France fought; if Russia co-operated; if the USA lent its moral authority to resistance; if smaller nations acted together; if the League could be effective; and the biggest 'if' – if Hitler could actually be deterred.

2. If not, then Britain would have to back up its deterrence with war. Was this possible in 1938? Churchill did not consider all the claims on Britain's defence – what if Japan and Italy took advantage of a war? What if the Chiefs of Staff were right in warning against war when Britain's army was weak and its navy overstretched. What if the French did not fight successfully or if Russia did not join in?

3. Was British public opinion really ready for war in 1938? Or did it agree with Chamberlain that the issue of Czechoslovakia – 'a far off country of which we know nothing' with serious problems of restless national minorities – was not worth fighting for? Had that changed by 1939 because it was clear that everything had been done for peace but still had failed?

4. Did Churchill underestimate the need to build up British arms and did the gap between 1938 and 1939 give it the chance to develop vital Spitfires, Radar, a larger conscripted army and air raid defences? Would a war in 1938 without these elements have been a disaster?

5. Was Churchill, in fact, offering the only alternative feasible, since negotiation with Hitler was quite impossible in the way Chamberlain had attempted? Did Churchill have a clearer and more realistic view of Germany than Chamberlain? Did he propose alliances that in the end were responsible in the war for the defeat of Germany and might have deterred Hitler?

6. Did Churchill sum up the justifiable moral case for supporting smaller countries against aggression and for standing up to international aggression that Britain as great imperial power had a duty to follow?

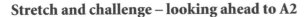

Stretch and challenge – looking ahead to A2

Look at the views by historians in Sources A–C below. It is clear that there is no more agreement now than there was when Churchill was advocating alternative policies in the 1930s. This looks forward to A2 work, which focuses on historical interpretations by historians.

Remember however that you will not need to have knowledge of detailed historiographical debate. You may be asked to look at the view expressed by an historian in a short source.

Views arising from the sources

Put each of the historians below in a 'hot seat' and ask as many difficult questions as you can about their views. A team of two should research the views and represent and defend 'their' historian. For example, Charmley could be asked whether an alliance was such a bad idea; the Charmley team might point out that Soviet Russia in the 1930s was very distrustful of the West and would not have been likely to join capitalist powers even in a war against their ideological enemy.

Sources

A Shen's views on British foreign policy in the 1930s.

In order to avoid facing three enemies at the same time, Britain should, in cooperation with America, France, Russia and other powers in the League have checked Japan, Italy and Germany one by one.

It should have tried to prevent Germany from developing her military capabilities instead of acquiescing in her rearmament. During the Rhineland crisis if Britain had backed up France and forced Germany to withdraw it would have spoiled Hitler's plans and prevented Germany from threatening world peace as well as the interests of the British Empire. If Britain had responded to France in firmly resisting the Anschluss, this would have seriously hindered Hitler's ambitions in Czechoslovakia. And if Chamberlain had taken a hard line at Munich, Hitler might have been overthrown by his opposition.

From: Shen, P. (1999) *The Age of Appeasement: The Evolution of British Foreign Policy in the 1930s*, pp. 272–3.

B Parker suggests that if Churchill's policy of opposing Hitler had been carried out in 1938, Hitler might have been overthrown.

The British policy advocated by Churchill in the second half of 1938, so Halder claimed [Halder was a leading German general who gave evidence after the war at the Nuremberg Trial] would have enabled the plotters against Hitler [among high-ranking German army officers] to proceed Whether they would have done so or not or whether they would have restrained or removed Hitler we cannot tell. Nor can we confidently say whether Hitler's conduct would have been different if he had been faced with the certainty of British and French action in the west and the certainty of Soviet hostility in the east. What we can safely assert is that Churchill's policies gave the only chance of restraining Hitler in 1938 or 1939.

Parker, R.A.C. (2000) *Churchill and Appeasement*, pp. 258–9.

C Charmley's critique of Churchill's policy on establishing a 'Grand Alliance'.

Churchill's ideas on how to contain Germany did not inspire members of the Government with confidence about his judgement. He wanted to gather together, under the aegis of the League of Nations, the Baltic States, Holland, Belgium, France, Italy, Switzerland, Austria, Russia and Poland in an effort to deter Germany from aggression.

This idea, which by 1938 was being dignified by the title 'the Grand Alliance', remained a feature of Churchill's thinking right up to the outbreak of war. But attractive as it sounded, it ignored two questions: whether the other countries would collaborate, and whether such a league was more likely to drive Germany in the direction of a war against Britain.

Charmley, J. (1993) *Churchill: The End of Glory*, pp. 308–9.

EXAMINER'S ADVICE

During this chapter you have been looking at a wider range of sources and considering their provenance and how well they support a particular argument.

It is a good idea in the examination to start with the debate implied by the question. There will be an element of discussion involved and you have to be aware that there can be more than one view or 'interpretation'.

It is likely that you will be able to group the sources, as some will agree with the view and others will not.

You should make clear how the sources relate to the view – what is in them that could confirm or challenge the interpretation.

When you have made this clear, look at the nature of the sources and use your own knowledge to consider how convincing is the support or challenge they offer to the interpretation.

Then make a clear judgement about the view in the question.

In the Exam Café section there is an exam question on Churchill and appeasement for you to practise.

Conclusion

How many Churchills were there in this period? It could be said that there was the old-fashioned, war-like, romantic and unrealistic Churchill, overestimating the chances of effective action against Hitler and disregarding the practical problems of rearmament, international diplomacy and popular aversion to war. The alternative picture is of the visionary who clearly saw the nature of the Hitler regime, the only ways to stand up to it and the duty that Britain had to maintain the balance of power and the sheer integrity of its position as a great power. A third interpretation is the practical politician who shared many of the same ideas as his Conservative colleagues, did not push opposition too far and was always keen to return to office, but was careful after the war to rewrite history in much more dramatic and clear-cut terms. It is up to you to make up your own mind based on the evidence and your own further reading.

By the end of this chapter, we saw Churchill on the verge of being once again a major figure in policy making. The period from 1931–39 was a controversial one and judgements have to be made about a number of issues concerning Churchill's relationship with those in power, the alternatives he put forward to policies and how realistic his view of international politics and Britain's interests were. Sources not only have to be compared, but evaluated in the light of their nature as evidence and in the light of contextual knowledge.

At this point you should be familiar with the need to consider different interpretations, to look at issues, rather than merely a sequence of events, and to use sources critically. These skills will be extended in Chapter 4.

Exam Café

At this point, it would be useful to undertake an audit to see what skills you are comfortable with and what you need more support in developing. Go to page 164-73 of the Exam Café and complete the activities there.

Bibliography

Charmley, J. (1993) *Churchill: The End of Glory*, pp. 161, 227, 271, 304–5 308–9, 360–61. Hodder.

Churchill, W.S. (1948) *The Gathering Storm*, pp. 106, 244, 246. Penguin.

Herman, A. (2008) *Gandhi and Churchill: The Epic Rivalry That Destroyed an Empire and Forged Our Age*, p. 513. Bantam Dell.

Nicolson, H. (collection edited 1967) *Diaries and Letters*, (ed: Nigel Nicolson), Collins, 1967.

Parker, R.A.C. (2000) *Churchill and Appeasement,* pp. 143–4, 155–7, 258–9. Macmillan.

Pelling, H. (1999) *Winston Churchill*, pp. 381–82. Wordsworth Editions.

Ponting, C. (1994) *Churchill,* p. 698. Sinclair-Stevenson.

Ramsden, J. (2003) *The Man of the Century: Winston Churchill and his Legend Since 1945,* p. 208. HarperCollins.

Reynolds, D. (2004) *In Command of History*, pp. 99, 102. Allen Lane.

Rhodes James, R. (1973) *Churchill: A Study in Failure*, p. 298. Penguin.

Rhodes James, R. (ed) (1980) *Churchill Speaks*, p. 313. Chelsea House.

Shen, P. (1999) *The Age of Appeasement: The Evolution of British Foreign Policy in the 1930s*, pp. 272–3. Sutton Publishing.

Wavell A.P., Moon, P. (ed) (1973) *Wavell: The Viceroy's Journal*, pp. 22–23. Oxford University Press.

Churchill as a Great Wartime Prime Minister

In this chapter, we will look at why and how Churchill became Prime Minister after such an inauspicious decade prior to 1940. The main elements of the specification content dealt with in this chapter relates to the key issue of 'How far does Churchill deserve his reputation as a great wartime Prime Minister?' The stance he took in 1940 and how his personal style affected his leadership skills are discussed. Also, his relations with his generals and his impact on strategic decisions made in the war about the Mediterranean, plus the bombing of Germany and the war in Europe 1944–45 will be covered. Churchill then lost the 1945 election and we will look at why. Finally, his view of post-war reconstruction is touched on.

Key Questions

Areas of study are:

1 Why did Churchill become Prime Minister?
2 What was Churchill's style of leadership?
3 How justified is the view that Churchill in 1940 was a great wartime leader?
4 What was Churchill's relationship with his generals?
5 How did Churchill's relationships with his senior commanders impact on the war?
6 What were the plans for reconstruction and why did Churchill lose the 1945 election?

In this chapter there will be more comparison and evaluation of sources and more opportunities to practise making supported judgements about issues. There will be opportunities to combine more of what you know about the provenance of Sources with your own knowledge in order to make judgements.

Sources

Two very differing opinions of Churchill. Source A is from Hitler and B is from an historian.

Churchill is the most bloodthirsty of amateur strategists that History has ever known. He is as bad as a soldier as he is as a politician. Like a madman, Churchill has always been running all over Europe to look for a country to become a battlefield. His May Day speech was symptomatic of a paralytic disease, or the ravings of a drunkard.

Quoted in Charles Eade, *Churchill by his contemporaries*, 1953, Hutchinson, p. 142

I now put Churchill with all his idiosyncrasies, his indulgences, his occasional childishness, but also his genius, his tenacity and his persistent ability, right or wrong, successful or unsuccessful, to be larger than life, as the greatest human being ever to occupy 10 Downing Street.

Jenkins, *Churchill*, 2001 p. 912.

These opinions in Sources A and B are about as far apart as possible and an analysis could compare the date, purpose, situation and intention of these comments by a bitter wartime enemy, and an admiring peacetime biographer. However, there was more criticism of Churchill at the time than wartime propaganda and post-war reminiscences might suggest. The post-war reputation of Churchill surged and his own account of the Second World War put a highly favourable view of his leadership forward as objective history. The diaries of those who worked with Churchill offer, sometimes, a more critical view and there have been some very hostile historical accounts of his leadership as well as many favourable ones, so there is a considerable debate about many of the issues in this chapter.

Why did Churchill become Prime Minister?

The answer might seem obvious. Once war started, then who more suitable to lead Britain than the greatest critic of appeasement and the politician who had been willing to risk war in order to deter aggression? Who else had wartime leadership experience and actual knowledge of fighting which went back so far?

However, there were a number of limitations. Firstly, Churchill's age and the history he had of military misjudgements. Secondly, his uneasy relations with his own party and with the opposition over a range of issues before the war. Thirdly, the respect that senior ministers, particularly Lord Halifax, had in political circles. There was much more consensus about Churchill being valuable in the War Cabinet than there was about him being Prime Minister as Churchill's record before May 1940 did not necessarily inspire confidence.

Norway

Churchill was eager for action, but not by invading Germany. Instead he urged action in Scandinavia. Germany imported important Swedish iron ore via Norway. Germany moved the iron ore from Sweden by land to Norwegian Narvik and then by sea, hugging the Norwegian coastline. Both Sweden and Norway were neutral. Britain needed to have a route for supplies to reach Finland, then being attacked by Russia. It also needed to prevent metal ores reaching Germany. Churchill's initial idea was to mine Norway's waters to force the German ships into the North Sea where the Royal Navy could sink them.

There were however, problems. Firstly, interference would be likely to result in German occupation of Norway, for which a German military plan already existed. It would also make German occupation of Denmark likely. Secondly, supplying Finland could provoke Russia into joining Germany against Britain.

Such a campaign in Norway would have many difficulties such as keeping lines of communication protected against German planes and U-boats in the North Sea, and also those forces would have been better deployed in Northern France.

Churchill cared little for Norwegian neutrality, as was shown when British forces raided the German supply ship *Altmark* in a Norwegian fjord to rescue 300 allied prisoners on 16 February 1940. This rescue killed six crew members and overawed the Norwegian coastal vessels. This action was popular in Britain but hastened German action against Norway.

Case Study: The Norway campaign

On 28 March the operation (*Operation Wilfred* – so named after a naive character from the popular comic strip 'Pip, Squeak and Wilfred') to mine Norwegian coastal waters was approved to begin on 8 April. The Germans were aware of British plans and there was poor secrecy. In early April Churchill chaired the Ministerial Defence Committee, effectively running the military operations of the war.

There was little preparation made for the German attack on Norway which set out on 7 April. The German invasion of Denmark began on 9 April and on the same day German forces landed in Norway. There were two naval engagements in Narvik, and, from 14 April, there were allied landings at Trondheim, Narvik, Namos and Harstad. On 17 April the British landed at Andalsnes. The campaign went badly and allied evacuations began on 30 April.

Though Narvik was taken from the Germans, the final decision to evacuate was taken on 1 June. By that time, German advances through the Low Countries and into France had made the campaign irrelevant. Norwegian resistance ended on 10 June and the country remained occupied.

Churchill was the main initiator of the Norway campaign, yet did not take the blame for its failure. He told Chamberlain that he had not had enough of a free hand and could not bear responsibility for the continuing situation. He blamed the Norwegians. Yet he has had a lot of criticism subsequently. However, contemporaries did not blame him as much as historians. Chamberlain took overall responsibility and suffered for the failures.

Criticisms of Norway

The burden of the criticism is that:

- the consequences of mining Norwegian waters and breaking Norwegian neutrality were not considered properly and there were no plans to meet German counter-measures.
- the campaign was at best a side show with limited results. The idea of helping Finland was misguided and may have been a justification for the campaign rather than a real motive.
- Churchill, as with the Gallipoli campaign of 1915, with which Norway was compared at the time, took valuable resources that were needed in the Low Countries and France when the Germans invaded.
- Churchill interfered ineffectively with the conduct of war, often changing his mind and not providing his forces with proper equipment and plans.
- Britain lost the moral high ground by ruthless action – especially in view of the *Altmark* incident.

Why then did Churchill not only survive the debate, but end up as Prime Minister?

The answer may be that even if the campaign had been a poorly-managed failure as a whole, it had showed that Britain was being active in opposing Hitler. The *Altmark* affair was a popular success. The Royal Navy had shown its worth in the campaign sinking ten German destroyers and badly damaging many more as well as sinking the battleship

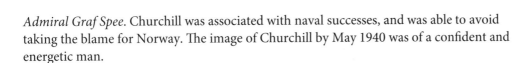

Admiral Graf Spee. Churchill was associated with naval successes, and was able to avoid taking the blame for Norway. The image of Churchill by May 1940 was of a confident and energetic man.

Sources

 A modern historian assesses Norway

A French officer complained 'The British have planned this campaign on the lines of a punitive expedition against the Zulus'.

The Norway campaign was uncoordinated, flawed in concept and massively mismanaged by Churchill, who hardly seemed to be able to make up his mind, and when he did make it up, invariably undermined an almost unwinnable campaign by making decisions as if he were the commander-in-chief and by violated cardinal principles of war. Churchill's habits of micromanagement and of bullying his subordinates did nothing to improve his capacity to understand the consequences of his actions. As he had been over the Dardanelles, Churchill was unrepentant over the failure of the Norway Campaign, blaming it on 'the impotence and fatuity of waging war by committee'.

The great irony of the campaign is that instead of crushing his career, its negative repercussions hardly touched him.

From Carlo d'Este: Warlor, *A Life of Churchill at War* p.418.

 Churchill's verdict

Failure at Trondheim! Stalemate at Narvik! Such in the first week of May 1940 were the only results we could show to the British nation, to our allies and to the neutral world, friendly or unfriendly. Considering the prominent part I played in these events and the impossibility in explaining the difficulties with which we had been overcome, or the defects of our staff and government organization and our methods of conducting war, it was a miracle that I survived and maintained my position in public esteem and Parliamentary confidence.

From: W. Churchill, *The Gathering Storm*, p. 583.

ACTIVITY

Compare the content, nature, purpose and reliability of Sources A and B on Norway.

Note: In the AS examination you will not be required to compare a primary with a secondary source.

The puzzle is why Churchill was able to become Prime Minister with such a doubtful record. One reason is the impact that his speeches had. Already his oratory was making him a famous figure. Another may be that he stood out in a government of rather colourless personalities as a recognisable and dynamic figure. On 8 May 1940 he was defending the government in a debate on the failures of the Norway campaign which turned into a major attack on the ministerial decisions. Chamberlain won the debate but decided that he could not go on. Churchill was not the first choice to replace him, but rather Lord Halifax. Halifax's reluctance to stand was a key decision. He was concerned that he should not be able to lead the government from his seat in the House of Lords, but King George VI, who favoured him, thought that he could be given special permission to sit in the House of Commons. Halifax would certainly have been a popular choice and both Labour and Liberals would have served under him. However, he did not stand and it was with some reluctance that the King sent for Churchill. Churchill made it clear to Chamberlain and Halifax that he depended on their support and high standing with most of the Conservatives and the nation to be able to operate as Prime Minister.

Therefore, it is wrong to assume that once war broke out Churchill was the clear choice to lead. The following source is from someone who was initially quite sceptical of Churchill, though later Sir John ('Jock') Colville, was to become one of Churchill's closest advisers and greatest admirers. Colville began the war as one of Neville Chamberlain's private secretaries.

He listened to Churchill's first wartime broadcast of 1 October 1939, and commented:

> 'He certainly gives one confidence and will, I suspect, be Prime Minister before this war is over. Nevertheless, judging from his record of untrustworthiness and instability, he may, in that case, lead us into the most dangerous paths. But he is the only man in the country who commands anything like universal respect, and perhaps with age he has become less inclined to undertake rash adventures.'

Reservations were expressed in the diary of Sir Alexander Cadogan, Permanent Under-Secretary at the Foreign Office, 9 May 1940:

> 'I'm not at all sure of WSC [Churchill]…I don't think they'll get a better PM than Neville [Chamberlain].'

Sources

A **Colville's diary entry for Thursday 25 April 1940. Colville was Assistant Private Secretary to Churchill 1940–41 and 1943–45.**

The trouble about Winston, which has been brewing for the last few days, arises from his demand to be appointed Chairman of the Chiefs of Staff Committee. This would not only annoy the other service ministers but would also probably cause chaos among the Chiefs of Staff and planning experts, because, as was shown when Winston presided over the Military Co-ordination Committee, his verbosity and restlessness make a great deal of unnecessary work, prevent any real practical planning from being done and generally cause friction.

B **From the diary of Leo Kennedy, diplomatic editor of *The Times*, 4 May 1940.**

There is a drive against Chamberlain. I can't quite see who can advantageously take his place. Curiously enough what is really needed is that Winston should be made to take a rest. He is overdoing himself and taking the strain by stoking himself unduly with champagne, liqueurs etc; Dines out and dines well almost every night. Sleeps after luncheon, then to the House O' Commons, then a good and long dinner, and doesn't resume work at the Admiralty till after 10pm, and goes on till 1 or 2am. He has got into the habit of calling conferences and subordinates after 1am, which naturally upsets some of the Admirals who are men of sound habits. So there is a general atmosphere of strain at the Admiralty which is all wrong. Yet Winston is such a popular hero and so much the war-leader that he cannot be dropped. But he ought somehow to be rested!

C **Chamberlain's opponents managed to make the debate on Narvik on 8 May, a debate in which Churchill had to defend the Government and his own involvement as First Lord of the Admiralty, into a vote of confidence in the administration's conduct of the war to date. Churchill, writing later in his war memoirs, described the moment.**

From the benches behind the Government Mr Amery [Leo Amery, a leading Conservative opponent of Chamberlain] quoted amid ringing cheers Cromwell's imperious words to the Long Parliament: 'you have sat too long here for any [of the?] good you have been doing. Depart, I say, and let us have done with you. In the name of God, go!' These were terrible words coming from a friend and colleague of many years, a fellow Birmingham Member, and a Privy Councillor of distinction and experience.

D **For many, this was a difficult situation. Quentin Hogg, later Lord Hailsham, was the young Member for Oxford University who had won his seat in Parliament in a 1938 by-election supporting Chamberlain's foreign policy against an anti-appeasement candidate. In an unpublished, hand-written memoir that survives in the Churchill archives in his papers, he describes his own personal dilemma.**

The Speaker rose and put the question. I did not alter. I sat in one of the little cross benches by the Sergeant of Arms, with a colleague also in uniform. What should I do? Abstain,

as many subsequently did? Vote against and perhaps bring my country as well as the Government down? I was never more lonely in my life. As the Speaker rose a second time to tell the Sergeant to lock the doors, I brushed past the attendant with my colleague and got into the opposition lobby as the door closed behind me. I felt like a traitor…'.

In a later hand he has added, 'I was one of the minority, 281 ayes to 200 noes. My disloyalty, I thought, has not even succeeded in its object.'

(E) From a paper by Allen Packwood, the Keeper of the Churchill Archive in Churchill College Cambridge where these sources can be found, entitled 'A Week in London', 2008.

Churchill became Prime Minister on 10 May 1940. It was not a result that had been wanted by all, it emerged rather suddenly from a specific crisis, and Churchill began his famous Premiership in a rather precarious political position. He was dependent upon the good will of Chamberlain and Halifax, who at this stage continued to command more loyalty and support than Churchill from the Conservative rank and file. His ability to form a Government rested upon the support of the Labour and Liberal opposition parties. Moreover, there were many in Whitehall and the establishment who were sceptical about the new Prime Minister and with a massive unfolding military crisis in France, even his large public support could easily turn against him if things did not improve. The archives show how seriously Churchill prepared for his speeches to his political colleagues and the British people. By stripping away the layers of hindsight, the archives also reveal just how important these speeches were to his position, and quite how fragile that position was.

All sources taken from the Churchill Archives.

ACTIVITY

The following exercise is based on Sources A–E above from the Churchill Archive.

Using these sources consider the view that Churchill did not have overwhelming support in 1940 and only became Prime Minister because of doubts about Chamberlain.

1 Take each of the sources and comment on their usefulness by reference to their provenance.

   a   Consider when they were written.

   b   Consider the position of the authors.

   c   Think about how typical the authors were and whether they were in a position to know.

2 Now consider what knowledge you might bring to assess the value of these sources.

Churchill was not only in a difficult position politically, but the war had taken a dramatic turn for the worse with the invasion of France by Germany and the retreat of British forces. The rapid advance of the Germans and the failure of the French to hold them led to a major crisis and British forces had to be evacuated from Dunkirk (1940).

Britain faced the loss of its major ally, France, and the danger of invasion from Germany. The control of the air seemed to be the key element in preventing defeat, but even if Britain were not invaded, it still faced a powerful enemy without the support of allies. The nightmare of the military chiefs had come true: Britain faced a huge danger from Germany, Italy and Japan simultaneously.

What was Churchill's style of leadership?

The traditional view

The traditional picture is that Churchill's qualities now came into their own:

- His oratory rallied the nation and his personality persuaded his Cabinet and his military commanders.
- His courage and blind faith in Britain sustained him when logic suggested an end to the war and some sort of deal with Hitler.

By surviving 1940 and managing to get some US aid, Britain stayed in the war. Then, when Hitler invaded Russia and Japan attacked America, this created the platform for the Grand Alliance that Churchill had dreamed of, and which proved to be the main element in the Allies eventual victory.

Does this mean that whatever doubts politicians and civil servants, not to mention the royal family, had about Churchill in May 1940 were proved to be invalid? Certainly his stand in the face of disaster meant that he was seen as a great war leader by the end of the year. But were his policies the right ones?

Churchill's oratory: the speeches of 1940

Churchill's speeches remain the most famous and important examples of inspirational oratory in British history. They have been seen as a key element in keeping up British determination to resist under very difficult circumstances and a major element in Churchill's greatness as a leader. The speeches can still be heard online.

Three speeches give a flavour of the power of Churchill's oratory:

---

1 Blood, toil, tears, and sweat

Churchill became England's Prime Minister on 10 May 1940. On 13 May, he addressed the House of Commons for the first time as Prime Minister:

'We are in the preliminary stage of one of the greatest battles in history. I would say to the House as I said to those who have joined this Government: I have nothing to offer but blood, toil, tears, and sweat. We have before us an ordeal of the most grievous kind. We have before us many, many long months of struggle and suffering…You ask, what is our aim? I can answer in one word: Victory. Victory at all costs—victory in spite of terror—victory, however long and hard the road may be, for without victory there is no survival.'

2 We shall fight on the beaches

4 June 1940: British forces had had to be evacuated from Dunkirk following a massive and successful German attack.

> *'I have myself full confidence that if all do their duty, if nothing is neglected, and if the best arrangements are made, as they are being made, we shall prove ourselves once again able to defend our island home, to ride out the storm of war, and to outlive the menace of tyranny, if necessary for years, if necessary alone. Even though large tracts of Europe and many old and famous States have fallen or may fall into the grip of the Gestapo and all the odious apparatus of Nazi rule, we shall not flag or fail. We shall go on to the end, we shall fight in France, we shall fight on the seas and oceans, we shall fight with growing confidence and growing strength in the air, we shall defend our island, whatever the cost may be, we shall fight on the beaches, we shall fight on the landing grounds, we shall fight in the fields and in the streets, we shall fight in the hills; we shall never surrender!'*

3 This was their finest hour

On 18 June 1940: Churchill again addressed the House of Commons. The collapse of France was likely, and with it the only substantial army that stood against the Germans.

> *'I expect that the Battle of Britain is about to begin. Upon this battle depends the survival of Christian civilization. Upon it depends our own British life, and the long continuity of our institutions and our Empire. The whole fury and might of the enemy must very soon be turned upon us. Hitler knows he will have to break us in this Island or lose the war. If we can stand up to him, all of Europe may be free and the life of the world may move forward into broad, sunlit uplands. But if we fail, then the whole world, including the United States including all that we have known and cared for will sink into the abyss of a new Dark Age made more sinister, and perhaps more protracted, by the lights of perverted science. Let us therefore brace ourselves to our duties, and so bear ourselves that, if the British Empire and its Commonwealth last for a thousand years, men will still say, "This was their finest hour."'*

These speeches were all delivered to the House of Commons. Churchill did not personally broadcast them and the first was not broadcast at all. Churchill was not interested in direct addresses to the nation. Harold Nicolson describes a very reluctant performance on 19 June. Nicolson was then working for the Ministry of Information. He knew Churchill well and was an eminent former diplomat and MP.

> *'When we bullied him into speaking he just sulked and read the House of Commons speech over again. Now as delivered in the House of Commons, that speech was magnificent, especially the concluding sentences. But it sounded ghastly on the wireless (radio). All the great vigour he put into it seemed to evaporate.'*
>
> (Harold Nicolson's Diaries)

Churchill did not address the nation between 14 July and 11 September 1940 at all. The impression was given of a united nation. The famous Low cartoon is the generally accepted picture of the mood of 1940 (Figure 4.1).

ALL BEHIND YOU, WINSTON

Figure 4.1   'All Behind you, Winston', by David Low and appeared in the *Evening Standard*, a London newspaper

Churchill's blind faith in Britain

The Ministry of Information was collecting reports of public opinion:

'There is great restlessness, great depression at the fall of France. Home morale is still bungled. The appeals of the leadership are failing to register. The reasons are partly that persons responsible for propaganda and morale have no sympathy with the majority of the masses.' (Report: 24 June 1940, quoted Ponting, p. 448.)

Churchill's popularity increased when he became the symbol of the defence of Britain. Gradually there were more successful attempts to rally the nation: the creation of the Home Guard; the success of the 'Battle of Britain'. Churchill's visual impact in photographs (Figure 4.2) and posters with his cigar, V-sign for Victory and publicised walkabouts were just as important as his speeches.

Figure 4.2   Churchill disliked this portrait and thought it humourless, but it represented defiance.

Timeline – 1940

10 January	Mechelen Incident: A German plan carrying secret plans for the invasion of western Europe force lands in Belgium.
16 February	Altmark Incident: A British destroyer rescues 303 British POWs from the German transport *Altmark* in neutral Norwegian territorial waters.
9 April	Germany invades Denmark and Norway. The British campaign in Norway begins.
10 May	Battle of France begins – German forces invade Low Countries; Iceland is invaded by the United Kingdom; Winston Churchill becomes Prime Minister.
15 May	The Dutch army surrenders.
17 May	Brussels captured by German forces; the Belgian government flees.
26 May	The Dunkirk evacuation of British Expeditionary Force begins.
10 June	Italy declares was on France and the United Kingdom; Norway surrenders to German forces.
14 June	Paris is occupied by German forces; the French government flees.
17 June	France asks Germany for peace terms.
18 June	Winston Churchill makes speech in the House of Commons stating that "The Battle of France is over. The Battle of Britain is about to begin.
30 June	German forces land in Guernsey.
10 July	The Battle of Britain begins.
2 September	50 US destroyers are transferred to Great Britain in return for use of a number of British naval bases.
7 September	The Blitz aerial bombing attack on London begin.
27 September	Germany, Italy and Japan sign a joint alliance treaty.
14 November	Coventry is bombed by 500 German aircraft. 60,000 of the city's 75,000 buildings are destroyed and over 500 people are killed.
20 November	Hungry, Romania and Slovakia join the Axis Powers.

Did the speeches and the images of unquestioned defiance reflect the truth?

It is not exactly true that Churchill never considered negotiating peace terms. Churchill, of necessity, had to consider negotiation, even if it was just a fall-back plan. Before the Grand Alliance became fact Britain was losing the war through lack of resources. Churchill's government was running out of time.

Consider Sources A and B. How far do they confirm or challenge the view that there was no thought of compromise or defeat by Churchill in May 1940?

Britain supported France's idea of approaching Mussolini through Roosevelt (Source A, page 96) with a view to bringing the Italians into the alliance against Nazi Germany. However, by 28 May it was clear that Roosevelt was not interested. The British Cabinet decided that it might be better to store up concessions such as giving Mussolini Malta or Gibraltar in case they should have to be given to Hitler later on. As the USA was not interested in supporting negotiations with Italy, it became clear that Britain had little option but to continue fighting; especially as Churchill felt that the terms Britain would get from Germany on surrendering the war would be similar if not the same whether they went on fighting or not (Source B). This very secret discussion was certainly not the public face. Churchill did not accept Halifax's suggestion on 27 May that Britain should find out what Hitler's terms might be, but Churchill argued not from any moral imperative, but because he had no hope that Hitler would settle for anything as limited as overlordship of central Europe.

Sources

A A telegram from Churchill on 24 May 1940 to the British ambassador in Paris.

The idea put forward by the French Prime Minister and the Minister for Foreign Affairs to approach Signor Mussolini through the President of the United States is welcome to His Majesty's Government.

We are aware that the Italian government entertains certain grievances in regard to the Italian position in the Mediterranean. We are prepared to consider reasonable Italian claims at the end of the war.

Would welcome Italy's participation at the peace conference with a status equal to the belligerents.

The offer would be more attractive to the Italian government if the US government would not only sponsor but guarantee it.

Public Record Office, *Cabinet Minutes*.

B Colville's diary 28 May 1940 (though not the Cabinet minutes) records Churchill as saying:

We should get no worse terms [from Germany] if we went on fighting, even if we were beaten, than were open to us now. A time might come when we felt that we had to put an end to the struggle, but the terms then would not be more mortal [severe] than those offered to us now.

We felt that we had resources left to us which we could make good use. If, as we believed we could hold out, we should be able to obtain terms which would not affect our independence.

Ponting, p. 446.

The Cabinet records, which now can be downloaded from the public office website, reveal that even if Churchill's words were not the ones he used in public or in his later accounts, he nevertheless advocated continuing resistance. In retrospect the likelihood of a German invasion was never very strong, largely because any German landings would have been destroyed by the navy, but at the time there was a genuine fear that Germany would invade Britain. Nevertheless, the maintenance of air superiority in an extended air campaign from August to September was the first real defeat of a German force and the Battle of Britain boosted morale. The decision to send a force to North Africa to protect Egypt and the Suez Canal was a brave one when the army had barely recovered from being evacuated from France. It was rewarded by victories against the Italians who had joined the war in June 1940 in the wake of French defeats.

ACTIVITY

Re-read the chapter so far and consider how far you agree with the view expressed below.

A.L. Rowse, Churchill's friend and the biographer of the family, wrote in *The Later Churchills* published in 1958:

> *'By the end of the year 1940 a remarkable transformation had come over the outlook for us. The Battle of Britain had defeated all serious threat of invasion. Suez was firmly held and one of the Axis partners (Italy) had been started on the road to defeat…For us the year 1940 must ever rank with the other annus mirabilis 1588. Transcendent as were the services yet to come from Churchill, 1940 must rank as his finest hour, along with the nation's, for in that year, his contribution made the difference between defeat and survival.'*

Stretch and challenge

What if? A debate to consider

There is an alternative view. **IMPORTANT**: *This is a view for consideration; many reject it and some consider it as an insult to those who fought in the war.*

The argument runs that Chamberlain had been right in a political if not a moral sense in appeasing Hitler because there was no real British interest involved in a German conquest of Eastern Europe: this is a very expedient view and certainly not a moral one.

When Russia dominated Eastern Europe after 1945 our national existence was not threatened, and it would not have been by Hitler creating 'Lebensraum'. In the end we made more concessions to both the USA and the USSR than we ever did to Hitler. Instead of saving Poland we consigned it to Russian domination. Instead of preserving the British Empire we weakened ourselves so much that it was lost. As a Great Power we felt obliged to make a stand in 1939, but the war ended our Great Power status as much as a Nazi victory would have done.

In *Mein Kampf* there is little that was hostile to Britain. Hitler could not understand why Britain was so concerned with Eastern Europe. The German navy was not a threat to Britain as it had been before 1914 and the German air force had no plans for war against Britain. Hitler was not interested in the return of pre-1914 German colonies or in eradicating the British Empire. His geopolitical aims were targeted on Russia, a country with which Britain had had poor relations since 1917 and of whose ideology its rulers disapproved. In the event of a massive struggle between Germany and the USSR, Britain could have remained neutral and benefited from the exhaustion of two bloodthirsty regimes battling against each other. Actually, Britain attempted to do this for much of the war, delaying the Second Front until 1944 and restricting the use of large-scale land forces to the minimum.

Without British participation in the war, it would have had the resources to stop the Japanese assaults on South-East Asia in co-operation with America and would have prevented the humiliating defeats of 1942, which saw the beginning of the end for the Empire.

It would have been better if Churchill had not pressured the government into war. It would even have been better if negotiations had been made with Hitler after Dunkirk. Churchill did not understand what Britain's true interests were.

ACTIVITY

There are a number of counter-arguments possible here. Read the analysis of those views on page 98, and then answer the following question:

How justified is the view that Churchill fought an unnecessary and harmful war?

Historians have debated the effects of Churchill's speeches. Cabinet records have shown more doubts about the outcome of events than Churchill's public statements revealed and the degree of national unity has been challenged by evidence from surveys and reports about public opinion. However, the forceful and determined approach taken by Churchill to waging war and the belief that Britain had everything to gain by maintaining resistance and waiting for the Soviet Union and the USA proved to be the right one in ensuring the survival of British independence and the eventual defeat of Nazi Germany.

ANALYSIS

Analysis of counter-arguments

Firstly, the sudden collapse of the French forces in 1940 was not foreseen by either Britain or Hitler. There was no reason to base policy on a very large army collapsing so quickly, though Chamberlain had seen the French as potentially weak.

Secondly, the maintenance of a balance of power in Europe was a long-standing British policy and could be justified. If Germany had controlled Poland, then the prestige of Hitler and the army would have been so great that other conquests would have followed, especially as Nazi Germany was a state devoted to armed expansion. A war against Russia without the German forces being distracted by Britain and a campaign in the Mediterranean might have been more successful. As it was, the Germans nearly won in 1941. The assumption that the long struggle that did take place between Germany and Russia between 1941 and 1945 would have taken place if Britain had not been fighting Germany is not justified. Had Russia been conquered then Britain's position would have been very dangerous. There was no certainty of US support and no certainty that France and Britain would not have been completely dominated by a German empire stretching from Cologne to Vladivostok.

Thirdly, critics of Churchill assume that it would have been possible to have some sort of meaningful agreement with the Hitler regime based on mutual self-interest. But Hitler's allies did not do well. They were forced into supporting anti-Semitic policies and into helping with Germany's war effort. Also, the Third Reich had a massive irrational agenda of racial purification which made it an unreliable partner. What guarantee would there have been that Britain would have been able to sustain her independence after a successful campaign by Germany in Russia?

Fourthly, the arguments that Britain was forced into concessions to the USA and Russia anyway are flawed. There was a world of difference in the USA pressuring Britain to follow economic policies after 1945, and not supporting the British Empire, to the type of pressure that an all-powerful Hitler would have exerted. The antagonism between Russia and America, too, prevented any joint pressure being put on Britain.

The whole idea that Churchill might have been wrong in wanting to fight and defeat Hitler would have been impossible to debate until relatively recently. It is certainly now a valid debate and has opened up interesting issues. It may affect judgement about whether Churchill was a great wartime politician in 1940 if a view is taken that his basic aim was flawed.

How justified is the view that Churchill in 1940 was a great wartime leader?

It might be better to end this section with an account of a meeting Churchill called of those Cabinet ministers not in the War Cabinet on 28 May 1940; Churchill said to them 'Of course, whatever happens at Dunkirk, we shall fight on'. In *The Gathering Storm*, Churchill described their enthusiastic reaction, running up to him and patting him on the back.

Earlier in the War Cabinet, there had been talk of terms. Later that day Churchill was resolute (Source A, on page 99).

The diary of Leo Amery confirms the incident if not the actual wording. Later Churchill met the War Cabinet again and confirmed his view that, given the enthusiasm of the other ministers, there would be no negotiation. Halifax mentioned the possibility of approaching the USA and received a final put down (Source B).

Sources

(A) **Hugh Dalton, a Labour member of the Cabinet wrote down what was said by Churchill.**

"It is idle to think that if we tried to make peace now we should get better terms from Germany than if we went on and fought it out. The Germans would demand our fleet...We should become a slave state though a British Government which would be Hitler's puppet would be set up..."

On the other side, we had immense resources and advantages, Therefore, he said "We shall go on and we shall fight it out, here or elsewhere and if at last the long story is to end, it were better it should end not through surrender but only when we are rolling senseless on the ground."

Dalton added a marginal note "when each of us lies choking on his own blood."

Dalton's memoirs.

(B) **Churchill's response to Halifax on approaching the USA (see also page 98).**

The Prime Minister thought to appeal to the United States at the present would be altogether premature. If we made a bold stand against Germany, that would command their admiration, but a grovelling approach would have the worst possible effect.

The Public Record Office, *Minutes of War Cabinet meeting*, 28 May 1940.

ACTIVITY

'To what extent do Sources A and B confirm the view that Churchill was a great wartime leader in May 1940?'

Discussion points:

- Did Churchill actually know what terms Hitler proposed?

- Was Halifax right to want to know what Hitler might have wanted or was Churchill right to avoid giving any impression of weakness to the USA?

- Was Churchill right to use his sense of drama to win over the ministers not of Cabinet rank?

- Was Churchill being a clever politician to use the support of the lesser ministers to win over doubters in the War Cabinet or should he have pursued suggestions for negotiations?

Churchill and the Battle of Britain

'*Never in the field of human conflict was so much owed by so many to so few.*' Churchill's words sum up the huge importance that contemporaries saw in the British maintaining air superiority over Britain in August and September 1940. It was believed that the RAF had prevented a German invasion. Churchill himself gave the name to this conflict in the air on 18 June 1940:

'The Battle of France is over. I expect the Battle of Britain is about to begin...'

The French had been defeated and there was every expectation that Britain would be invaded and that a struggle for national survival would begin. Sir Hugh Dowding, the head of Fighter Command must take much of the credit for victory in the Battle of Britain. Not only was the organisation of the RAF defences his responsibility, but he had opposed Churchill in two crucial decisions.

1. He had urged on 15 May that Churchill's promise to commit another ten squadrons of fighters to aid the French army, then beyond any real help, should not be honoured. These aircraft were available for home defence in August.

2. Then he resisted Churchill's suggestion that an all out attack should be made on the German Luftwaffe following the first day of the Battle of Britain on 13 August 1940, when the Germans had suffered heavier losses than the RAF.

It was vital that Dowding kept his forces intact in order to go on defeating the Germans and not risk them in the early stages of the battle. It was the strategy of using radar intelligently, and being careful to keep the loss of trained pilots and aircraft to a minimum, which was to be successful. That, together with the German decision to switch air attacks to British cities away from airfields on 7 September 1940, ensured British victory.

The very effective British aircraft, the Hurricanes and Spitfires, had been developed under Churchill's much-criticised predecessors, MacDonald and Baldwin. Churchill had played little part in this or in the growth of radar. His operational advice was unsound and he failed to prevent Dowding falling victim to rivalries within the top RAF command and being virtually sacked after the battle. The Labour leader, Attlee, was asked what Churchill's contribution to the battle was and he replied 'just words'. However, Churchill's memorable and splendid oratory was indeed inspirational and gave the RAF pilots their place in history.

The Second World War, 1941–45

At the start of 1941 Britain and her Empire stood alone and was fighting a three-front war.

■ One was at sea, where the navy had to keep the supply lines from North America open and to maintain the defence of Britain.

■ The other was in the air where the RAF had to maintain the defence of Britain and to carry the war to Germany by bombing.

■ Thirdly there was the war in North Africa to defend Egypt and the Suez Canal and beyond that the oilfields of the Middle East.

Churchill was committed to total warfare, as the sinking of the French fleet at Oran in 1940 had shown, to prevent it being taken by either Germany or Italy. However, there was little prospect of fighting in Europe. The invasion by Hitler of Russia in June 1941 transformed the war and Churchill had no hesitation in putting his hostility to the Soviet Union behind him. There was increasing co-operation between Britain and the USA but little possibility of Roosevelt joining the war until Japan attacked the US base at Pearl Harbour in December 1941.

The Japanese followed this up with invasions of all the European and American colonies in South-East Asia and Britain suffered a huge defeat when Singapore fell in 1942. German reinforcements under Rommel's brilliant leadership had reversed Britain's victories in North Africa. Churchill blamed his generals and took a leading part in strategic discussions and in appointments. Despite the mostly respected work of General Claude Auchinleck in Africa he was replaced by General Montgomery who defeated the Germans at El Alamein in October 1942 and began a drive through North Africa. The American forces joined this campaign in Tunisia and in 1943 the long awaited assault on mainland Europe began by an invasion of Sicily, which led to a lengthy campaign in Italy. When Mussolini fell later in 1943, German troops took over the resistance, which was maintained until 1945.

In the Far East, India was defended against Japanese attacks and counter-attacks begun in Burma while the Americans took on the main burden of regaining South-East Asia. The Japanese advance was finally halted in the Solomon Islands in 1943 and an extended two prong drive was undertaken, which finally reached the outer islands of Japan itself.

The Germans had failed to take Moscow and Leningrad in 1941. A 900-day siege of Leningrad achieved little and a drive to the south was held by the Russians at Stalingrad. Huge Russian counter-attacks in 1943–44 drove the Germans back.

The British war effort was focused on the defeat of the U-boats in the *Battle of the Atlantic* and bombing campaigns against Germany, which intensified with US assistance, culminating in massive raids on Dresden in 1945 and the large-scale destruction of most major cities, especially Berlin and Hamburg. Land warfare was restricted to the Far East and the Mediterranean until June 1944 when British and American forces landed in Northern France. From this point losses in the British army mounted to First World War levels, though the campaigns were more mobile. Churchill and his generals resisted Soviet calls for a second front and only when there was an overwhelming Allied accumulation of men and equipment was invasion attempted.

By May 1945 Germany had been invaded by ruthless application of superior force. An attempt to speed up the process by an attack on Arnhem to take a crossing point of the Rhine proved a costly failure. Control of the war had effectively passed to the USA and the USSR by 1944 because of the much greater contribution of US resources and men and the sheer scale of fighting in the east.

The naval power of the US had destroyed the Japanese navy by 1944 and the US had air superiority and the ability to bomb Japan at will by spring of 1945. British forces had been successful in Burma but the bulk of the Japanese army was still intact. However there was no chance of Japan winning or avoiding complete surrender. Even so the danger of massive loss of life in an invasion of the main islands of Japan remained and was one of the factors behind the use of atomic weapons in August 1945 at **Hiroshima and Nagasaki**, which ended the Second World War.

Hiroshima *and* Nagasaki

The British had been part of the development of atomic weapons by the USA. This is not the place to outline the controversy about why they were used. In context, Japan had been heavily bombed and there was concern about the losses that might be incurred if an invasion of the main Japanese homeland took place. It was decided to demonstrate the destructive power developed by the allies by dropping an atomic bomb on Hiroshima. The bomb had its origins in the Manhattan Project set up in 1942. The bomb was tested in the USA on 16 July 1945. The first bomb to be used was dropped on Hiroshima on 6 August 1945. It produced the equivalent of 15 kilotons of energy and killed between 130,000 and 200,000 people. A second bomb was dropped on Nagasaki on 9 August. The Japanese government had no alternative but to accept surrender. The potential damage of future warfare was expanded in a way unthinkable in 1940.

By this time Churchill was out of office. Against all his expectations he lost the election of 1945.

There are three issues to consider from this very complex story:

1. Does Churchill's relationship with his generals indicate that he was a great wartime Prime Minister?

2. What judgement is to be made about Churchill and the bombing campaign against Germany?

3. What measures of reconstruction emerged during the war and why did the electorate reject Churchill as the leader to take forward post-war change in Britain?

What was Churchill's relationship with his generals?

Chiefs of Staff Committee

A Committee of the senior army, navy and air force leaders.

Churchill not only became Prime Minister in 1940 but also Minister of Defence. Unlike previous civilian war leaders, he was directly involved by his membership of the two leading committees which ran military affairs: the Defence Committee of the Cabinet and the Chiefs of Staff Committee.

He was very concerned not to repeat the situation in the First World War in which responsibility for the war was handed over to military experts such as Field Marshall Sir Douglas Haig. He was one of the few prime ministers to have direct military experience – even if this was limited to junior command in colonial wars and a brief period as a lieutenant-colonel on the Western Front in 1916. His writings had led him to a study of military history and he had great confidence in himself as a strategist. Like Hitler, however, he was an amateur working alongside highly-trained professional soldiers. The results were not always harmonious. The most famous criticisms came in the diaries of Lord Alanbrooke, Britain's most senior soldier from 1941–45, who worked closely with Churchill. He was temperamentally very different from Churchill and found the older man's style difficult to cope with.

On 10 September 1944 he wrote in his diary (an entry omitted in the published version):

'[Churchill] *has only got half the picture in his mind, talks absurdities and makes my blood boil to listen to his nonsense. I find it hard to remain civil. And the wonderful thing is that 3/4 of the population of this world imagine that Winston Churchill is one of the Strategists of History, a second Marlborough, and the other 1/4 have no conception what a public menace he is and has been throughout the war! It is far better that the world should never know and never suspect the feet of clay on that otherwise superhuman being. Without him England was lost for a certainty, with him England has been on the verge of disaster time and again…Never have I admired and despised a man simultaneously to the same extent.*'

Churchill believed in direct supervision and detailed questioning of his military leaders. On 30 March 1941, for example, Churchill sent General Sir Hastings Ismay a note regarding an exercise called *Victor*, which had occurred from 22 to 25 January of that year, under the auspices of the then-commander of Home Forces, General Sir Alan Brooke. Churchill's query went as follows:

1. *In the invasion exercise VICTOR, two armoured, one motorised and two infantry divisions were assumed to be landed by the enemy on the Norfolk coast in the teeth of heavy opposition. They fought their way ashore and were all assumed to be in action at the end of forty-eight hours.*

2. *I presume the details of this remarkable feat have been worked out by the Staff concerned. Let me see them. For instance, how many ships and transports carried these five Divisions? How many armoured vehicles did they comprise? How many motor lorries, how many guns, how much ammunition, how many men, how many tons of stores, how far did they advance in the first forty-eight hours, how many men and vehicles were assumed to have landed in the first twelve hours, what percentage of loss were they debited with? What happened to the transports and store-ships while the first forty-eight hours of fighting were going on? Had they completed emptying their cargoes, or were they still lying in shore off the beaches? What naval escort did they have? Was the landing at this point protected by superior enemy daylight Fighter formations? How many Fighter airplanes did the enemy have to employ, if so, to cover the landing places?*

3. *All this data would be most valuable for our future offensive operations. I should be very glad if the same officers would work out a scheme for our landing an exactly similar force on the French coast at the same extreme range of our Fighter protection and assuming that the Germans have naval superiority in the Channel.* (Source: for both documents Prof. Eliot A. Cohen Churchill and his Generals, *Proceedings of the International Churchill Society*, 1992–93.)

This could either be seen as an essential function of leadership – to be a critic and to ensure that military leaders were up to scratch; or it could be a sign of irritating micro-management and undermining of professional soldiers.

Debate about military strategy is often more intense than about any other aspect of history. The generals were prolific after the war in writing their memoirs, and Churchill produced his own very one-sided account in a multi-volume *History of the Second World War*. To give an objective account is difficult. What follows is by and large a critical study of some key points and you must form your own opinion based on the sources and your own further reading.

The Blitzkrieg

Churchill's suggestions (see below) for continuing the conflict by establishing alternative fronts during the confused situation following the German invasion of France in May 1940 seemed to the men on the spot unrealistic, prompting Chief of Staff Pownall to make the comment, '*The man's mad. I suppose these figments of the imagination are telegraphed without consulting his military advisers.*'

The British commander General Gort ignored Churchill's orders, and there is a view that Dunkirk was a success only because Gort had used his own initiative to cover the evacuation against Churchill's advice. Gort did not commit his forces to further support of a defeated French army but concentrated on saving them.

On 24 May the French Prime Minister Reynaud telegraphed London:

'*You had instructed General Gort to continue to carry out the Weygand plan* [i.e. support the French generals]. *The British army instead carried out on its own initiative a retreat of 25 miles towards the Channel ports when our troops moving up from the south are gaining ground.*'

This shows a lack of understanding of the situation from both Reynaud and Churchill, who was complaining about the evacuation of Calais. On 24 May Churchill wrote angrily to the Chief of the Imperial General Staff:

'*Pray find out who was the officer responsible for sending the order to evacuate Calais... Are you sure that there is no streak of defeatist opinion in the General Staff.*'

Blitzkrieg

This is the name given to the German attacks on Poland in 1939 and France and the Low Countries in 1940. It means 'Lightning War': A swift, sudden military offensive, usually by combined air and mobile land forces.

Churchill was reluctant to accept the defeat and overruled his generals and decided to start another British Expeditionary Force (BEF) in France under the command of General Sir Alan Brooke. The 52nd Division, and 1st Canadian Division, which was in reserve in England, were to embark for Cherbourg, sending Brooke ahead to co-ordinate operations. By this time, it was unrealistic to retrieve the situation and Brooke confirmed that another front was impossible. He faced a stubborn Churchill and had to put it bluntly:

> *'He told me...I had been sent to France to make the French feel we were supporting them. I replied that it was impossible to make a corpse feel and that the French army was, to all intents and purposes, dead.'* (Quotes taken from: Knight, *Churchill*, pp. 128–30.)

Oran (3 July 1940)

The surrender of France and the creation of a pro-German regime in the south of the country called Vichy France offered a real danger to Britain. The French fleet at Oran in French North Africa was theoretically under the control of a neutral independent power, but might have been taken by the Germans and used by them against Britain. Therefore Churchill ordered it destroyed.

British military leaders had great doubts about Churchill's orders to sink the French fleet. To destroy it would mean heavy loss of life among former allies and would seem to world opinion to be ruthless.

The decision was opposed by many of those involved, especially Admiral Cunningham who wrote after the war that '90 per cent of senior naval officers, including myself, thought Oran a ghastly error, and still do' (quoted Knight, p. 154). They believed that negotiation could have won the French fleet over to the British side, but orders had to be obeyed and the British Navy reluctantly sunk the French ships, killing 1,297 naval personnel.

The situation leading up to the Dunkirk evacuation and the sinking of the French fleet do demonstrate Churchill's awareness of the bigger picture, however. At Calais in May 1940 Churchill decided to sacrifice several excellent British units to shore up the French defences and to show them that Britain would support them. It was an attempt to keep France in the war and on-side.

At Oran, with France no longer in the war he took a decision that he personally hated having to make, to sink the fleet. Many historians have commented that the powerful message this act sent to the US had a positive impact on opinion there. In both instances it demonstrates Churchill's ruthless desire to win and defeat Germany.

North Africa (Wavell, Auchinleck and Montgomery)

With Italy's entry into the war in June (1940), attention shifted to the Mediterranean. The Desert War produced a flurry of controversy where Churchill took great personal interest in the war and in its generals.

Wavell (Commander-in-Chief Middle East, 1939–41)

Churchill was not an admirer of General Wavell, the Commander-in-Chief of the Middle East. When the Italian forces drove the British forces out of British Somaliland in 1940, Churchill had clashed with Wavell in insisting on the dismissal of the British commander there. Wavell argued that he had conducted a highly competent retreat, the only course of action possible since he had been so outnumbered.

Wavell and his subordinate O'Connor inflicted a spectacular defeat on Italian forces in Libya, driving them back hundreds of miles and capturing 11,000 men. The British drove the Italians out of East Africa. However, Churchill was not seen as being very appreciative,

Figure 4.3 Montgomery (left) and Wavell

criticising the ratio of support troops to actual fighting men in a way that seemed unrealistic.

Initial successes were reversed by the arrival of the German Afrika Korps under Rommel.

Defying British expectations, Rommel attacked immediately in March and drove the British back. Wavell was blamed, but had had to divert men to Greece in an unsuccessful attempt to stop a German invasion there. British forces were overstretched in the Middle East. They could not meet German attacks in Libya, Greece and Crete *as well as* conduct operations in Syria and Iraq. There was an inability to prioritise which meant that early victories by Germany were sustained and British Forces were driven back to Egypt.

Wavell wanted to build up more materials and reinforcements before counter-attacking, but was pressured into a premature attack on Rommel in May 1941 in Libya, which failed.

BIOGRAPHY

Rommel (1891–1944)

Erwin Johannes Eugen Rommel (a.k.a. the 'Desert Fox', *Wüstenfuchs,* for his skills of desert warfare), was the commander of the *Deutsches Afrikakorps* in North Africa and later in command of the German forces fighting the allied cross-channel invasion at Normandy.

Rommel's military successes earned the respect not only of his troops and Adolf Hitler, but also that of his enemy Commonwealth troops in the North African Campaign. Rommel was known to be a chivalrous and humane military officer. His famous Afrikakorps was not accused of any war crimes and captured Commonwealth soldiers during his Africa campaign were largely treated humanely. Furthermore, orders to kill captured Jewish soldiers and civilians out of hand in all theatres of his command were defiantly ignored. But, following the defeat of Axis forces in North Africa, his luck changed. He was suspected of involvement in the failed 20 July plot of 1944 to kill Hitler and was forced to commit suicide.

Auchinleck (July 1941–Aug 1942)

General Sir Claude Auchinleck took over as Commander-in-Chief of the Middle East on 4 July 1941. 'The Auk' was a thoughtful leader, who had realised the importance of taking advantage of German concentration on invading Russia to build up a superiority of weapons, men and supplies in Egypt before attacking. Churchill found him too cautious and also clashed with the RAF leaders. In the event the attack, operation *Crusader*, was successful against a weakened Afrika Korps, which had lost men and weapons to the Russian campaign. However, when Rommel gained vital fuel and tanks he counter-attacked in January 1942, took the port of Benghazi and then later the Port of Tobruk. Auchinleck faced him at Marsa Matruh, 170 miles inside Egypt.

If Rommel had been successful, then Suez and the Middle East oil fields would have fallen and the British link to India and the Far Eastern theatre of war would have been cut off. It also might have been possible for the Germans to link up the Middle Eastern troops with those in southern Russia. Auchinleck thought it vital to have back up defences and not to rely on a last-ditch stand. Churchill saw this as defeatism.

In the end Auchinleck's careful defences held Rommel at the first battle of *El Alamein*. The Auk used the secret information about German movements intelligently, the so-called 'Ultra' transcripts. However, it had been Churchill's prominent backing of the intelligence services that had led to the breaking of the German codes. Rommel was halted and faced very long and vulnerable supply lines and shortage of fuel and vehicles.

Auchinleck and his Chief of Staff, Major General Dorman-Smith drew up plans for an offensive from El Alamein which were sent to London, and later used to great effect at the second battle of El Alamein.

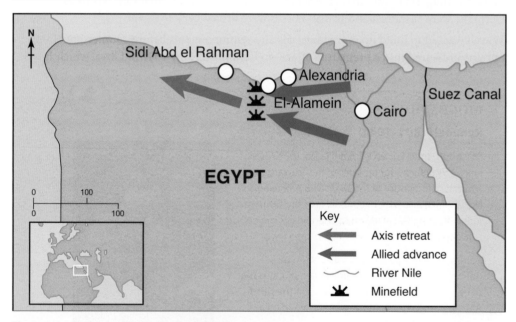

Figure 4.4 The battle of El Alamein, October 1942.

Sir Harold Alexander and Montgomery (August 1942–May 1943)

Meanwhile, Churchill arrived in Egypt on 3 August and replaced Auchinleck with General Sir Harold Alexander as new Commander-in-Chief of the Middle East and **Montgomery** took over as Commander of the Eighth Army. Churchill was impatient to begin an offensive, which Auchinleck was reluctant to do. In the event Montgomery, delayed by bad weather and an unexpected German withdrawal, waited until he was well supplied and, building on Auchinleck's work, attacked at El Alamein in October 1942. The initial plan failed and Montgomery was lucky that the sheer energy of his New Zealand division carried the day in a hastily revised plan. Given Rommel's weaknesses and the information available from Ultra, Montgomery's victory was not a brilliant one and he delayed following it up for no very clear reasons. Nevertheless, he was praised highly by Churchill while Auchinleck and Wavell had been, some claimed, treated poorly.

BIOGRAPHY

Montgomery (1887–1976)

Bernard Law Montgomery, 1st Viscount Montgomery of Alamein, often referred to as 'Monty', was an Anglo-Irish British Army officer and the son of a bishop. He famously commanded Allied forces at the *Battle of El Alamein*, a major turning point in the Western Desert Campaign during the Second World War. The troops under his command played a major role in the expulsion of German Axis forces from North Africa. He was later a prominent commander in Italy and North-West Europe, where he was in command of all Allied ground forces during *Operation Overlord* until after the Battle of Normandy. All through his career, Montgomery stirred up the resentment of his superiors for his arrogance and dictatorial ways, and also for his disregard of convention when it obstructed military effectiveness. For example, he set up a battalion brothel in Tripoli, Libya, during the Second World War, regularly inspected by the medical officer, for the 'horizontal refreshment' of his soldiers rather than forcing them to take chances in unregulated establishments. He was quoted as saying that his men 'deserved it'. On taking up command of the Eighth Army in North Africa, he ordered all contingency plans drawn up by his predecessor, Auchinleck, for retreat to be destroyed. 'I have cancelled the plan for withdrawal,' he told his officers at the first meeting he held with them in the desert. 'If we are attacked, then there will be no retreat. If we cannot stay here alive, then we will stay here dead.' His major talent was in inspiring confidence – his actual plan for the attack at El Alamein was flawed and he was slow to follow up his victory. Montgomery visited his troops as often as possible, making himself known to the men, often arranging for cigarettes to be distributed. His relationship with his American counterparts and his superiors was often strained. Montgomery died in 1976 at his home in Alton, Hampshire aged 88 years.

ACTIVITY

Consider the question 'why was Churchill led to change the command of the Middle East so frequently?'.

Think about his motivation and his character.

Give evidence to support your answer.

The Mediterranean strategy

Britain was not able to regain the initiative until 1942 when Rommel was defeated at the *Battle of El Alamein* and British Commonwealth forces advanced through North Africa. The Mediterranean continued to be the focus of the British war effort and a joint Anglo-American invasion of Sicily and then Italy took place in 1943. The British assisted anti-German forces in Yugoslavia and British troops were involved in a civil war in Greece in 1944 between royalists and communists.

The whole Mediterranean strategy has come in for criticism from some. While Russian forces were meeting the brunt of the fighting and destroying the German army, a great deal of British and American effort was being put into peripheral areas of Europe where there were traditional British interests. The fighting in Italy degenerated into slow and costly campaigns more redolent of the First World War warfare which Churchill had wanted to avoid.

However, others have argued that the Mediterranean strategy was genius on Churchill's part. It lured the Germans into a conflict where the British could fight on favourable terms and make use of their superior sea power and logistics. The Germans were forced to commit large numbers of vehicles due to the requirements of desert combat, vehicles that could have been used in the Russian campaigns to greater effect. The defence and subsequent victories in North Africa also prevented German seizure of the Middle East oilfields and German troops possibly linking up with forces invading southern Russia.

The Far East

Churchill had given little attention to South-East Asia. He did not think in 1940 that the Japanese were a threat or would attack Singapore. He believed in the power of the British naval presence, the great battleships, the *Prince of Wales* and the *Repulse* (both sunk by Japanese aircraft) and overestimated the ability of inexperienced troops to hold Malaya. Though understandable, these miscalculations resulted in considerable human, strategic and political disaster when Japan overran British colonies in early 1942 (see Chapter 5). Churchill was furious at the surrender of Singapore by General Percival in 1942. Churchill made the situation worse by attempts to reinforce Singapore shortly before its fall, doing what military theorists call 'reinforcing failure'.

Operation Overlord: the invasion of Normandy

Montgomery pursued Rommel slowly, and it was not until May 1943 that the North Africa Campaign finally came to an end. The entry of America into the war had taken much of the decision making effectively out of Churchill's control. During the long build up to the invasion of France, Churchill wanted Sir Alan Brooke to be Supreme Allied Commander but the Americans decided that, as ultimately they would be supplying most of the men and material, an American, General Dwight D. Eisenhower, would fill that post. Montgomery got the job of Ground Forces Commander.

D-Day

On 6 June 1944 British and American forces launched the greatest seaborne invasion of the war. 156,000 troops were involved; 7000 ships and 11,590 aircraft. The huge losses expected did not materialise, with fewer than 10,000 casualties (though a third were killed) and only two ships hit and 127 planes grounded.

Churchill was eager to land with his troops as soon as possible and only the King's intervention prevented him accompanying the expedition. However, he had been unwilling, because of memories of Gallipoli and the Somme and his wariness of the sheer quality of the German army, to embark on an invasion earlier. The opening of the Second Front in Northern France had been urged by Churchill's allies, but he had resisted this, preferring what has been called a 'dispersionist' strategy focused on the Mediterranean. Even when addressing the D-day leaders on 15 May 1944 he used the odd phrase '*Gentlemen, I am hardening towards this enterprise*', rather than expressing his total confidence in it.

In 1942 Churchill's views about a cross-Channel invasion were clear. He had told Roosevelt on 14 July that '*I have found no one who regards Sledgehammer* (the US plan to invade Northern France) *as possible*'.

But just one month later British and Canadian forces attacked Dieppe on 19 August 1942. Despite making it clear that an invasion of Northern France was impossible, Churchill approved this raid on Dieppe, which had little chance of success and left 4000 dead and lost 106 aircraft and a destroyer.

The Germans did not begin the massive fortification of the Channel coast until November 1943 when they started to construct the Atlantic Wall. While this was underway, massive allied forces were taking part in a campaign in Italy, which tied down 25 American and British divisions. There is a view that the Americans were right to press for concentration of forces in Northern France in 1943. Certainly, once Rommel was put in charge in 1943, there was a considerable increase in German fortification and troops in Northern France – 39 divisions (200,000 men) by May 1944. Delay had enabled the Germans to prepare for an attack more effectively.

Churchill's fears of casualties on a First World War scale were proved justified in the phase after the initial landings when operations in Normandy cost 1,800 casualties a day. As Richard Holmes has pointed out (Holmes p. 264) the British attack at Passchendaele, one of the bloodiest battles of 1917 accounted for 2,121 casualties a day. Many of the German forces were highly trained veterans, superior to the inexperienced forces of the US and British armies. The German troops were however undermined by their own command structure. The High Command too often felt the need to refer decisions back to Hitler which hindered the Commanders in the field. This factor combined with allied air superiority and overwhelming superiority in war material ensured victory.

Two facets of Churchill: amateur strategist and skilled military adviser

Churchill was highly enthusiastic about 'setting Europe ablaze' by clandestine sabotage operations and links with European resistance movements. The Germans were efficient in repressing these activities. They led to considerable hardship for local populations, for example the destruction of the Czech village of Lidice in reprisal for the British-inspired assassination of the Nazi chief, Heydrich which in turn led to a ban on such plans. The military value of the efforts made was doubtful. The larger scale daring raids fared little better. A raid on Dieppe in 1942 achieved nothing of value and was costly in terms of lives and the attempt to shorten the war by striking at the Rhine crossing at Arnhem was a costly failure.

Against this view, an insider, Sir Jack Peck, one of Churchill's secretaries wrote:

> *I have the clearest possible recollection of General Ismay* [General Sir Hastings Ismay, Churchill's closest liaison officer] *talking to me about a meeting of the Chiefs of Staff Committee at which they got completely stuck and admitted they had not known what*

was the right course to pursue; so on a purely military matter, they had come to Churchill for his advice. He introduced some further facts into the equation that had escaped their attention and the solution became obvious. The point of the story is one of the reasons for the success of the working relationship between Churchill and the Chiefs of Staff was their deep respect, even on the frequent occasions when they disagreed with him, for his military talents if not genius.' (Quoted: John Keegan, *Churchill's Generals* p. 234.)

How did Churchill's relationships with his senior commanders impact on the war?

Churchill was unusual as a political leader to have had military experience, but it was not always relevant. Sir Alan Brooke often stopped mistakes but in essence the two men agreed on a basic principle. The British war effort would be:

- to control the seas and oceans;
- to inflict damage on Germany by bombing; and
- to fight for as long as possible in the Mediterranean to avoid the bloodbath which would occur once the main German army in northern Europe was engaged.

To that extent there was harmony about the way in which the war was to be fought but there was plenty of disagreement on lesser matters.

There were two men that Churchill dealt with as senior soldier or CIGS (Chief of the Imperial General Staff). The first until December 1941 was Sir John Dill (Figure 4.5).

Senior commander

The role of senior commander during the Second World War was the Chief of the Imperial General Staff (CIGS). He was in overall charge of all British armed forces.

Figure 4.5 Sir John Dill (centre) – Chief of the Imperial General Staff (1940–41).

Sir John Dill

Dill was a highly intelligent and gentlemanly figure but he and Churchill established no warm bond.

After the evacuation from Dunkirk, Dill thought the army needed to be built up and trained. He also saw the defence of the *whole* empire as his responsibility. However, Churchill wanted action and he was especially concerned with the Mediterranean.

Dill infuriated Churchill by a memo of 6 May 1941:

> *'The loss of Egypt would be a calamity which I do not regard as likely and one which we should not accept without a most desperate fight; but it would not end the war. A successful invasion (of Britain) alone spells our final defeat. It is the United Kingdom...and not Egypt that is vital and the defence of the United Kingdom must take first place. Egypt is not even second in order of priority, for it has been an accepted principle in our strategy that in the last resort the security of Singapore comes before that of Egypt.'*

A week later Churchill replied:

> *'I gather that you would be prepared to face the loss of Egypt and the Nile Valley together with the surrender or ruin of the Army of half a million we have concentrated there, rather than lose Singapore. I do not take that view, nor do I think the alternative is likely to present itself.'*

A week after the Japanese had captured Singapore in February 1942 the British General Pownall, the Chief of Staff in South-East Asia wrote:

> *'There is no doubt we underestimated the Japanese. But suppose we'd made a better shot,* [referring to the surrender of 130,000 troops under General Percival to 30,000 Japanese troops in February 1942] *would it have made any real difference? Our policy was to avoid war with Japan as long as we could and we gambled on that policy succeeding. With all other commitments I don't believe that however highly we had rated the Japanese as fighters we could have improved the condition of our forces in the Far East. We just hoped it wouldn't happen, and it did.'* (Quotes taken from: Keegan, *Churchill's Generals.*)

Churchill was eager to give Japan priority after the disasters of 1942 and Brooke (Figure 4.6) who had replaced Dill in December 1941, now fought an opposing battle. Brooke remained as CIGS throughout the rest of the war.

Sir Alan Brooke

Sir Alan Brooke (later Lord Alanbrooke) had clashed with Churchill in 1940 but was such an outstanding personality that Churchill could not get rid of him in the way that he had ousted 'Dilly Dally' as he called Dill, by sending him as his representative to Washington. Brooke was highly practical and intelligent and the working relationship of two opposite personalities was one of the greatest wartime partnerships. Lord Alanbrooke's diaries, however, reveal the strains (see Source A, page 112).

Brooke was still arguing with Churchill through 1944 and 1945. Churchill wanted a substantial British role in recapturing the lands lost in 1942 even though the Americans were engaged in this battle with huge resources. Brooke persuaded Churchill that Britain should concentrate on defeating the Japanese in Burma. The hugely successful campaign by General William Slim in Burma was not recognised or understood by Churchill.

Source

A Two extracts from Lord Alanbrooke's diary.

On 23 August 1943, Lord Alanbrooke wrote:

> [Churchill] *has been more unreasonable and trying than ever this time. He has in a few idle moments become married to the idea that success against Japan can only be secured through the capture of the northern tip of Sumatra! He has become like a peevish child asking for a forbidden toy.*

On 1 October Lord Alanbrooke wrote:

> *…An hour's pitched battle between me and the PM on the question of withdrawing troops from the Mediterranean for an Indian Ocean offensive, I was refusing to impair our amphibious potential in the Mediterranean for adventures in Sumatra. He was prepared to scrap our basic policy and put Japan before Germany. However, I defeated most of his evil intentions in the end.*

War Diaries, Field Marshal Lord Alanbrooke, Danichev and Todman, Weidenfeld and Nicolson 2001

B Churchill telegram to General Wavell, in overall command of Far East 15 January 1942.

How many troops would be needed to defend this area? [Singapore] *What means are there of stopping landings such as were made in Hong Kong* [which fell to Japan on Christmas Day 1941] *What are defences and obstructions on the landward side* [The Japanese did not attack Singapore by sea but landed in Malaysia and attacked from the north through the Malay peninsula] *Is everything being prepared? It has always seemed to me that the vital need is to prolong the defence of the island to the last possible minute.*

Everyone here is very pleased with the telegrams you have sent which give us all the feeling how buoyantly you are grappling with your tremendous task.

Knight, *Churchill, The Greatest Briton Unmasked*, pp. 225–56.

Where earlier he had enthusiastically endorsed plans for a new naval base in Singapore, now he mercilessly struck it from his list, he opposed the admiralty's cruiser programme and vetoed the increase in submarine strength at Hong Kong. He wrote, *'I do not believe that Japan has any idea of attacking the British Empire or that there is any danger of her doing so for a generation to come.'* Instead he wanted to know more about defence of Singapore. This is borne out by Source B.

Singapore surrendered on 15 February 1942. The troops rushed to the island in January and fell into Japanese captivity. The fall of Singapore was the greatest blow to the British Empire in its history and

Figure 4.6 Sir Alan Brooke [CiGS].

showed how vulnerable Europeans were to Asian forces with inferior numbers but much greater confidence and organisation. Singapore's great naval guns were useless against an enemy attacking from land. The British forces had a bitterly divided command and an ineffectual overall chief in General Percival. They lacked air cover and the two great ships intended to protect South-east Asia, the *Prince of Wales* and the *Repulse* had been sunk by Japanese aircraft on the way to Singapore.

There has been some discussion as to Churchill's responsibility for the fall of Singapore.

The historian Nigel Knight has written:

'In the Second World War Churchill wrote "...it had never entered my head that no circle of detached forts of a permanent character protected the rear of the famous fortress. I cannot understand how it was that I did not know this....My advisers ought to have known and I ought to have been told, and I ought to have asked." The eminent historian A.J.P. Taylor said of this passage "I am sorry to say that the records show his advisers told him and Churchill pushed their warnings aside" ' (From: Knight, p. 228.)

The subsequent strategy in the Far East was one of the causes of disagreement between Brooke and Churchill. Brooke's diaries are a fascinating insight into the strains of war, but need careful interpretation.

The diary entry for May 24 May 1943 is typical (see Source A and commentaries B and C below).

Source

(A) Lord Alanbrooke's diary entry for 24 May, 1943.

Churchill thinks one thing at one moment and another at another moment, At times the war may be won by bombing and all must be sacrificed to it. At others it becomes essential for us to bleed ourselves dry on the continent because Russia is doing the same. At others our main effort must be in the Mediterranean, directed against Italy or the Balkans, alternatively with sporadic desires to invade Norway. More often he wants to carry out ALL operations simultaneously, irrespective of shortages of shipping.'

Commentary (B)

Lord Alanbrooke's diary reveals the weakness of Churchill as wartime Prime Minister. He could not establish good relations with his generals and this frustration is typical of that felt by senior officers about the Prime Minister's lack of consistency. Sir John Dill complained in much the same way. Churchill often treated his generals badly, sacking Auchinleck and interfering with operations. Churchill's limited military experience in no way prepared him for the massive task of preparing modern armies for war and he was too taken with 'bright ideas' such as the invasion of Norway referred to here and another plan that Brooke grappled with in 1943 to invade Sumatra. He wasted time and demoralised his military leaders by foolish ideas and ignored the practicalities. The source is useful in showing Churchill's failure to come to terms with the reality of Britain's military limitations.

Commentary (C)

Lord Alanbrooke's diary certainly shows that his relations with Churchill were strained at times. However, there were few occasions when Churchill overruled his generals. He and Brooke agreed on vital elements like delaying D-Day until Britain was well prepared. Though Churchill pressed Brooke and Montgomery to begin the attack on Rommel in 1942 quickly, in fact he accepted that they needed to build up forces. The PM regarded it as his job to question and urge on his generals, but they were tough men and understood the situation. After a long day and with a lot of responsibility to cope with, it was understandable that Brooke became frustrated, but diaries reveal the emotions of the moment, not the long term considered view. Churchill had bad ideas but also good ones, such as the backing of Wingate in irregular operations in the Desert and Burma, the great support given to intelligence gathering and the Bletchley Park decoding of German signals, not to mention the successful deceptions which preceded D-Day. The diary does not give the whole picture – by 1943 the situation was difficult and there were various possibilities; it was Churchill's job to stimulate and provide ideas and Brooke's to assess them and advise. It would not be right to draw too many conclusions from the diary.

ACTIVITY

1   Consider these two commentaries on this diary entry by Lord Alanbrooke.

2   Which do you find more convincing and why?

3   Look at all the sources and quotes in this section. What impression do you get from these about Churchill's understanding of the situation in Singapore and the subsequent war against Japan?

4   What do they tell you about Churchill's relationship with his most senior military commanders?

Stretch and challenge

Some of the bitterest controversies have arisen about the Desert Campaign and about the relative merits of Montgomery and Auchinleck. At A2 level you will have the chance to explore a historical controversy in more depth. In the meantime, you might like to try your hand at this one.

(i)   Montgomery alleged that he scrapped a defeatist plan and inspired his troops to confident and aggressive actions which resulted in the victory at El Alamein.

(ii) Churchill and Brooke both thought that new leadership was needed in 1942 and wanted to get rid of Auchinleck. Brooke championed Montgomery.

1   Were their estimations valid and was El Alamein and Montgomery's leadership over-praised?

2   Was the contribution of Auchinleck and Wavell unfairly underestimated?

3   How justified was Churchill's view of his Desert generals in 1942?

(See also the *Further Reading* list on page 122)

The Bombing Campaign

The newspaper article opposite offers a summary of the debate however many would consider calling Churchill a 'war criminal' extreme. There is strong feeling about the role of the head of Bomber Command, Sir Arthur Harris, and about the whole bombing strategy. Harris can be seen in a film clip on the website of the *Daily Telegaph*. See www.heinemann.co.uk/hotlinks for details.

Churchill was uneasy about the bombing but made his position clear. On 30 June 1943 he spoke at the Guildhall in London on receiving the freedom of the City of London:

Three years ago, Hitler boasted that he would 'rub out' – that was the term – the cities of Britain and certainly in the nine months before he abandoned his attack we suffered very heavy damage to our buildings and grievous hindrance to our life and work, and more than 40,000 people were killed and more than 120,000 wounded. But now those who sowed the wind are reaping the whirlwind. In the first half of the year which ends today, the RAF has alone cast upon Germany thirty five times the tonnage of bombs which has been discharged on this island in the same six months. Not only has the weight of our offensive bombing grown and its accuracy multiplied, but our measures of defence, tactical

GERMANS CALL CHURCHILL A WAR CRIMINAL

By Kate Connolly in Berlin
19 Nov 2002, The Daily Telegraph

Winston Churchill was effectively a war criminal who sanctioned the extermination of Germany's civilian population through indiscriminate bombing of towns and cities, an article in the country's biggest-circulation newspaper claimed yesterday.

In an unprecedented attack on Allied conduct during the Second World War, the tabloid, *Bild*, has called for recognition to be given to the suffering inflicted on the German population during the strategic air campaign of 1940–45.

The newspaper is serializing *Der Brand* (*The Fire: Germany Under Bombardment 1940-45*) by the historian Jorg Friedrich, which claims to be the most authoritative account of the bombing campaign so far.

Mr. Friedrich claims the British government set out at the start of the Second World War to destroy as many German cities and kill as many of their inhabitants as possible. Civilian deaths were not collateral damage, he says, but rather the object of the exercise. He argues that Churchill had favoured a strategy of attacking the civilian population centres from the air some 20 years before Hitler ordered such raids.

The debate is certain to anger those in Britain who see the strategic air campaign as a necessary evil.

Yesterday Antony Beevor, the British historian and author of the bestselling *Berlin: The Downfall, 1945*, criticised the German claim that Britain's war of attrition was unnecessarily brutal. "The trouble is this argument is removed from the context that they were the ones who invented terror bombing," he said, referring to German attacks on Coventry, Rotterdam and Warsaw. "They literally obliterated whole cities and that certainly preceded what the British did," he said. "What we did was more terrifying and appalling, but it was a natural progression in this war. One can certainly debate the whole morality of bombing, but for Germans to say Churchill was a war criminal is pushing it a bit," he said.

Friedrich, J. (2006) *The Fire: The Bombing of Germany, 1940–1945*.

---

and scientific have improved beyond all compare. In one single night, nay in one single hour, we discharged upon Düsseldorf, to take an example, 200 tons of terrible explosive and incendiary bombs. (Stewart, *His Finest Hours*, p. 149.)

RAF Bomber Command had been founded in 1936. Three years later, there were 480 aircraft. Blenheim, Wellington, Whitley and Hampden bombers were the main weapons until 1942 and there was mostly night bombing with variable equipment. Then Sir Arthur 'Bomber' Harris, was given command. Harris believed implicitly that Germany's morale could be broken and its capacity for waging war wrecked by the systematic destruction of its industrial base, production facilities and city centres. It was a ruthless policy of **Total War**.

Total war

Harris (see Figure 4.7, page 116) saw the potential of four-engined heavy bombers such as the Stirling, Halifax and Lancaster: the larger aircraft had better navigation and could be used for more accurate bombing. The Lancaster became the main weapon of the bombing war. Targets were identified and the scale of warfare increased. On 31 May 1942, 1,000 bombers raided Cologne.

In May and June 1943, the saturation bombing of the Ruhr and Hamburg had a serious effect on war production and took vital Luftwaffe planes away from the Russian front. Around half a million Germans lost their lives as a result of the 955,044 tons of bombs that were dropped by the Allies during the war. There is some debate about the economic impact, but post-war evidence indicates that bombing was a major factor in the German defeat.

ACTIVITY

1 Read the article by Kate Connolly (above). It could be interpreted as a very extreme argument. What evidence is there to dispute this claim?

Total war

This is when civilians and residential areas are targeted *as well as* military targets.

Figure 4.7   Sir Arthur Harris

This was at a cost – 55,000 members of Bomber Command were killed in action. There were spectacular actions, such as the 'Dambusters' raid on the Ruhr dams. The destruction caused by the firebombing of Hamburg and the raids on the Ruhr industrial areas 1943-4 was considerable. Bombing supported the D-Day landings and also took a toll on German shipping.

On 13 February 1945 Dresden was hit. It was seen as an industrial centre but there were heavy casualties – the figures are disputed but up to 40,000 died partly as a result of poor defences and the concentration of refugees in the city. The railway yards and factories were destroyed. The destruction of this major cultural centre and the heavy casualties so late on in the war has made it a controversial decision. In the context of so much destruction of German cities, it may have had less significance at the time than subsequently.

In March 1945 Churchill wrote in memo to senior RAF commanders:

> 'It seems to me that the moment has come when the question of bombing German cities simply for the sake of increasing the terror, though under other pretexts, should be reviewed. Otherwise we shall come under control of an utterly ruined land – the destruction of Dresden remains a serious query against the conduct of allied bombing. I feel the need for more precise concentration upon military objectives rather than on more acts of terror and wanton destruction, however impressive.' (Knight, p. 294, quoted from Probert's biography of Harris.)

What seems clear from the evidence of Albert Speer, Hitler's main armaments minister, and post-war reports such as that by Sir Solly Zuckerman, is that when bombing targeted communications and supplies there was a real danger to the Nazi war machine. When it concentrated on terror and civilian death, then morality apart, it was a lot less effective (Source A, opposite).

Source

A

Speer wrote:

> *The attack on the traffic was certainly the most effective one. First of all I could no more produce anything regularly. Then the whole German economy came to a standstill because we hadn't any more coal.*

Zuckerman wrote:

> *The crucial blow inflicted to Hamburg's economy was…the transportation difficulties that resulted from…raids against railway and canal installations.* (Report on the effects of the bombing campaign, both quoted Knight, pp. 297–98)

There is a view that had Harris been given more resources and focused them on transport, then bombing might have achieved victory. However, Churchill's strategy before 1944 was to disperse the war effort with campaigns in the Mediterranean and Balkans and then D-Day (Knight, p. 300).

There is also a view that for the resources that went into it, the bombing campaign was not especially effective, partly because terror could not alone win the war. Even if the civilian population were terrorised (see Figure 4.8), then it is difficult to see what they could do with the frightening prospect of a Russian advance and a very effectively enforced Nazi police state.

Figure 4.8 Dresden after the bombing.

This moral debate continues. Harris was an embarrassment to Churchill despite the delight he seemed to take earlier in the war in the Germans suffering for the destruction they had caused. Harris was not given a peerage and gets scant mention by Churchill in his later volumes about the Second World War. Only recently was there a statue to him in London.

The effectiveness and morality of the bombing campaigns remains the vexed issue that it became by the end of the war.

ACTIVITY

Look carefully at Source A and the newspaper article on page 115.

Discuss whether Churchill's support for civilian bombing in Germany reduces the claim that he was a great wartime Prime Minister.

SUMMARY ACTIVITIES

■ Was Churchill's greatness his willingness to wage war with determination and win whatever the costs?

■ Was his greatness his uncompromising determination for Germany's 'Unconditional Surrender'?

■ Or do elements of his strategy such as his dispersal of efforts in the Mediterranean, his delay of the invasion of France, his over-reliance on bombing and his interference with his generals somehow detract from that greatness?

What were the plans for reconstruction and why did Churchill lose the 1945 election?

The domestic scene and the election of 1945

Churchill was defeated in the British election in May 1945 and Labour returned to power for the first time as an independent party since 1931. Clement Attlee had been deputy Prime Minister since 1942 and well known Labour leaders had been in Churchill's government. So the change was not as great as it appeared. The vote was against the Conservatives and their pre-war domestic record as much as for Labour, and the popular vote was not as decisive as the change in the number of seats. However, it was a vote for a degree of domestic change that Churchill was not thought likely to deliver.

Churchill had fought the war to defend Britain and its Empire. However, the Britain that he believed in was not necessarily the Britain that had emerged as a result of the war. A visit to Chartwell, Churchill's country home, is instructive here. Its ample grounds and comfortable rooms, while not on the scale of Blenheim Palace, nevertheless evoke a world of upper-class weekend parties, servants and solid comfort. Churchill worked hard to maintain it through his writings and never minded helping with its upkeep by roofing and bricklaying. But it was a world away from the day to day lives of ordinary English people.

The common effort through years of war, the rise of many to positions of responsibility in the services through their own abilities, the sacrifices of millions which seemed to deserve rewards in terms of better health, housing and job security led to a huge belief that peace would mean change. It was widely thought that peace in 1918 did not deliver the promises made by Lloyd George during the First World War. This time, Labour seemed determined to deliver reforms. There was a large degree of agreement among the parties that there should be an end to poor health, poverty, bad housing and poor education. The turning point was the **Beveridge Report** of 1942.

Case Study: The Beveridge Report

Sir William Beveridge produced a report on Social Insurance and Allied Services on 1 December 1942. He argued that poverty could be abolished if there were an extended social insurance scheme. He recommended child allowances and foresaw a national health service and an end to mass unemployment. Not really revolutionary, it nevertheless promised an end to the bad conditions of the 1930s and sold over 600,000 copies. It was a the symbol of a desire for greater social welfare and became immensely important and influential in the creation of the post-1945 Welfare State.

Churchill had seemed uninterested in post-war domestic planning and his interests in home policy were confined to matters affecting the war itself. He urged greater censorship; he disliked any criticisms of pre-war conditions; disapproved of the Army Bureau of Current Affairs, which encouraged discussion among the troops and delegated reconstruction plans to a committee. When the Beveridge Report came out, Churchill thought it the work of 'an awful windbag and a dreamer'. Churchill made it clear that the recommendations were not to be put into effect during the war:

> *'Ministers should in my view be careful not to raise false hopes as was done last time by speeches about 'homes fit for heroes'. It is for this reason of not wishing to deceive the people by false hopes and airy visions of Utopia and Eldorado that I have refrained from making promises about the future.'* (Ponting p. 707.)

('Homes Fit for Heroes' had been promised by Lloyd George in the First World War and not, on the whole, delivered, even though council houses were built after 1918.)

In the parliamentary debate on the Beveridge Report on 18 February 1943 there was considerable opposition to Churchill's view and 121 MPs voted against the government and for immediate implementation. Churchill took a similar view to the Uthwatt Report, which had recommended that the government should have powers to take over land for development schemes and was the basis of modern town and country planning.

Churchill put a Conservative, W. S. Morrison in place as Minister of Town and Country Planning to ensure nothing was done and also appointed another Conservative, Henry Willink, as Minister of Health to stop any schemes for a national health policy.

The *Butler Education Act* was another conservative measure, which was rendered even more traditional by Churchill, insisting that women teachers should not receive equal pay.

The White Paper on Health was quite a way from the eventual National Health Service created after the war, the idea that Labour had huge influence on post-war policy is not justified – the main reconstruction planning was in the hands of Conservatives and there was growing public discontent about post-war policy. The government was losing by-elections from 1942 and the coalition was strained from 1944. Finally, in the campaign of 1945, Churchill made no commitment to employment policy and his main theme was his war record (source A, page 120).

There are a number of reasons for the Labour victory of 1945. Labour's experience in the coalition and the familiarity of their leaders as ministers is one. Another is Labour's election campaign which promised social reforms and the full implementation of wartime plans such as the Beveridge Report. Another is the poor record of the Conservatives before the war in dealing with social and economic problems. By 1945 there was a great awareness of domestic issues, helped by institutions such as the Army Bureau for Current Affairs and wartime discussions in the press and on radio of the post-war world. There was also

considerable admiration for Soviet planning which seemed to have allowed Russia to win the war. Because so many US troops had been stationed in Britain, and there had been frictions with the local population, there was rather less admiration for the free market capitalism of America. Then there was the line taken by Churchill that conflict was likely to be prolonged, that Britain needed to preserve her Empire and remain a great power and that 'Socialism' threatened liberty. To many, little of this seemed as relevant as the need for social change. The resurrection of the 'Red Menace' when Churchill had worked with Labour ministers and had been an ally of Stalin did not seem to make sense.

Sources

A On 4 June 1945 Churchill broadcast:

I declare to you, from the bottom of my heart, that no socialist system can be established without a political police. No Socialist Government could afford to allow free, sharp or violently-worded expressions of public discontent. They would have to fall back on some form of Gestapo, no doubt very humanely directed at first.

Socialism is an attack on the right of an ordinary man or woman to breathe freely without having a harsh, clumsy, tyrannical hand clapped across their mouth and nostrils.

The general consensus was that this speech did enormous harm. However, the tide had been turning against Conservative policies for some time and Churchill's wry and humane resignation to the Labour victory which subsequently emerged on 26 July has impressed many.

B Churchill's reaction to his loss of political power.

A hitherto subconscious conviction that we were beaten broke forth and dominated my mind...The power to shape the future would be denied me. The knowledge and experience I had gathered, the authority and goodwill I had gained in so many countries would vanish.

...the first results had begun to come in. They were, as I expected, unfavourable. By noon it was clear that the Socialists would have a majority. At luncheon, my wife said to me "It may well be a blessing in disguise." I replied, "At the moment, it seems quite effectively disguised".

Sources A and B from: *Triumph and Tragedy*, the final volume in Churchill's *The Second World War*, p. 253.

C To His friend Duff Cooper he wrote in a different vein:

There are some unpleasant features in this election which indicate the rise of bad elements. Conscientious objectors were preferred to candidates of real military achievement and service. All the members of Parliament who had done most to hamper and obstruct the war were returned by enormously increased majorities. None of the values of the years before were preserved. The soldiers voted with mirthful irresponsibility. Also there is the latent antagonism of the rank and file for the officer class.

From: 17 September 1945, quoted Gilbert, Volume 8: p. 148.

D A correspondent of Harold Nicolson, Raymond Mortimer expressed a contemporary view. Mortimer was literary editor of the *New Statesman*, a left-wing weekly magazine which supported a Labour victory in the election. Nicolson was an MP in Churchill's coalition.

10 July 1945

I think that Churchill more than anyone else was responsible for the squalid lies in these elections. He started the rot with his talk of Mr Attlee's Gestapo. These Hogarthian spatterings are inseparable from the parliamentary system. The gloomy result is to make sensitive people keep out of politics. I should like to see Churchill retire. I think him quite the wrong man for directing the reconstruction of England. Our debt to him is probably greater than to any other politician in our history, but I could not feel on that account any obligation to vote for him.

Nicolson who was an MP in Churchill's coalition lost his seat to Labour in the election of 1945.

Nicolson's *Diaries and Letters*, 1945.

Conclusion

In this chapter, there has been a lot of stress on offering judgements about issues to do with Churchill's leadership using sources and taking into account their provenance and contextual knowledge.

In the Churchill Museum attached to the Cabinet War Rooms in London – an essential visit for all interested in Churchill – there is a film clip showing Churchill being given the freedom of Portsmouth after the war. The Lord Mayor refers to Churchill as the greatest man in the world. Churchill smiles and says *'There are some things no man ought to hear until he is dead... .'*

There is no doubt that hero worship of Churchill reached enormous heights after the war and was bolstered by the publication of his own account *'The Second World War'* in 1948.

Churchill's wartime leadership is a much more controversial topic than it would have seemed in 1965 at the time of his death. The nation mourned and any criticism of Churchill would have been very difficult. Now, there is a far greater range of interpretations. A balanced judgement is called for on these issues. Look again at Roy Jenkins's overall verdict in the quote on (page 86) Do you think that it is valid? Was Churchill a great war leader and did the victory owe more to him than anyone else?

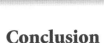 *At this point, it would be useful to undertake an audit to see what skills you are comfortable with and what you need more support in developing. Go to pages 164–173 of the Exam Café and complete the activities there.*

Bibliography

Churchill, W. (1985) *History of the Second World War, Volumes 1–6,* Penguin Books.

Churchill, W. (1985) *The Second World War, Volume 6: Triumph and Tragedy*, p. 253, Penguin Books.

Churchill, W. (1948) *The Gathering Storm*, p. 583. Penguin.

Cohen, E.A. *Churchill and his Generals*: The Tasks of Supreme Command Proceedings of the International Churchill Society 1992–3. URL www.winstonchurchill.org [accessed 24.3.09]

Danchev, A., Todman, D. (eds) (2001) *War Diaries 1939–1945, Field Marshal Lord Alan Brooke*. Weidenfeld and Nicolson.

Eade, C. (1953 *Churchill by his Contemporaries*, p. 142, Hutchinson.

Friedrich, J. (2006) *The Fire: The Bombing of Germany, 1940–1945*. Columbia University Press.

Gilbert, M. *Winston Spencer Churchill, Never Despair*, Volume 8: p. 148. Heinemann-Minerva.

Holmes, R. (2005) *In the footsteps of Churchill*, p.264, BBC.

Jenkins, R. (2001) *Churchill: A Biography,* p. 912. Pan Books.

ACTIVITY

Using the Sources A–D and the information in this section how far do you agree that Churchill must bear the responsibility for his defeat in 1945?

EXAMINER'S ADVICE

Remember to consider the nature of the sources and remember to use your own knowledge to reach a judgement.

Keegan, J. (ed) (2005) *Churchill's Generals,* pp. 7, 234. Orion.

Knight, N. (2008) *Churchill: The Greatest Briton Unmasked*, pp. 128–30, 225–6, 228, 294, Chapter 10. David and Charles.

Packwood, A. (2008) *A Week in London*, Churchill Archives Centre, CHPC

Ponting, C. (1994) *Churchill,* pp. 446, 448. Sinclair-Stevenson.

Rowse, A.L. (1958) *The Later Churchills,* Penguin edition.

Stewart, G. (2007) *His Finest Hours*, p. 149, Quercus.

Further reading

Barnett, C. (1999) *The Desert Generals.* Phoenix.

Connell, J. (1965) *Auchinleck.* Cassell & Co. Ltd.

Hamilton, N. (2002) *The Full Monty.* Penguin Books.

Keegan, J. (ed) (1991) *Churchill's Generals.* Adam and Charles.

Knight, N. (2008) *Churchill: The Greatest Briton Unmasked.* David and Charles.

Pitt, B. (1981) *Churchill and the Generals,* republished Pen and Sword Military Classics, 2004.

How Successful was the International Diplomacy of Churchill During the Second World War?

5

The Second World War brought about the Grand Alliance that Churchill had hoped for, and changed the nature of British foreign policy. After 1941 Churchill was faced with negotiating with allies whose political systems differed very greatly from each other, and whose war aims were different. It was crucial for Churchill to maintain good relations with them, but the task became increasingly difficult as the war went on, and it was clear that Britain was less powerful than either of the two 'superpowers': Russia and the USA.

The international conferences held during the war were of increasing importance in shaping the post-war world. Churchill wanted Britain to play a leading part in war-time decisions and to be a major influence on any post-war settlement. This chapter helps you to decide how far these aims were met.

Key Questions

Areas of study are:

1. How did Churchill interact with the Grand Alliance (Roosevelt, Stalin, de Gaulle)?

2. How far was the image presented of Churchill's friendship with Roosevelt matched by the reality?

3. What was Churchill's overall strategy and his view of Britain's world role?

4. Was Churchill right to fear the power of the USSR?

5. What was the significance of the Moscow Conference of 1944 and the 'Percentages agreement'?

6. Why were the relations between Churchill and de Gaulle so stormy?

In terms of skills, there will be opportunities to consider source material and to evaluate a series of sources. There will also be the chance to review and practise source analysis skills: comparison, considering the value and utility of evidence, and relating contextual knowledge to Sources.

The Exam Café (pages 158–73) will give you the opportunity to consolidate knowledge by considering answers to real OCR questions at different levels.

This chapter deals with Churchill's relations with the other wartime leaders, Roosevelt, Stalin and de Gaulle. It begins with an analysis of the disagreements that have arisen among historians about Churchill's wartime diplomacy.

In the course of the study of how Churchill interacted with Roosevelt, Stalin and de Gaulle, Churchill's views about Britain's world and imperial role will be considered. He was eager to maintain both the Empire and traditional areas of British interest, particularly the Eastern Mediterranean, and assumed continuing British control of her Asian possessions, particularly India. As it will emerge, the US view was somewhat different.

Churchill's plans for post-war Europe had to be substantially revised in the course of the war and by the time of the conferences of 1945 were very different from 1940. The one

consistent element was that there would be no place for Hitler and Nazism in post-war Europe. In that aim he was successful and delivered his best service to Britain and the world.

How did Churchill interact with the Grand Alliance (Roosevelt, Stalin, de Gaulle)?

Churchill's relations with the other leaders should be considered within the context of the time (see the Analysis below). There is some debate about Churchill's dealings with all three of the leaders above and before studying this topic in detail it is helpful to understand the issues.

ANALYSIS

Churchill had urged a Grand Alliance in the 1930s, but Chamberlain had thought it impossible. This is why:

1   The French were unreliable in military terms and might not survive an invasion by Germany. The French also had severe political upheavals and frequent changes of government.

2   The USSR was under a very brutal dictator, Stalin, and its communist ideology might lead to attempts to expand its influence. In addition it had lost lands in 1919 and might well wish to recover its 1914 boundaries. All this made it a dangerous and morally repugnant potential ally. As well as this, the huge disruptions of the 1930s and the purging of the military leadership made it doubtful whether Russia would endure a modern war or be a valuable ally.

3   The USA had an unfavourable view of the British Empire; it had done little to stop any international aggression, for example by Japan in the Far East, and had small armed forces. Its isolationism was evident and it would be unlikely to help Britain. Roosevelt was seen as an unreliable leader by Chamberlain, who did not trust him.

Chamberlain's solution was to avoid war, come to an understanding with the dictators and to build up Britain's defences. Germany had no territorial claims on Britain and Hitler had not been hostile in his writings or speeches to Britain or its Empire. There was a more direct threat from Italy and Japan, and Germany could act as a restraining impulse. In the meantime, Britain's armed forces did not have to worry about Germany and they could easily defend the Empire against Mussolini and the Japanese.

The Second World War had reversed Chamberlain's strategy. However, the issue is whether his surmises were proved wrong.

1   France did collapse in 1940, much more quickly than expected. Churchill was amazed when France surrendered and appalled that his calculation that France would do the bulk of the fighting had been proved wrong so quickly.

2   As for the USSR, the initial defeats when Germany invaded in 1941 seemed to prove Chamberlain's view as right. At first, the USSR was a drain on Britain because supplies were diverted to help it. However, the determined resistance by the Soviet forces and the huge losses inflicted on the Germans defied expectations. What was proved right was the USSR's desire to expand, which was evident from Stalin's stated war aims given to Britain in 1941. Stalin wanted to return to the frontiers of 1914, including Poland, the Baltic States and Bessarabia and a security zone, which would mean dominating its Eastern European neighbours. This intrusion into Europe would upset the balance of power and offer a potential threat equivalent to that of Germany.

3   The view that the USA was isolationist and would do little to stop aggression seemed in retrospect to be wrong. Roosevelt did help Britain before 1941, and then played a leading role in the defeat of Germany, Italy and Japan despite campaigning on a 'no war, no involvement' platform. From 1941, after the collapse of the first alliance between Britain and France, a much more significant Grand Alliance occurred between Britain, the USSR and the USA. Other countries joined, but the Grand Alliance did prove to be the key to defeating the Axis powers of Germany and Italy.

The accepted view

The accepted view has been that Churchill's vision had been proved right. He had forged a personal bond with Roosevelt and he had the faith that the USA would join the war. Indeed he worked assiduously to that end because it was his only policy to win the war. He had been practical enough to see that alliance with Russia was essential and had made huge efforts to keep contact with his allies throughout the war by a series of hazardous journeys and difficult summit meetings (see Table 5.1, page 126). The *Atlantic Charter* of 1941 was a noble document setting out war aims for freedom. However, he had seen the dangers of Russian expansion and had done his best to warn the West of the dangers.

In short, Churchill's personal diplomacy, his belief in ultimate victory and his vision of a world united against the horrors of Nazism had brought victory. His own account put a great deal of emphasis on the warm relationship between himself and Roosevelt. If there was a key element in victory it was this '**Special Relationship**' between Britain and America. He knew he had to cultivate this relationship at all costs.

The alternative view

Not everyone was convinced by the accepted view. Historians and commentators have raised some objections that may be summarised briefly:

1   The Americans did not share Britain's concern to preserve its Empire; their policy was to weaken European empires and institute an 'open door' trading policy with free trade that would benefit American economic strength. The help that Roosevelt gave to Britain before 1941 was quite limited and Britain got a bad deal (see page 127). Churchill's appeals achieved relatively little.

2   If Japan had not attacked the USA in December 1941 it is doubtful whether Roosevelt would have joined the war against Germany. Congress would not have allowed it. Even then it was by no means certain that the USA would not have restricted itself to fighting Japan alone had not Hitler declared war on the USA. Churchill's influence and diplomacy has been exaggerated.

3   During the war, there were considerable strains about strategic issues. By 1943 relations were much less warm between Churchill and Roosevelt, and the US military chiefs were critical of Churchill's overall strategy. Increasingly, Britain lost influence over the war.

4   The USA was not influenced by Churchill to oppose Russia later in the war and had a different view of Stalin.

5   In order to keep Stalin in the war, Britain was ready to appease him about control of Eastern Europe to a greater extent than it had been prepared to appease Hitler. The USA disapproved of this policy, but neither Britain nor the USA could stop Stalin expanding into Eastern Europe and shifting the whole European balance of power.

6   If Churchill's aim was to preserve the security of the British Empire and Britain as a great power, then he failed. If the aim was to protect Eastern European independence, then it failed. If the aim was to protect France, then it failed. If the aim was to preserve a balance of power in Europe, it failed. If the aim was to fight for a democratic Europe, then it failed.

Special Relationship

This term is still in use suggesting that a common language, background and belief in democracy gives Britain a uniquely close bond to the USA. Churchill emphasised his personal links to Americans through his mother and the ties of shared values between the two countries. Post-war leaders in Britain have used the term extensively, but it has not always accurately described relations between the two countries.

8 If Russia's aim was to defeat the threat from Germany, restore its borders and establish its power in Eastern Europe and prove that a communist power could be a superpower, then these aims were met.

9 If the US aim was to re-establish and even extend its influence in the Pacific and open the world to US economic influence, and to increase the amount of self-governing and independent people, then it was successful – not in Europe, but in the world at large. The independence of India, and later the rest of the British, French, Dutch and Portuguese empires, were in accord with the Atlantic Charter, even if Eastern Europe was not.

Table 5.1 Churchill's travels 1941–45 (with the main conferences in bold). This extraordinary wartime itinerary shows Churchill's travels and the major summits. He braved wartime dangers and often uncomfortable conditions to keep in touch personally with Roosevelt and, whenever possible, with Stalin. It shows the enormous effort he put into wartime diplomatic and strategic discussions.

Venue and date	Who met	Codename	Also visited
Placentia Bay, Newfoundland, Canada 8–11 August 1941	Roosevelt and Churchill	Riviera	
First Washington Conference, Washington DC 9–12 August 1941	Roosevelt and Churchill	Arcadia	
Second Washington Conference, Washington DC 20–25 June 1942	Roosevelt and Churchill		
Second Moscow Conference, Moscow, USSR 12–17 August 1942	Churchill and Stalin		
Casablanca Conference, Casablanca, Morocco 14–24 January 1943	Churchill and Roosevelt	Symbol	Algiers, Gibraltar and Tunis
Third Washington Conference, Washington DC 12–27 May 1943	Churchill and Roosevelt	Trident	
Quebec Conference 17–24 August 1943	Churchill and Roosevelt	Quadrant	
First Cairo Conference, Cairo, Egypt 23–26 November 1943	Churchill and Roosevelt	Sextant	
Tehran Conference, Tehran, Iran 28 november – 1 December 1943	Churchill, Roosevelt and Stalin	Eureka	Cairo, Tunis and Marrakesh
Second Cairo Conference, Cairo, Egypt 4–6 December 1943	Churchill and Roosevelt	Sextant	
Second Quebec Conference 12–16 August 1944	Churchill and Roosevelt	Octagon	New York
Fourth Moscow Conference, Moscow, USSR 9–19 October 1944	Churchill and Stalin	Tolstoy	Naples, Cairo, Athens
Malta Conference, Malta 30 January–2 February 1945	Churchill and Roosevelt	Argonaut and Cricket	
Yalta 4–11 February 1945	Churchill, Roosevelt and Stalin	Argonaut and Magneto	Malta and Cairo
Potsdam Conference, 17 July–2 August 1945	Churchill, Attlee, Truman and Stalin	Terminal	

How far was the image presented of Churchill's friendship with Roosevelt matched by the reality?

American help before December 1941

Churchill had met **Roosevelt** in 1918 and apparently made a bad impression. The next time they met was in 1941. Churchill believed that the USA would never allow Britain to be defeated and the whole basis of the policy to fight Hitler alone depended on eventually gaining US support, a policy that he would stick to and that would prove to be successful. Victory in 1918 had depended on the USA not in terms of armed force, but in terms of credit and supplies from North America. However, there was no certainty of US intervention and Churchill ran an enormous risk. He had to; he had no other effective policy. Roosevelt was very conscious of US public opinion and the desire to stay out of the war. He was also conscious of problems in the Far East and did give Britain support before December 1941: firstly by giving her 50 redundant US destroyers in return for rights in British bases in the Caribbean and secondly by providing supplies in a deal called **Lend Lease** in 1941. In both cases, Britain got poor terms. The destroyers would have been scrapped anyway and the USA got valuable concessions for virtually nothing. In the second case, British gold reserves in South Africa were taken – in US destroyers – as security for advancing credit for war supplies that made profits for USA industry. It is true that as U-boats became a menace, American navy vessels supplied protection for British convoys as far as Iceland.

Lend Lease

The Lend Lease Act of 1941 allowed the USA to supply war materials to any government whose defence the President deemed vital to the defence of the USA. In 1941 this included Britain, despite the fact that at that time the US was theoretically neutral. Britain was in urgent need of supplies. 'Lend Lease' aid was extended to other countries after the USA joined the war against the Axis powers in December 1941 and a total of \$50.1 billion worth of supplies was sent to US allies. Originally, the agreement aimed to ensure that Britain was able to maintain its war effort against Germany, possibly to avoid the USA being confronted with the decision as to whether defeat of Britain might lead to America having to consider entry into the war.

The agreement is seen as a decisive step away from American non-interventionism since the end of the First World War and towards international involvement.

Churchill praised these measures highly, but they were not necessarily indications that the USA would ever join in the war. Also, the USA had a clear agenda that, after the war, they expected an end to customs duties on goods being imported by foreign countries into the British Empire.

Roosevelt had disliked the British policy of Imperial protection – i.e. free trade between Britain and its Empire, but a tariff barrier against other nations. This had been established in the ***Ottawa Agreement*** (page 129), which Britain had signed in 1932, giving preference to British trade with its Empire and establishing customs barriers against other countries. It was US policy to end it. Indeed, many of Roosevelt's advisers disliked the whole idea of the British Empire and saw it as just as much against US interests as the closed economic systems of Nazi Germany and Soviet Russia.

BIOGRAPHY

Franklin Delano Roosevelt (1882–1945)

Roosevelt was a Democrat who was elected in 1932. He had polio as a young man but despite this setback he became a popular and energetic leader. Roosevelt was elected in 1936, 1940 and 1944 – the only US president to have served more than two terms.

During the Great Depression of the 1930s, he created the *New Deal*, a series of economic stimulus programs (1933–38) with the goal of giving aid to the unemployed, reform of business and financial practices, and recovery of the economy. Roosevelt was a very skilled communicator (he appealed to the nation by radio 'fireside' talks). He helped American farmers through projects such as the Agricultural Adjustment Administration and the National Recovery Administration which promoted public works. However, unemployment remained high.

US public opinion was not in favour of involvement in another European war. The USA did not have large armed forces and was conscious that Japan posed a threat to its interests in the Far East, namely its trade with China and its possession of the Philippines. Roosevelt's position was ambiguous. He sometimes appeared to be sympathetic to opponents of the Italian and German dictators, but he made it very clear that America was neutral and made promises in the election of 1940 that America would not become involved in the Second World War.

When European war broke out in 1939 the USA remained neutral, but in practice aided Britain through the Lend Lease and by supplying war materials. This strained relations with Germany. Also, Roosevelt was openly critical of the Japanese occupation of French Indochina. Relations between the USA and Japan worsened when Roosevelt imposed embargos on imports of oil and metal to Japan. However, he continued to assure the US public that the USA would not enter the war.

In the event, the Japanese attack on Pearl Harbor in December 1941 and the subsequent declaration of war by Hitler, made it unnecessary for Roosevelt to decide and his energies went into mobilising US resources for war. The powers of the federal government were extended further into large-scale conscription, control of resources, and internment of 'enemy aliens'. America became a major influence on world diplomacy and took a leading part in the war and the post-war settlement. Under Roosevelt the USA became 'the Arsenal of Democracy'. Along with Churchill, the President established the major principle behind the war – the *Atlantic Charter*; he planned the post-war United Nations and the division of post-war Europe.

By 1945 Roosevelt was suffering from ill-health and he did not live to see final victory against Germany and Japan; nor did he live to see the dropping of the atomic bombs or the establishment of communist rule in Eastern Europe and the escalation of the Cold War.

Ottawa Agreement 21 July and 20 August 1932

The Imperial Economic Conference or Ottawa Conference in 1932 of British colonies and the autonomous dominions was held to discuss the Great Depression. In it the group admitted the failure of the Gold Standard and abandoned attempts to return to it. The meeting agreed a zone of limited tariffs within the British Empire, but high tariffs with the rest of the world. This came to be known as 'Empire Free-Trade'.

So while Roosevelt spoke sympathetically about freedom and democracy, he was well aware that in huge areas of the world ruled by Britain these were no more apparent than in Germany, Italy or Russia. As a result, when Hitler invaded Russia in 1941, Roosevelt was keen that Britain should not do any deals with Stalin to promise him territory; to keep him in the war, for example, to recognise his right to the Baltic States.

Latvia, Estonia and Lithuania had been part of Russia before 1918. Stalin's troops occupied them in 1940 as part of the agreement made with Nazi Germany in 1939, which divided Poland between Russia and Germany. In fact, Stalin was reclaiming the Tsarist frontiers – he also took Bessarabia from Romania. Britain was more willing to recognise this return to pre-1914 boundaries than the USA. The USA saw it as the USSR violating the rights of the independent countries which America had done so much to establish at the *Treaty of Versailles* in 1919 (see page 63).

Figure 5.1   Roosevelt and Churchill aboard the HMS *Prince of Wales*.

The first summit and the *Atlantic Charter*

The first wartime summit meeting took place in Newfoundland, Canada in August 1941. There is no doubt about the personal bonds established between Churchill and Roosevelt, but also no doubt about tensions under the surface. The *Atlantic Charter* (see Source A) was agreed, which is often portrayed as a noble statement of belief in democracy and freedom. However, more critical historians have argued that it had a distinct message for Britain:

- that Free Trade was expected;
- that the USA wished democracy to be established in all areas, and
- that there should be no deals between the USSR and Britain regarding Eastern Europe.

Churchill had to appease Roosevelt by explicitly stopping Foreign Secretary Eden from making any agreements with Stalin about post-war frontiers in Eastern Europe. He accepted the free trade ideas to please the USA, hoping that they would never have to be implemented and being careful to insert qualifications to protect existing British arrangements with the Empire.

Sources

 A The *Atlantic Charter*

The President of the United States of America and the Prime Minister, Mr. Churchill, representing His Majesty's Government in the United Kingdom, being met together, deem it right to make known certain common principles in the national policies of their respective countries on which they base their hopes for a better future for the world.

First, their countries seek no aggrandizement, territorial or other;

Second, they desire to see no territorial changes that do not accord with the freely expressed wishes of the peoples concerned;

Third, they respect the right of all peoples to choose the form of government under which they will live; and they wish to see sovereign rights and self government restored to those who have been forcibly deprived of them;

Fourth, they will endeavour, with due respect for their existing obligations, to further the **enjoyment by all States, great or small, victor or vanquished, of access, on equal terms, to the trade and to the raw materials of the world** which are needed for their economic prosperity;

Fifth, they desire to bring about the fullest collaboration between all nations in the economic field with the object of securing, for all, improved labor standards, economic advancement and social security;

Sixth, after the final destruction of the Nazi tyranny, they hope to see established a peace which will afford to all nations the means of dwelling in safety within their own boundaries, and which will afford assurance that all the men in all the lands may live out their lives in freedom from fear and want;

Seventh, such a peace should enable all men to traverse the high seas and oceans without hindrance;

Eighth, they believe that all of the nations of the world, for realistic as well as spiritual reasons must come to the abandonment of the use of force. Since no future peace can be maintained if land, sea or air armaments continue to be employed by nations which threaten, or may threaten, aggression outside of their frontiers, they believe, pending the establishment of a wider and permanent system of general security, that the disarmament of such nations is essential. They will likewise aid and encourage all other practicable measures which will lighten for peace-loving peoples the crushing burden of armaments.

Signed by: Franklin D. Roosevelt & Winston S. Churchill.

B Churchill recalls the making of the *Atlantic Charter*.

Considering all the tales of my reactionary, Old World outlook, and the pain this is said to have caused the President, I am glad that it should be on record that the substance and spirit of what came to be called "The Atlantic Charter" was in first draft a British production cast in my own words. The only serious difference from what I had written was about the fourth point [in Churchill's draft] the access to raw materials. The President wished to add "without discrimination and on equal terms" … With regard to this, I pointed out that the words "without discrimination" might be held to call into question the Ottawa Agreements [of 1932 establishing preferential trading terms within the British Empire] and I was in no position to accept them…Mr Sumner Welles [from the US State Department, or foreign office] pointed out that this was the core of the matter.

I then said that if the words "with due respect for their existing obligations" could be inserted … I should be able to refer the text to Her Majesty's government with some hope that it might be accepted. The President was obviously impressed. He never pressed the point again.

Churchill's *The Grand Alliance*, 1950.

C A modern historian questions Churchill's account, using the diary of Sir Alexander Cadogan, a leading foreign office official who accompanied Churchill to Canada in 1941 to meet Roosevelt.

On the first night of the conference, 9 August 1941, FDR suggested they concoct a joint declaration of principles. Next morning Churchill demanded an immediate draft, telling Sir Alexander Cadogan of the Foreign office in broad outlines the sort of shape the latter should take. Over the eggs and bacon, Cadogan worked up a text, about which Churchill "expressed general but not very enthusiastic approval". Churchill's reference to "my text" is therefore economical with the truth.

For months he had resisted pressure … for a statement of British war aims. His enthusiasm for the Atlantic Charter was something of a volte-face [about turn] he needed something to show from the meeting and the Atlantic Charter could be represented as a tacit alliance.

Reynolds, (2004) *In Command of History*, pp. 260–61.

D Roosevelt's son recalls his father's attitude to the *Atlantic Charter*, the British Empire and Free Trade.

They must never get the idea that we're in the war just to help them hang on to their archaic, mediaeval empire ideas….I hope they realise we're the senior partner, and we're not going to sit by, after we've won and watch their system stultify the growth of every country of Asia and half the countries in Europe to boot…Great Britain signed the Atlantic Charter, I hope they realize that the US government intends to make them live up to it.

Elliott Roosevelt, *As He Saw It*, New York 1946.

ACTIVITY

Britain, America and post-war aims

1 In what ways could Source A be seen as an inspiring document of war aims?

2 In what ways could it be seen as a problem for Britain?

3 How does Reynold's account (Source C) differ from that of Churchill's (Source B)? Why do you think this is?

4 What justification is there for the view in Source C that Churchill only enthused about it because the conference with Roosevelt had been disappointing and he needed something to show for it?

5 How reliable as evidence are the two memoirs – Churchill's in Source B and Elliott Roosevelt's in Source D?

6 Using all these sources and your own knowledge, how good were US relations by September 1941?

The Second World War after December 1941

The situation was transformed in December 1941 by two events which were not necessarily connected.

The first was the Japanese attack on the US Pacific base at Pearl Harbour. For the Japanese this was a way out of the deadlock created by US hostility to their war in China and the freezing of assets and supplies of oil and metal ore. Churchill was frantic with joy, anticipating that now the USA would *have* to join the war. However, there was no certainty that Roosevelt would have done more than fight a war against Japan. This option was taken out of his hands when the second event took place and Hitler declared war on the USA. This bizarre decision has never received the attention that it deserves and, more than anything else in the war, justified Churchill's policy of waiting for something to turn up to push America into war. Churchill and Britain were very lucky that this occurred; it was entirely outside of British control and exceeded British expectations. Churchill rushed, uninvited, to see Roosevelt again in Washington.

Figure 5.2   Roosevelt and Churchill at Casablanca

What was Churchill's overall strategy and his view of Britain's world role?

By 1941, Churchill had a very clear idea of how the war should go. At the heart of his strategy was a belief that there could be no invasion of France to create a second front to help the USSR in the immediate future. They would have to bear the brunt of the land war. Britain should contribute by fighting in the Mediterranean against what he later described to Stalin as 'the soft under belly of the Axis'. This would protect British possessions in the Eastern Mediterranean and oil supplies in the Middle East and keep the Suez Canal open as a link to India and Australasia. It would also open up the chance of a Balkan campaign. Once Britain had established control of North Africa, then it could consider attacking through Greece and Yugoslavia. This would take the pressure off the USSR and also bolster Britain's influence in south-east Europe. It would also be much less costly than an attack over the Channel against strong German defences. Britain would also fight at sea to keep its links with North America and the Empire open, and it would bombard Germany by air to weaken the industrial capacity of the Nazi regime. Churchill's view was based on a clear aim that Britain would continue to be a major imperial power with vital worldwide interests which it needed to protect.

The Mediterranean strategy

Despite all Churchill's rows with the generals, this strategy was exactly what they wanted. The Chief of the Imperial General Staff, Sir Alan Brooke especially supported this from December 1941. It had several advantages.

1. It would avoid the bloodbaths of the First World War in France.

2. It would negate the need for a very dangerous seaborne invasion of France over the Channel by Britain. A cross-Channel invasion was a very risky venture and even if successful would involve British forces in what was considered likely to be a long drawn out war in Northern France with heavy casualties.

3. The Germans had not thought a cross-Channel invasion possible in 1940 and the British did not think it would work easily for them. Brooke did not want to attempt this until 1946, by which time it was hoped that the USSR would have bled Germany dry on the Eastern Front. The USA was to play its part by providing a stream of supplies and by joining in with the Mediterranean actions.

There were problems with this approach.

1. Russia might not actually survive the German attack – though this was less likely when the German attacks lost momentum in the winter snow in late 1941 and Russia began to revive after the initial disasters of the German invasion.

2. Stalin might, without a second front being opened in France, make another deal with Hitler.

3. The USA might insist on a second front in France rather than dispersing their efforts in the Mediterranean to serve British interests. If Britain refused, they might merely concentrate on Japan.

Stalin was writing angrily to demand a second front. The US generals, mainly Marshall, the steely and determined Chief of Staff, and Stimson, the Secretary of War, were arguing for landings in France as soon as possible.

What Churchill achieved was to persuade the USA to postpone the Second Front and to support his view of the war. But in return, he had to agree to American demands not to discuss territorial gains for the USSR.

Would the Mediterranean strategy work?

The British were wedded to this strategy, but it is difficult to see how Germany would actually be defeated by it. Bombing alone would not destroy the German army. Attacks in

the Mediterranean might distract Germany but would not easily lead to an invasion of
Germany itself. In 1918 Germany had stopped fighting even though there were no allied
troops on German soil but there was no certainty that this would happen again, and that
Germany would go on fighting for every inch of the German homeland. With the USA
raising large forces and US generals eager to invade France, it was difficult to see why they
should be persuaded not to. The entire strategy was based on the USSR engaging the bulk of
the German army until Britain was ready, with considerable financial and military
assistance from the USA, to invade Northern France. After this, Britain, despite not having
contributed nearly as much to the war, would want to:

- retain its status as a world leader;
- keep its Empire, and
- maintain its trading policies intended to protect its supply of imperial food and imperial
  markets.

In the event, expectations of casualties on a First World War level were proved to be
entirely justified, but the numbers were different. The 'Western Front' only lasted from June
1944 to May 1945 (see Figure 5.3) and victory was achieved without the tragic
consequences suffered by British forces in the First World War.

Throughout the entirety of the war the Soviet Union bore the brunt of military casualties
amongst the Allies. They would lose 8 to 10 million military personnel compared with
380,000 British and 416,000 US casualties.

Figure 5.3   D-Day 6 June 1944: US troops at Utah beach prepare to land in Normandy. British and Canadian forces
made simultaneous landings at other points on the French coast.

Sources on the situation by the time of Tehran in November 1943

(A) General Marshall wrote to Roosevelt:

France is the only place in which a powerful offensive can be prepared and executed by the United States in the near future....It is the only place where the bulk of the British ground forces can be committed to a general offensive in cooperation with US forces. It is impossible, in view of the shipping situation, to transfer the bulk of the British forces to any distant region, and the protection of the British Isles would hold the bulk of the divisions in England. The USA can concentrate and use larger forces in Western Europe than in any other place, due to seas distances and the existence in England of base facilities. In other localities the enemy is protected against invasion by natural obstacles. Time would be required to reduce these and to make the attack effective.

Michael Howard, *Grand Strategy* HMSO (1972) p. xiv, quoted: in C. Barnett in *The Rise and Fall of the Grand Alliance,* eds Lane and Temperly, p. 179, Macmillan 1995.

(B) Churchill's view in 1942 as expressed to Sir Alan Brooke (later Lord Alanbrooke) the leading British soldier.

If we move from Torch [the invasion of North Africa]

northwards into Europe a new situation must be surveyed. The flank attack may become the main attack and the main attack a holding operation in the early stages. Our second front will in fact comprise both the Atlantic and the Mediterranean coasts of Europe, and we can push either right-handed or left-handed or both handed as our resources and circumstances permit.

Howard (see left).

(C) Lord Alanbrooke wrote in his diary in November 1943.

The "drag" [desire to avoid commitment] of the Americans has seriously affected our Mediterranean strategy and the whole conduct of the war. If they had come wholeheartedly into the Mediterranean with us we should now have Rome securely, the Balkans would be ablaze, the Dardanelles would be open and we should be on a highway to get Rumania and Bulgaria out of the war.

Weidenfeld and Nicolson War Diaries 1939–45.

ACTIVITY

1   How far do Sources A, B and C show a difference of opinion about the war? (Comparing content.)

2   Which view do you think was the more realistic?

Make a judgement based on contextual knowledge and the nature of the sources.

After a highly successful speech to Congress and an amicable visit to Roosevelt, Churchill was in a buoyant mood at the start of 1942. Eden, however, was not, and thought that Britain would have to offer concessions to Stalin. In reality Churchill was now caught between two allies that were going to do a lot of Britain's fighting. Britain had become the junior partner and a lot of negotiation had to be done. As if to prove this point and highlight British weakness (now that most British forces were concentrated in the Mediterranean), the Japanese took Singapore in 1942 against a larger British force and destroyed the greatest symbol of British power in South-East Asia. Japan also took Burma and threatened India, which was vulnerable because of nationalist agitation. Initial British victories in North Africa were reversed by the German 'Afrika Korps' and a major port, Tobruk, fell, which left Egypt threatened. Roosevelt was sympathetic and offered help but it was clear that Britain was in no position to dictate strategy.

Problems in 1943

The high point of British influence was probably when Churchill persuaded Roosevelt, against the advice of his military advisers, to take part in an attack on the North African colonies of Algeria and Tunisia as part of the British strategy of controlling North Africa. After that, there was less agreement. With some justification, the Americans questioned the point of the whole Mediterranean strategy. It then seemed logical to launch an invasion of Sicily and subsequently of Italy in 1943. As a result, Mussolini fell in 1943 but instead of Britain tying down large numbers of German troops to help the USSR, the reverse happened. It was British and American troops who were tied down.

Germany poured troops into Italy and the Balkans. The British were pinned down in a long and costly advance in which smaller German forces took advantage of good defensive positions to occupy large numbers of allied troops. Meanwhile, the Russians were taking the brunt of the fighting and Stalin was increasingly determined to get his reward in territorial gains. Subsequently, Roosevelt felt that he had been driven by Churchill in the wrong direction and relations were much cooler in 1943.

Sources on the situation by the time of Tehran in November 1943

A **This historian takes a critical view of Anglo-American relations by 1943.**

The shift in the balance of power – intellectual and psychological as well as material and military – is reflected in the fortunes of the Anglo-American arguments over grand strategy. Whereas in 1941–42 the British generally prevailed, in 1943–45 they were almost brushed aside. The Tehran Conference in November 1943 marked a turning point. For by then the Americans had grown tired of the persistent British urging of a Mediterranean strategy at the expense of delaying a cross-Channel invasion…Churchill's special relationship with Roosevelt had faded into coolness and distance by Tehran….Churchill was no longer the dominating personality of the earlier war years, but a tired and worried man.

Corelli Barnett on Anglo-American strategy in Europe in *The Rise and Fall of the Grand Alliance,* Op cit, p.105, p.187.

B **From the diary of Sir Charles Wilson, later Lord Moran, Churchill's doctor who accompanied him to meet Roosevelt and Stalin at Tehran, 28 November 1943. It reveals what some have seen as a humiliation for Churchill and divisions between America and Britain.**

When the President [Roosevelt] was safely ensconced [settled] in his quarters, Stalin lost no time in calling on him. Harry Hopkins [Roosevelt's special adviser and friend] poured out the whole story. The president … made it clear that he was anxious to relieve the pressure on the Russian front by invading France. Stalin expressed his gratification and when the president went on to say that he hoped Malaya, Burma and other British colonies would soon be "educated in the arts of self-government" the talk became quite intimate.

Nov 29

When I saw the Prime Minister this morning he was plainly put out. It seems that he had sent a note to the President suggesting they should lunch together, but the President's answer was a polite "No". "It is not like him", the PM murmured. …This did not prevent the President seeing Stalin alone after lunch...Roosevelt poured out to Stalin his own idea of a new League of Nations. Stalin listened patiently, but when the conversation turned to the future of Germany, he became animated.

Lord Moran, *Winston Churchill, the Struggle for Survival, 1940–1965,* published in 1966 and based on Moran's diaries.

C Churchill's own account in *Closing the Ring*, volume 5 of *The Second World War.*

It has become a legend in America that I strove to prevent the cross-Channel invasion called 'Overlord' and that I vainly tried to lure the Allies into some mass invasion of the Balkans or a large-scale campaign in the Eastern Mediterranean which would kill it. Much of this nonsense ... has been exposed and refuted, but it may be worthwhile to set forth what it was I actually wanted....'Overlord' now planned in great detail should be launched in May or June (1944).

Closing the Ring, p. 304.

D Churchill's plan of 19 October 1943 to be brought to the Tehran Conference. This was omitted from *Closing the Ring*. The items are in order of importance.

(a) Stop all further movements of British troops and British and US landing craft from the Mediterranean...

(b) Use all possible energy to take Rome.

(c) Bring Turkey into the war...Prepare an expedition to take Rhodes before the end of January 1944.

(d) ... aid and animate the resistance in Yugoslavia and Albania and also to capture islands like Corfu and Argostolui.

(e) Continue and build up Overlord without prejudice to the above.

Reynolds, *In Command of History*, p. 383.

E Churchill in a first and unpublished draft to a section on 1943 in *Closing the Ring* explains why he supported the proposal of Roosevelt that an American general should command an invasion of Northern France. It shows his fears about an invasion. The *Battle of the Somme* resulted in 60,000 British casualties on the first day.

I had the fear that if a bloody and disastrous repulse were encountered [in Overlord] far bigger than the first day's battle of the Somme in 1916 there might have been an outcry in the United States. It would be said that another result would have attended the appointment of an American General.

Reynolds, *In Command of History*, p. 385.

ACTIVITY

1   Compare the content and nature of Sources C and D about Churchill's support for *Overlord* in 1943.

2   Use your own knowledge to assess how far Sources A–E support the interpretation that there were poor relations between Churchill and Roosevelt by November 1943.

EXAMINER'S ADVICE

These are **similar** to the questions asked in the OCR examination. Some hints:

■   What are they saying specifically about the key issue of relations between the USA and Britain by 1943, as opposed to what they are saying in general terms? This may need some thought and interpretation.

■   Look at the origins of the sources. Who wrote them? When? Why?

■   Which do you find convincing and why? (Try allocating each a mark out of 10 to rank them.)

Figure 5.4   Stalin, Roosevelt and Churchill at Tehran.

Source

(A) **A modern historian in a study of the differences between Churchill's account of events in his memoirs and opposing evidence.**

In 1948 Stimson's [The US Secretary for War'] *memoirs presented the Tehran Conference as the triumphal culmination of two year 'quarrel of brothers' over grand strategy, when outvoted by Stalin and Roosevelt, the Prime Minister finally had to agree a firm date for 'Overlord'* [the invasion of Northern France]. *The memoirs of the US Admiral Leahy published in 1950 stated bluntly that the British "finally fell into line" at Tehran.*

Reynolds, *In Command of History*, p. 383.

ACTIVITY

Look at this additional Source A. What does it show you about Churchill's attitude to the Second Front?

The American agenda

The **Tehran Summit** (Figure 5.4) of November 1943 (see opposite) was a low point: Roosevelt kept Churchill at a distance and in his first meetings with Stalin moved closer to Russia. Roosevelt discussed the partition of Germany after the war with Stalin. An invasion of Northern France was decided for summer 1944 and it was going to be under US command (*Operation Overlord*). An American general and not Sir Alanbrooke was to lead the invasion. By 1943 there were large amounts of US troops in Britain; US resources were considerably greater than those of Britain's and British influence was considerably less than the previous year.

Previously, Roosevelt had been set against deals with Stalin about post-war frontiers. Whereas Churchill, in a desperate bid to reduce pressure for a second front, had signed a treaty with Stalin and tacitly accepted the 1941 frontiers. However, by 1944 Churchill was determined to deal with post-war threats from the USSR directly. Once a second front in Northern France was underway Churchill no longer had reason to appease Stalin to explain away his postponement of it. Now he could consider directly the post-war threat of the USSR to Central and Eastern Europe. The USA did not help.

Tehran Summit *(28 Nov–1 Dec, 1943)*

Franklin Roosevelt, Winston Churchill and Joseph Stalin met in Tehran, Iran, during the Second World War to discuss military strategy and political issues. It followed the Cairo Conference with Chiang Kai-shek and was the first three-power war conference attended by Stalin. Stalin agreed to:

- Launch a military offensive from the east to coincide with 'Operation Overlord', the planned invasion of German-occupied France from the west.
- Commit Soviet forces against Japan after the defeat of Germany.

In return:

- Roosevelt and Churchill would have to support Stalin and the partisans in Yugoslavia.
- Allow for the manipulation of the border between Poland and the USSR.

Churchill up to this point had been trying to persuade the USA to join a UK/Commonwealth forces push through the Mediterranean that would have secured British interests in the Middle East and India. Roosevelt was determined to break up the British Empire and so the concessions to Stalin served this purpose.

Also discussed but not settled were Eastern Europe's post-war borders, including Poland's post-war status, and a post-war international organisation. A separate protocol pledged the three powers to maintain the independence of Iran.

BIOGRAPHY

Dwight David 'Ike' Eisenhower (1890–1969)

Born in Texas into a working class family, Eisenhower was brought up in Kansas and went on to study at West Point military academy. He did not have combat experience in the First World War but was a skilled trainer and staff officer. He rose in the army as an organiser and was widely read and respected for his managerial skills. He worked with General MacArthur in building up a Philippines Defence Force but was recalled to the USA by Chief of Staff Marshall, who needed his experience as a staff officer. He was put in charge of the Torch landings in North Africa and the invasion of Sicily and then given the overall command of the invasion of Europe on D-Day. He was a thoughtful leader who established good relationships with those around him and bore heavy responsibilities calmly. He continued a military career after the war and was the first supreme commander of NATO. He served as president from 1953 to 1961.

Churchill had not made headway with persuading Roosevelt to consider opposing a possible post-war Russian domination of Eastern Europe, which might threaten British interests in the Eastern Mediterranean (Suez, Egypt, Palestine, Iraq, Jordan, the route to India). Secondly, at a meeting with Roosevelt at Quebec in September 1944, Churchill had to implore Roosevelt to extend Lend Lease credit after the war to Britain. At one point he exclaimed: 'What do you want me to do? Get up on my hind legs and beg for you, like Fala?', (Fala was Roosevelt's dog). However, when he raised the need to push on to reach

Berlin before the Russians, the Americans were not convinced. **Eisenhower**, the commander of the invasion force, did not want to rush for Berlin at the expense of his strategy of advancing through Germany on a broad front and consolidating gains.

Churchill then turned instead to power politics similar to those of the previous century. He and Eden negotiated the famous *Percentages Agreement* with Stalin in Moscow in October 1944, which divided up Eastern Europe into spheres of influence and was a greater act of territorial appeasement than anything proposed by Chamberlain. Richard Holmes disagrees:

> 'It is nonsense to equate this with Munich. Winston had no power independent of the USA to affect post-war boundaries, and the issue is not what he lost, but that he managed to win with a very weak hand.' (*In the Footsteps of Churchill*, BBC 2005.)

As to whether or not this is convincing is questionable given Churchill's own comment to Stalin: 'Might it not be thought rather cynical that we had disposed of these issues so fateful to millions of people in such an offhand manner?'.

The Percentages Agreement

This was an agreement between Stalin and Churchill made on 9 October 1944 at Moscow to divide south-eastern Europe into 'spheres of influence'. This had been a term used in colonial agreements between great powers before 1914. Stalin would enjoy 90 per cent in Romania; Britain 90 per cent in Greece. Stalin had 75 per cent in Bulgaria; Britain and Russia would have 50 per cent each in Hungary and Yugoslavia. Churchill wrote the 'deal' on a piece of paper which Stalin ticked (see Figure 5.7, page 148).

The point is that by 1944 the USA had not acted to prevent any Russian expansion despite Churchill's concerns and there was no guarantee that the USA would not simply withdraw from Europe once the war against Germany had been won. The Americans were displeased about British policy in Greece which used British forces to bolster the royal government there against communist guerrillas and persuaded Stalin not to intervene by agreeing to his dominating other Eastern European areas. The US agenda favoured free trade policies in Europe and self-determination for all countries, including those in the British Empire.

The Yalta Conference

The Yalta Conference of February 1945 (Figure 5.5) was the last between Churchill and Roosevelt. There was little to be done except to accept Stalin's control of Eastern Europe and Roosevelt made it clear that US military forces would only be deployed for two years at most.

The war to protect Poland ended with the loss of its Eastern territories to Russia and political domination by Stalin. Stalin was determined to create a buffer zone in Eastern Europe and all Yalta did was to make vague promises about democracy, which could not be enforced. Roosevelt was eager to get Soviet help against Japan to minimise what were becoming very high casualties. Churchill agreed, though later gave the impression that it was largely an American plan.

Figure 5.5. Winston Churchill, Franklin D. Roosevelt and Joseph Stalin meet at the Yalta Conference. *This photograph reveals Roosevelt as a sickly man – compare it with that of Tehran.*

There was little by this stage that Britain could do to stop US initiatives or USSR expansion. Roosevelt's death in April 1945 produced a heartfelt reaction from Churchill (see Source A, page 142), but the hopes for a post-war world based on a special relationship were not really founded on reality.

Limitations on Britain's freedom of action by the end of the war

Churchill had driven Britain into an unavoidable dependence on the USA with the Lend Lease agreement and the domination by the USA of military policy during the war. Britain was financially dependent on America. To stand against Russia, Britain would need US support. There had been no certainty that it would help Britain against Hitler and now there was no certainty that it would help Britain against the USSR or support it financially after the war. There was every chance that US pressure would be applied against Britain's economic and colonial interests and every chance that bitter wartime divisions and suspicions would influence US post-war policy. On 9 June 1945 Churchill told his planners to consider how Britain could 'defend our island' if the Americans withdrew to the Pacific, leaving the Russians to advance to the North Sea and the Atlantic. He was already using phrases like 'iron curtain', 'veil of secrecy' and 'screen' to describe the Soviet control over Eastern Europe. He had not been fully able to persuade America to respond to the threat.

ACTIVITY

Different views on Churchill and the USA

1 How do the views in Sources A–C of Churchill's relationship with Roosevelt differ?

2 Which view do you find most convincing.

(Try ranking the views out of 10.)

Sources

A From Churchill's tribute to Roosevelt.

I conceived an admiration for him as a statesman, a man of affairs and a war leader. I had the utmost confidence in his upright, inspiring character and outlook and a personal regard – affection, I must say – for him beyond my power to express today.

He devised the extraordinary measure of assistance called Lend Lease, which will stand forth as the most unselfish and unsordid financial act of any country in all history.

We drew up together the Atlantic Charter which will, I trust long remain a guide for both our peoples and for other peoples of the world.

Nor need I speak of the plans which we made with our great ally Russia at Tehran, for these have been carried out for the world to see.

For us it remains only to say that in Franklin Roosevelt there died the greatest American friend who has ever brought help and comfort from the New World to the Old.

April 17 1945, Churchill in an Address to Parliament following Roosevelt's death on 12 April.

B From *Churchill* by Clive Ponting 1994. (Ponting is a modern historian who takes a generally unfavourable view of Churchill).

Throughout the war the USA kept the British economy and finances under close control.

During 1942, as American forces were stationed in Britain and other parts of the sterling area, Britain's dollar reserves, which had been exhausted at the end of 1940, began to rise again. Roosevelt was determined that Britain should not benefit from this. He wanted to keep Britain's dollar reserves at a level sufficient to stop them opting for an enclosed trading system at the end of the war, but not so high as they could ignore US demands. On 1 January 1943 he decided that the UK's gold and dollar balances should not be permitted to be less than $600 million nor above $1 billion.

The US was able to achieve this by taking out goods (such as tobacco) out of Lend Lease and forcing the British to pay for them. On 12 February 1944 Roosevelt virtually ordered Churchill to reduce British reserves to the $1 billion level. The Chancellor of the Exchequer warned that if this was accepted "we should have lost our financial independence and would emerge from the war victorious but quite financially helpless". Churchill protested to Roosevelt but American policy was unchanged.

Roosevelt reneged on his discussions with Churchill [to provide continued economic assistance after the war] at Quebec – he wanted to keep Britain in a dependent position. When the war ended, Lend Lease was cancelled within a few days.

{During Quebec} Roosevelt told Morgenthau "All they want is Singapore back". Britain had been deliberately excluded from the American war in the Pacific.

Roosevelt was determined to raise colonial issues at the Yalta Conference. He put three propositions to Stalin: Hong Kong should be given to China rather than being restored to Britain; Korea should be a trusteeship with Britain ignored and Indochina should be made independent instead of being restored to France. Stalin was cautious partly because of the Percentages deal [see page 140 on deal] that he had done with Churchill in October 1944.

C Another modern historian, Geoffrey Best, from his book Churchill, *A Study in Greatness*, 2001.

The Churchill-Roosevelt relationship was special, no doubt about that, but not … the Special Relationship of Churchill's imagination, it could never achieve as much as Churchill imagined. The questions that arose to disturb the harmony of Britain's alliance with the US would have done more damage than they did had the relations between the two national chieftains not been amiable, and on the whole trusting; an easy working relationship which Churchill went to endless lengths to create and sustain.

ANALYSIS

Historians views

In the end, the British and Americans did sustain an alliance which defeated Nazi Germany and launched together the greatest military invasion of all time on D-Day, 1945. America shared with Britain, largely as a result of Roosevelt, the greatest weapon ever produced – the atom bomb. Churchill put himself at great risk and inconvenience to keep the vital support of the USA going. There were US/British disagreements over:

■ China – which Churchill had little time for yet Roosevelt thought massively important;

■ the whole question of the British Empire and free trade;

■ aspects of strategy such as the Second Front disagreement;

■ financial and economic matters such as the *Atlantic Charter*;

■ the role of France (see pages 124–25), and

■ the threat of the USSR.

Churchill's pragmatism did not obscure his fears for post-war Eastern Europe, whereas US policy was to ignore the communist threat whilst the USSR could bolster their war in the Far East against Japan. Inevitably, there were disagreements. Whether the balance lies with 'revisionists' like Clive Ponting or with those who stress, like David Reynolds, the weaknesses of Churchill's own account of relations with America, or with those who see the relationship established with Roosevelt as one of the key elements for winning the war, which supports one of Churchill's claims to be thought of as a national saviour, must be a matter for personal choice. It may be Churchill's legacy to us that we are free to exercise that choice.

Was Churchill right to fear the power of the USSR?

In defence of Churchill's hostile view of the Russian Revolution after 1917 (see page 22), it could be argued that it did indeed, as he warned, create a bloodthirsty dictatorship under **Stalin**. When a greater threat arose from Hitler after 1933 Churchill proposed a Grand Alliance which would have included Stalin's Russia on purely practical grounds. He did not, however, alter his view that communism was an evil. In August 1939 Stalin agreed to a non-aggression pact with Hitler (a secret agreement which allowed Russia to recover land lost in 1918). Subsequently, the USSR's occupation of Eastern Poland, Bessarabia and the Baltic States was accompanied by violent repression in 1939 and 1940. In Poland, the areas occupied were of mixed population, not all occupied by ethnic Poles, and they had been under Russian rule before 1914. However, there was brutal repression of any potential opposition, with executions and deportations which might have even been copied from the Nazi occupation of Western Poland. It is disturbing to read of friendly meetings between the Nazi SS and Soviet NKVD torturers. The low point was the massacre of Polish prisoners in **Katyn** forest outside Smolensk in 1940 in which 4,253 (source: Chris Bellamy, *Absolute War*, 2007) people were executed, mostly with their hands tied behind them in a cold-blooded manner similar both to earlier Soviet internal purges and to Nazi ethnic killings. Stalin gave personal orders for this.

The Katyn Massacre

In 1943 the Germans announced to the world that they had found mass graves of Polish citizens killed by the Russians during their occupation of Eastern Poland in 1940. Though the USSR denied the massacre until 1990, it is clear that a decision was taken by the Soviet Politburo to eliminate Polish army officers, policemen and prominent officials and intellectuals in order to control Poland. Possibly 4,253 were killed by the Soviet security force – the NKVD – at a forest near Smolensk called Katyn and there were other murders at Tver and Kharkov. The victims were shot in the head. The Polish government in exile wanted condemnation of the killings, but both Britain and the USA had to be careful to maintain relations with Stalin. In private, Churchill admitted on 15 April 1943 during a conversation with General Sikorski:

> 'Alas, the German revelations are probably true. The Bolsheviks can be very cruel.'

According to the notes taken by Count Raczyński (a member of the Polish government in exile in London), on 24 April 1943 Churchill assured the Soviets:

> 'We shall certainly oppose vigorously any "investigation" by the International Red Cross or any other body in any territory under German authority.'

There is no doubt that Churchill's government knew about the Russian harshness even if the details of Katyn did not emerge until the Germans overran the area in 1942.

Thanks to an escape clause added to the 1939 guarantee to Poland, Britain was not obliged to declare war on Russia to defend Poland, as the treaty between Britain and Poland covered only Germany. There was concern about the Russian policy, but neither Britain nor the USA offered direct criticism.

BIOGRAPHY

Josef Vissarionovich Dzugashvili STALIN (1878–1953)

Stalin (his adopted name) was a Georgian born in 1879 who initially trained as a priest before joining the Bolsheviks. He came into his own during the Russian Civil War (1918–20) and became the Commissar of Nationalities. He exploited his position as Party Secretary and ousted his rival Trotsky to emerge as leader of the Communist party by 1928. He carried out a ruthless modernisation policy in both agriculture and industry in the 1930s and also established the greatest police state in world history of its time, imprisoning millions in a network of camps (Gulags). He signed a pact with Hitler in 1939 and divided Poland with the Nazis, but this did not prevent a German invasion of Russia in 1941. Stalin organised a relentless resistance to the Nazis and, despite high Russian casualties, defeated the Germans. USSR domination was then imposed on Poland, Rumania, Hungary, Czechoslovakia, Latvia, Lithuania, and Estonia. Stalin died in 1953.

The Grand Alliance – Russia

When Hitler's armies invaded Russia in June 1941, Churchill was quick to offer support. Even the most ardent anti-communist could not fail to welcome any chance that Hitler's forces would be distracted by a major war. There was little expectation that Hitler would lose. Russia had not done well in the war against Finland in the winter of 1939–40, and the rapid early German victories in Russia were thought likely to lead to a Russian defeat. However, in a famous comment Churchill made his view known: 'If Hitler invaded Hell, I would at least make a favourable reference to the Devil in the House of Commons'. This made it clear that Churchill was aware that the Soviet regime to which Britain was allying itself was maintained by brutal repression, but that the threat from Germany in 1941 was great enough to warrant such an alliance.

In the event, despite massive Soviet losses of men and equipment, the German advance was halted before Moscow and Leningrad. The prospect of a long and gruelling struggle in Russia emerged and was followed by the US entry into the war. Churchill now had his Grand Alliance, even if it did mean dealing with 'the Devil'. So, when the British ambassador to the exiled Polish government, Sir Frank O'Malley, produced a report making it clear that evidence pointed to the Soviet responsibility for Katyn, this was not made publicly available and remained top secret. Roosevelt was sent a copy but suppressed it and refused to entertain any opinion that Russian behaviour was so brutal. Perhaps it was simple necessity – to defeat the Germans. Both the USA and Britain had to maintain a favourable image in their countries of 'Uncle Joe' Stalin and the heroic Russian people.

First discussions between Britain and the USSR, 1941

After 1941, Churchill had clear aims:

1. Russia must stay in the war in order to weaken Germany.
2. Russian demands that a second front should be opened in France should not be met for as long as possible.

Stalin had clear aims, too, which involved a restoration of the 1941 frontier, including the gains of 1939–40 and the establishment of 'friendly' powers on Russia's borders. As this was a war fought for freedom and whose idealistic aims had been set out in the *Atlantic Charter* (see page 130), this presented moral problems for Churchill. Stalin's aims were in direct contradiction to the wishes of the countries of Eastern Europe who had no desire to have a brutal dictatorship forced on them by the USSR. In the first meeting with the British, attended by the British Foreign Secretary Eden in December 1941, Stalin made these claims clear and demanded a second front by the invasion of northern France.

At this stage, Roosevelt was completely against any promise of territorial gain. When Eden suggested negotiating possible USSR post-war frontiers, Churchill issued a considerable rebuke. All territorial decisions should wait until the war had been won. Appeasing the USA was more important than appeasing Stalin. However, if Russia did not co-operate, then difficulties might arise. There was no certainty that Stalin would not negotiate with Hitler, as he had done in 1939 or simply fight his own war. Convoys were sent to Northern Russia carrying supplies, with considerable loss of life among British seamen, to assure Stalin of Britain's goodwill. And Churchill decided to see Stalin personally.

Churchill in Moscow, August 1942

This first meeting with Stalin in Moscow in 1942 did not go at all well at first. Stalin bluntly demanded a second front. Churchill's explanation of 'the soft underbelly' strategy, which included drawing a crocodile to represent Germany and Italy to show why a Mediterranean

strategy was vital, was met with Russian scepticism. Churchill felt he was not being treated as the hero of 1940 but as some sort of cowardly weakling. Tempers were frayed. Only the direct talking of Archibald Clark-Kerr, the ambassador in Moscow, to Churchill prevented him from leaving in a huff. Eventually, and with a large consumption of alcohol, Stalin and Churchill became more friendly and Churchill seemed to warm to him. However, little was actually settled. Stalin did not get a second front, only promises of one, and there was still the unresolved issue of the post-war territory. The treaty between Britain and Russia contained a strong hint that Britain would recognise the 1941 boundaries, which included Soviet gains as a result of the pact with Hitler. However, fear of Roosevelt's displeasure prevented further agreement.

Churchill in Tehran, November 1943

By 1943 the attitude of the Americans had changed (see pages 136–139). Strains between themselves and Britain over the Mediterranean strategy were apparent at the Tehran Conference where the 'big three' met for the first time together. Stalin lured Roosevelt into staying in the Russian area and Roosevelt was sure he could charm Stalin if he talked with him man to man. Churchill was left out in the cold. Roosevelt supported a second front and he gave secret verbal agreement to Stalin's wish for a new division of Poland (see Figure 5.6). The conference was the first step into dividing Germany after the war and – possibly Roosevelt's main aim – Stalin agreed at Tehran to join the war in the Far East after the German defeat.

Churchill now faced exclusion from a Stalin-Roosevelt relationship. He was under pressure to agree to a second front which he was sure would fail and lead to unacceptably high casualties. However, the delay in implementing a second front gave the Germans time to reinforce the 'Atlantic Wall'. Also, the prospect of Soviet power in the Far East went against British interests, and Roosevelt did not appear to see how dangerous Stalin was. After all, if Russia expanded in Europe it would be Britain that would be threatened, not the USA.

The situation by 1944

Concerned about these developments, Churchill flew to Moscow in October 1944. By now his own reservations about discussing post-war settlement had gone; and there was less need to worry about offending the USA if these were discussed. The invasion of France had been successful – but Churchill could not really set the 156,000 troops who went into action on the 6 June 1944 (D-day) against the 2 million Russian troops who were fighting the Nazis in the simultaneous battle of Kharkov and pretend that the war was being fought equally by Russia and the West. Here is the essence of the problem. For Britain, D-Day was and remains a monumental and heroic enterprise. For the USSR, it was a long-delayed and relatively under-resourced diversion. Churchill had also lost a bargaining tool, since Stalin had gained the Second Front and his own campaigns were going well. The fact is that Stalin did not particularly need Churchill. In any negotiation, Churchill did not have a strong hand. Indeed, it could be said he really had no hand at all as it is probable that the USSR could have defeated Germany without the Second Front. However, at least the Second Front was established, which generated more good will, and some negotiation could take place before Russian troops broke through into Europe. Given the relatively weak hand that Churchill had in 1944, he did well to maintain the relationship with the USSR, keeping the door open for future negotiations with Stalin.

Why were the Moscow Conference of 1944 and the *Percentages Agreement* perceived as radical?

Churchill, Stalin, Molotov and Eden attended the fourth Moscow conference. Churchill produced, according to his memoirs, a piece of paper (Figure 5.7) which he described as 'naughty'. It proposed dividing Eastern European countries into spheres of influence. Churchill gave the impression that it was a somewhat casual and almost improvised suggestion. However, the detailed negotiations between Molotov and Eden that followed suggest it was considered foreign policy, aimed at ensuring British influence in Greece to bolster its position in the Eastern Mediterranean, though Eden claimed to have been taken by surprise by it. It is difficult to see what Churchill hoped to gain by the agreement. Stalin was likely to take territory simply as a result of Soviet military force. These talks did not appear in Churchill's later account which also omits a lot of the conversations before and after the percentages discussion. These concerned dividing Poland and the statement by Churchill that Romania was a Russian affair, 'But in Greece it was different. Britain must be the leading Mediterranean power.' (Quoted: Gardner.)

Poland would be radically altered – Churchill used a box of matches to show Stalin how – by giving the state German territory in the west in compensation for losing its eastern areas to Russia (see Figure 5.6). Eighteenth century Prussian, Austrian and Russian statesman had divided Poland in this 'great power fashion. The dictators had divided it in 1939. However, here was a democratic British leader agreeing to divide another country, on whose behalf Britain had gone to war in 1939, with one of the most violent dictators in world history. Utmost pressure was placed on the Polish government in exile to agree.

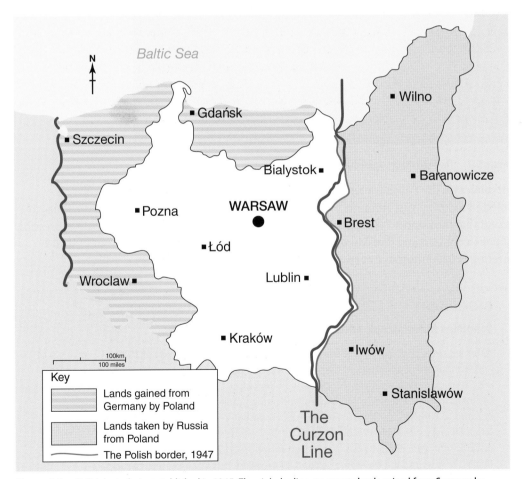

Figure 5.6   Polish boundaries established in 1945. The pink shading represents lands gained from Germany by Poland. The grey areas are land taken by Russia from Poland. The Curzon line of 1920 which was the original settlement which the Poles did not accept is shown in blue. The grey area was originally Russian territory.

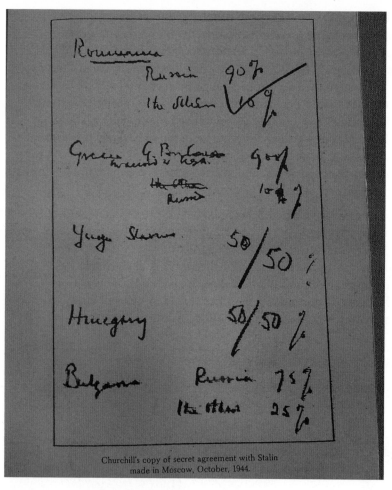

Churchill's copy of secret agreement with Stalin made in Moscow, October, 1944.

Figure 5.7   The Percentages Agreement.

Mikolajczyk, the Polish leader, was summoned and Churchill railed at him when he objected to losing vast amounts of his country to the USSR. Churchill wanted the Poles to accept that the puppet Polish government Stalin had established was a legitimate expression of Polish opinion and that Mikolajczyk should work alongside it. The account of this meeting is uncomfortable even sixty years on (see Source A, opposite).

BIOGRAPHY

Stanislas Mikolajczyk 1901–1966

A farmer's son, born in 1901, he fought against the Russians in the war of 1920 and went on to be a prominent member of the democratic Polish Peoples Party, critical of increasingly authoritarian rule in Poland after 1935. He fought against the Germans in 1939 when they invaded Poland, and escaped to Hungary. From there he went to Paris to join General Sikorski's government in exile. He became the leader when Sikorsky was killed in a plane crash in 1943. His democratic anti-communist government was called the 'London Poles' as opposed to the pro-Soviet 'Lublin Poles'. He resented the division of Poland by the allies, but attempted to participate in post-war Polish politics, but as the communists took over with Stalin's support, he was forced to flee in 1946. He died in the USA in 1966.

ACTIVITY

How do sources A and B agree and disagree about Churchill's attitudes to the Poles in 1944?

Compare them as evidence, looking at their origins, nature and purpose.

Hint – try reading the first source as a dramatic dialogue to catch the tone of the conversation.

Sources

(A) **A modern historian has considered the Russian and Polish records of the meetings between the leader of the Polish government in exile in London, Mikolajczyk, and Stalin and Churchill, 10 October 1944.**

Churchill could not believe that the Poles would not do as they were told. That is to join with the Soviet puppet government and accept the loss of Eastern Poland and the reconstituted Poland arranged by Britain and Russia and accepted by Roosevelt.

Churchill: "You must do this" he said, "If you miss this moment, everything will be lost!"

"Should I sign a death sentence against myself"? asked Mikolajczyk.

Churchill: "I wash my hands of it. As far as I am concerned we shall give the business up. Because of quarrels between Poles we are going to wreck the peace of Europe. In your obstinacy you do not see what is at stake. It is not in friendship that we shall part. We shall tell the world how unreasonable you are. You will start another war in which 25 million lives are lost, but you don't care."

"I know that our fate was sealed in Tehran."

Churchill: "It was saved in Tehran."

"I am not a person completely devoid of patriotic feeling, to give away half of Poland."

Churchill: "What do you mean by saying you are not devoid of patriotic feeling? Twenty five years ago we reconstituted Poland although in the last war more Poles fought against us than for us. Now, again, we are preserving you from disappearance, but you will not play ball. You are absolutely crazy."

"But this solution [The new frontier] does not change anything."

Churchill: "Unless you accept this frontier you are out of business for ever. The Russians will sweep through your country and your people will be liquidated. You are on the verge of annihilation."

Lawrence Rees, *World War Two: Behind Closed Doors*. This is based on *Documents on Soviet-Polish Relations 1939–45*, Volume II, Sikorski Institute.

(B) **Churchill to King George VI, 16 October 1944.**

The day before yesterday was "All Poles Day". Our lot from London (i.e. the Polish government in exile led by Mikolajczyk) are, as your majesty knows, decent but feeble, but the delegation from Lublin could hardly have been under any illusions as to our opinion of them. They appeared to be merely tools and recited their parts with well-drilled accuracy. ...We shall be wrestling with our London Poles all day and there are some hopes that we shall get a settlement. If not we shall have to hush the matter up and spin it out until after the American presidential election.

Churchill, *Triumph and Tragedy*, p. 209.

Was Churchill right?

Eden's suggestion that Stalin's demands be met in 1942 could be seen as a necessary gesture to keep Stalin as a member of the alliance at a difficult time in the war. The proposed agreements of 1944 can also be seen as realism, but the situation had changed and many think they are less defensible. The justification in 1944 was that Stalin could take what he liked; the USA did not seem willing to prevent him, so perhaps it was better to keep some

Western influence in Eastern Europe, particularly in Greece. Britain needed to protect the Eastern Mediterranean, Suez and the route to India and its south-east Asia Pacific Empire. Stalin appeared to keep his word and did not aid the Greek communists in their war against the Greek royal government. This allowed Britain to support the Greek royalists against communist forces after 1944. Greece did not become an 'iron curtain' country. Against this is the view that Churchill's acquiescence in the new frontiers in Eastern Europe caused huge and tragic movements of Eastern European people. He helped to consign millions to Soviet tyranny and showed considerable cynicism in agreeing with the demands of one of the worst dictators in modern history. Churchill could have been in no doubt of the brutal way in which Stalin was likely to treat any Eastern Europeans that came under his control.

The dealings between Stalin and Churchill have become as controversial as Chamberlain's dealings with Hitler. Both prime ministers bowed to what they saw as the realities of Britain's power and the strengths of a dictator. Churchill was fortunate not to have the same strong and articulate criticisms made about him that he had inflicted on Chamberlain. However, historical comment has been increasingly critical. Nor were all contemporaries prepared to accept Churchill's policy, and there was considerable unease expressed by Conservative MPs.

When the *Yalta Agreement* of 1945 confirmed the division of Germany and the new arrangements for Poland, Churchill faced his worse criticism of the war in the House of Commons from some Conservative MPs. He himself had considerable moral qualms, but this did not prevent British troops assisting in the return of Russian refugees in the Balkans to the Soviet Union where they faced at least captivity and probably death. Neither did the criticism prevent Russia from not only taking large areas of Eastern Poland, but controlling the rest of the country. Stalin had allowed the anti-Soviet resistance to be crushed in a brave but futile rising in 1944 against the Germans and when Soviet forces took Warsaw, or its remains, survivors of the Polish resistance found themselves being brutally treated by the Russian secret police. Churchill had shown sympathy with these Polish resisters and ordered a drop of weapons and supplies to them. However, nothing was done to prevent brutal Russian occupation of Poland except to get a futile undertaking from Stalin at Yalta that there would be elections. By the time of the last conference of the war at Potsdam, it was clear that this meant little and there was little goodwill between Stalin and the West. Churchill never met the Russian dictator again.

By 1946, out of office and free to express opinions, Churchill rallied America by speaking out against communism in his famous 'iron curtain' speech in Fulton, Missouri. He had used the phrase or equivalents before. He had returned to the anti-communist rhetoric of 1918.

ACTIVITY

Use your own knowledge to assess how far Sources A–D (page 151) support the interpretation that Churchill's policy on Eastern Europe 1944–45 was motivated by a selfish concern for British interests.

Sources

A Churchill gives the first published account of the *Percentages Agreement*, dictated in 1950 and published in 1954.

The moment was apt for business, so I said, "Let us settle about our affairs in the Balkans. Your armies are in Romania and Bulgaria. We have interests, missions and agents there. Don't let us get at cross purposes in small ways. So far as Britain and Russia are concerned how would it do for you to have ninety per cent predominance in Romania, for us to have ninety per cent of the say in Greece and go fifty-fifty about Yugoslavia? I wrote out on a half sheet of paper

Romania	Russia 10%
Russia 90%	Yugoslavia 50–50%
The others 10%	Hungary 50–50%
Greece	Bulgaria
Great Britain 90%	Russia 75%
(in accord with the USA)	The others 25%

I pushed this across to Stalin who had by then heard the translation. There was a slight pause. The he took his blue pencil and made a large tick upon it, and passed it back to us.

It was all settled in no more time than it takes to set down.

I said "Might it not be thought rather cynical if it seemed that we had disposed of these masses of people in such an offhand manner. Let us burn the paper." "No, you keep it." said Stalin.

I also raised the question of Germany, and it was agreed that our two foreign ministers…should go into it.

Churchill, *Triumph and Tragedy*, p. 198.

B Churchill's later reflection on the Percentage Agreement.

As I said, they [the percentages] *would be considered crude and even callous if they were exposed to the scrutiny of the Foreign Offices and diplomats all over the world. Therefore they could not be the basis of any public document, certainly not at the present time. They might however be a good guide for the conduct of our affairs. If we manage these affairs well, we shall perhaps prevent civil wars and much bloodshed and strife in the small countries concerned. Our broad principles should be to let every country have the form of government which its people desire.*

Gardner, *Spheres of Influence*, p. 203.

C A modern historian is critical.

The two leaders then moved on to discuss the future shape of much of the rest of Europe. It was during this discussion that Churchill produced what he called a 'naughty' document. This has become an infamous moment in the history of the war. As he took the paper out, Churchill said to Stalin that 'the Americans would be shocked if they saw how crudely he had put it [But Marshall Stalin was a realist]' *(British ambassador to Moscow, Clarke Kerr's notes on the meeting)*

Here was one of the leading statesmen of the democratic world secretly bandying percentages of 'influence' over countries of Eastern Europe with a man who was recognised as a tyrant. It seemed almost reminiscent of the first meeting between Stalin and Ribbentrop in August 1939, when the Soviets had bargained with the Nazis.

Rees, *World War Two: Behind Closed Doors*, p. 311.

D A former supporter of appeasement, the future Prime Minister Sir Alec Douglas-Home was critical in the debate on the Yalta agreement, 28 February 1945, in the House of Commons.

In a tense debate…I criticised our government's capitulation [to Stalin]. *In it Churchill had used a phrase which I could not let go by. He had seemed to accept a Russian occupation* [of Eastern Europe] *after victory as "an act of justice" – to use his words. I could recognise it as a fact of power but I repudiated any suggestion of* [it as] *an act of justice.'*

Broadcast, 1974; quoted: Knight, p. 324.

Why were the relations between Churchill and de Gaulle so stormy?

BIOGRAPHY

Charles André Joseph Marie de Gaulle (1890–1970)

A headmaster's son from Lille, de Gaulle became a professional soldier and served bravely in the First and Second World War. He commanded a tank unit against the Germans in 1940, launching one of the few successful French attacks. He was made Minister of War and opposed the armistice but had to flee to England in June 1940 where he became leader of the 'Free French'. Churchill admired his courage, but found him difficult to work with. There were disagreements about control of captured French colonies and when the USA entered the war, there were problems because official US policy recognised the pro-German Vichy regime in France, which de Gaulle condemned. However, de Gaulle was recognised as the leader of the French Provisional Government after 1944. He retired from politics in 1946 but returned to form a new Fifth Republic in 1958, of which he was President until 1969.

In common with many of Britain's pre-1914 ruling class, Churchill loved France. He had fought for it in the First World War, was a frequent visitor, and able to converse freely in French. He had no doubt that the French would rise to the challenge of war in 1939 and expected the large French army to sustain a long war against Germany. He was amazed by the French collapse in 1940 and did his utmost to keep France in the war, even proposing a union with Britain. He was particularly shocked at the failure of France's military leaders to sustain the campaign. He despised the creation of **Vichy France**. This led to the British destruction of the French fleet at Oran. Fearful that it would fall into German hands, the British destroyed the fleet of Vichy France, a nominally neutral country.

When de Gaulle appeared in London claiming to represent France and acting with almost visionary self-confidence, Churchill was impressed. This tall and imposing French officer won his imagination with his presence and total faith in France. However, there were considerable problems later when the USA and Britain became allies, in that the USA recognised Vichy France and showed no inclination to support what came to be called the 'Free French'. Churchill was torn between his desire to aid heroic resistance and his need to avoid alienating Roosevelt whose advisers favoured dealing with Vichy French leaders.

It was a delicate situation and de Gaulle was not sympathetic: 'I am too weak to make concessions' was his brilliant phrase. He held out for recognition of himself and his supporters in exile as the true representatives of France. Churchill veered between admiration and utter frustration. His encounters with de Gaulle were stormy. At first Churchill overrode advice and gave de Gaulle an expedition to take the French West African port of Dakar from its Vichy occupiers. Lacking secrecy and effective leadership, the result was a fiasco. The USA favoured dealing with Vichy leaders to reduce fighting when French North Africa was invaded. This led to frictions as de Gaulle was unwilling to meet the US favourites. A great effort was made to unite all the French opposition to Hitler

Vichy France

This was a semi-independent state in the South allied to the Germans but having diplomatic relations with other countries.

but de Gaulle was reluctant and by sheer stubbornness overcame his rivals. On the surface, France was freed in 1944 by a united alliance of Britain, America and the Free French. The reality was very different.

Again, Churchill did not have a free hand. He had to work with the Americans who did not share his respect for de Gaulle's sheer strength of character. He also had to endure a great deal of criticism from de Gaulle who was suspicious of British ambitions in the Mediterranean and unimpressed by the help given to France in 1939–40, and subsequently. This accounts for the often contradictory views of de Gaulle held at different times by Churchill and also for the less than smooth relations between Britain and France after 1945. The issue between de Gaulle, Churchill and the Americans was whether the free French of de Gaulle were the 'real' government of France or whether a wider selection of French opinion should be consulted.

> **ACTIVITY**
>
> Look at Sources A–C and answer the question:
>
> *'Which of these sources do you think is the most useful for understanding the relations between de Gaulle and Churchill?'*
>
> *Note*: Consider their origin and the context of the war.

Sources

(A) **de Gaulle recalls a meeting with Churchill, 25 September 1942.**

Mr Churchill attacked me in a bitter and highly emotional way. When I pointed out that the establishment of a British-controlled administration in Madagascar would constitute an interference with the rights of France, he exclaimed furiously "You claim to be France! You are not France! I do not recognise you as France! ..."

I interrupted him, "If in your eyes, I am not the representative of France, why, and with what right, are you dealing with me…?" Mr Churchill did not reply.

Memoirs, Vol. 2, translated by Richard Howard Caroll and Graf 1998 NY (Original 1956).

(B) **Churchill's doctor recalls the Prime Minister's admiration for de Gaulle during the Casablanca summit 1943.**

The Prime Minister watched de Gaulle stalk down the garden with his head in the air. Winston turned to us with a smile. "His country has given up fighting, he himself is a refugee and if we turn him down he is finished. Look at him! He might be Stalin with two hundred divisions behind him…France without an army is not France; de Gaulle is the spirit of that army, perhaps the last survivor of a warrior race."

Lord Moran, (1966) *Churchill, the Struggle for Survival*. Quoted in: Berthon, C. (2001) *Allies at war*, p.242.

(C) On 4 June 1944 de Gaulle came to Britain. Churchill was eager that he discuss the political future of France with the USA. De Gaulle was resentful at the thought of the American commander Eisenhower having any control over France after the forthcoming invasion. Churchill was exasperated. A modern historian describes the exchange:

There was now a crucial exchange that would have long lasting effects on Britain's future relations with de Gaulle. Churchill said, "I must tell you bluntly that if after every effort has been exhausted, the President is on one side and the French National Committee [which de Gaulle headed] is on the other, I will almost certainly side with the President. Anyway no quarrel will ever arise between Britain and the United States on account of France; Great Britain will side with the United States. To which de Gaulle replied 'I quite understand that in case of disagreement between the United States and France, Great Britain will side with the United States.'

Berthon, *Allies at War*, Op cit.

ACTIVITY

Churchill and the Grand Alliance

Create a timeline of the events in this chapter (see table below). It could emphasise the main events – or chart the rise and fall of Churchill's relationships with the Grand Alliance leaders. Look back at Table 5.1 as a reminder of the key conferences.

Copy and complete this table.

Date	Purpose of the conference	The significance of the meeting to Churchill's relationships with the Grand Alliance

Conclusion

In the Cabinet War Rooms of the Churchill Museum in London, visitors have the chance to offer their own views in writing on whether Churchill was a great wartime prime minister.

He faced a difficult task in building and then sustaining an alliance in which Britain was increasingly the junior partner in terms of resources. Within the alliance were competing political philosophies and very difficult personalities. It was difficult even for those very close to him to know what Roosevelt really thought: the Americans also had their own agenda which did not involve sustaining the British Empire. Stalin was and remains an enigmatic figure, with a history of destroying those who had thought themselves close to him. De Gaulle was an uncompromising and difficult figure who could not either be abandoned or fully supported. Churchill's astonishing energy in meeting these leaders and pursuing what he thought of as vital British interests, as well as being responsible for sustaining the war effort at home must be admired. Whatever criticisms are made about appeasement and whatever misjudgements are identified, the alliance *was* maintained and Nazism *was* destroyed.

However, the points at issue are worth considering with great care and judgements have to be made.

ACTIVITY

You have read the book. You have considered the debates. You have looked at some of the evidence. You have visited the Churchill Museum. You have decided to fill in the card:

'Was Churchill a great wartime Leader?'

What do you write?

Stretch and challenge

- Was Churchill unrealistic in expecting the USA to offer substantial help in 1940 and 1941?
- Was Churchill right to pursue a Mediterranean strategy rather than a second front?
- Did Churchill appease the USA too much?
- Did Churchill offer Stalin too little before 1944 and too much afterwards?
- How well did Churchill deal with de Gaulle?
- How far did Churchill achieve his aims by keeping Britain in the war and by negotiating with Stalin and Roosevelt?

Epilogue

Churchill continued to exert considerable influence on international events as Leader of the Opposition. His speech at Fulton, Missouri, in 1946 made the term 'iron curtain' famous.

He opposed the 'socialist' measures of the Labour government, though when he regained office in 1951 he did not dismantle the welfare state, though his government did denationalise iron and steel.

Churchill remained more interested in world politics than in the domestic scene. He had been interested in greater European unity, though Britain was not to be part of it, but little was done to increase integration with Europe after 1951. Britain acquired an independent atomic weapon in 1952 and Churchill was eager to ensure peace by a summit after Stalin's death in 1953. He wanted to broker some sort of settlement between the USSR and the USA to cap his career, though neither of these countries were interested in him performing this role. He hoped that the special relationship with the USA would continue with President Eisenhower. However, Churchill suffered a stroke in the summer of 1953. Weakened, he failed to make headway in persuading America to join in a new alliance for peace. Britain's war in Malaya against communist insurgents maintained a long tradition by Churchill of opposing communism and supporting the Empire.

He was knighted in 1953 and honoured with the Nobel Prize for his writings. His last ministry which ended in 1955 has not been seen as his finest hour:

> *'The fact was that at the end it was an octogenarian who presented the image of Britain to the world. It was an old man dressed in one more strange costume who amidst the pomp and pageantry of a Coronation* [of Elizabeth II] *in 1953 was the embodiment of a once great Empire now struggling ... against the ravages of time.'* (Robbins, *Churchill*, p.165.)

Churchill continued to write and he continued as an MP until 1964. He died on 24 January 1965. The most famous image is the dipping of the cranes along the Thames as Churchill's funeral barge went by. The author remembers the emotions of his own family and of the nation and the huge sense that this was the end of a truly great national figure. For all the reassessments and historical criticisms perhaps Attlee's words in 1965 ring true:

> *'Winston Churchill...was brave, gifted, inexhaustible and indomitable. He was, of course, above all, a supremely fortunate mortal...Winston was superbly lucky. And perhaps the most warming thing about him was that he never ceased to say so.'* (Quoted Holmes.)

Exam Café *At this point, it would be useful to undertake an audit to see what skills you are comfortable with and what you need more support in developing. Go to pages xx-xx of the Exam Café and complete the activities there.*

Bibliography

Lord Allanbrooke (2001) *War Diaries 1939–45*, Ed: Dancher and Todman. Weidenfeld and Nicolson.

Howard, R. (trans) (1998) *Memoirs Volume 2,* Caroll and Graf.

Berthon, S. (2001) *Allies at War*, p. 242. HarperCollins.

Best, G. (2002) *Churchill: A Study in Greatness,* Penguin.

Churchill, W. (1950) *The Grand Alliance*, Cassell.

Churchill, W. (1952) *The Second World War, Volume 5: Closing the Ring*, p. 304. Penguin Books.

Churchill, W. (1954) *The Second World War, Volume 6: Triumph and Tragedy*, pp. 198, 209. Penguin Books.

Gardner, L.C. (1993) *Spheres of Influence*, p. 203. John Murray.

Knight, N. (2008) *Churchill: The Greatest Briton Unmasked,* p. 234. David and Charles.

Lane, A. Temperely, H. (eds) (1995) *The Rise and Fall of the Grand Alliance*, pp. 105, 179, 187. Macmillan.

Lavery, B. (2007) *Churchill Goes to War,* frontpiece. Conway Maritime Press.

Moran, Lord (1966) *Winston Churchill: The Struggle for Survival 1940–1965*, Constable.

Ponting, C. (1994) *Churchill,* Sinclair-Stevenson.

Rees, L. (2008) *World War Two: Behind Closed Doors,* p. 311. BBC Books.

Reynolds, D. (2004) *In Command of History,* pp. 260–61, 383, 385. Allen Lane.

Robbins, K. (1992) *Churchill*, p. 165. Longman.

Roosevelt, E. (1946) *As He Saw It*, Dnell, Sloan and Pearce, NY.

PRO PREM 3 Records of Meeting quoted Gardner.

Attlee's Broadcast, 1974 Quoted Nigel Kight.

(quoted Holmes)

Exam Café
Relax, refresh, result!

Relax and prepare

Erica

I wasn't relaxed when I started the AS course because I had a lot of problems with the sources. The ones at GCSE were a lot easier and I couldn't see what the new ones were getting at. They didn't always start to talk about what was in the question and I used to just write down what they said. It took a while to get used to really reading them carefully. So my advice to anyone starting is not to get upset if you can't do it right away. I got the idea after a couple of weeks.

Anjali

I like to have lists of things when I revise and did really well at GCSE because I did work hard and knew a lot. I think it was good to know the main facts and events, but when I started I just put a lot of what I knew down – well, because I knew it and had done lots of work. It took a while to see that I wasn't getting marks just for facts but that I had to link them up with the sources and make sure I answered the question.

Marek

When I started to revise I realised that I hadn't caught up with some stuff that I missed when I was away. I got really worried that I had left it too late and asked Mr Lane for extra help. He was great, but it did make me realise that you do have to keep up. When I move on to A2, I am not going to make that same mistake and I am going to try and look at what we've done more regularly.

Student tips

Tom

Revision was a problem for me because there is a lo you just can't revise. I knew that I had to be able to deal with a set of sources that I hadn't seen before c sometimes I couldn't really see what to write about t evidence bit. I would do what I did at GCSE and say they were biased (see I spelt it right this time, Mr Dav or say they were from the time. But you have to do more than this and try and link them to what you kn about the time they were written and why they were written. But how do you prepare for this? Luckily my teacher gave me a list of the sort of things to look fo and kept saying that this was the skills bit. It must ha worked because I got an A.

Maria

My teacher hadn't given us a lot of notes and I got a bit upset when I came to revise and wasn't sure what to do. I tried making notes on my notes, but got fed up with this. I talked to the others and we talked to Miss Spendley. She told us to revise round the key themes rather than just learn a lot of facts. This was hard because we had to think quite a bit, but in the end it was better and I made sure that I covered all the 'key issues'. I was happier that I was making progress.

Amy

My teacher said we should enjoy revision because we can freshen up what we know, and see if what we thought is still OK. We gave him a hard time and really laughed about this. But I did try it. I didn't just go over my notes, I read some books I hadn't looked at before and used the Internet. I knew it was better to revise issues rather than just the story and I did think about my own views.

Jamie

I wasn't looking forward to revision – I'd had enough for the GCSE when I had to really shut myself away for hours. For this sources paper I decided that I would test myself a bit more than I did at GCSE. Looking back, I think I wasted quite a bit of time then and I didn't want to this time, so I made sure that whatever I learned I really knew. It was like when I was in the school play and had a lot of lines to learn, I had to make sure I knew them so I got someone to test me. I knew that I had to make sure that I knew about the issues, so I made sure that I learned about these and when I was sure that I understood them, I tested myself.

Anastasia

When I looked back at my first work in September I realised that I had come quite a long way. My teacher warned me not to rely too much on work I'd done at the start of the course, so I went through the earlier topics quite carefully to make sure they were at the same level as what I was doing by March. I really cringed when I read my first answers again, but it was useful to think what I would do now.

Kishan

My dad wants me to revise all day, but I don't do mornings. I like to work in the late afternoon and don't mind going on till quite late. But I did find that I was going on till 1 or 2 o'clock in the morning and then getting too tired. I think you do have to find the time of day that suits you, but I did change my approach and spread my revision out a bit more. I found that doing slots of an hour at a time was better than trying to do it all at night. More time for my Xbox now (only joking, dad!).

Mike

My house is very busy and my brothers and sisters make a lot of noise. I try putting the headphones on, but the problem is that this part of the history course needs a lot of thought – I can make lists of dates and events, but that's not enough. I really need to think about key questions. I decided to stay at school to revise and used the library. I even went to my local reference library sometimes. To be honest it was a bit too quiet, but as I really wanted to get home it did make me get on with my revision and not waste time. I had to think about reasons and ideas more than just sitting in front of the text book and my notes, because I wanted to go home!

Lou

I tried making notes on my notes, and also reading the text book again. The trouble was that I wasn't sure that I could remember it all. My teacher recommended using revision cards and I found that this was better. I have a strong visual memory – if things are in different shapes or patterns I remember them and I like to use different colours. I tried using cards for different issues – like Churchill's attitude to the General Strike. I put down key points about why he was pretty vicious on one side and why he wasn't so bad on the other – I couldn't get everything down but they were key ideas. I found some quotes and facts and did some more cards – using different layouts.

I know some people just write down their ideas, but it helped me.

Julia

I found it really hard to remember all those conferences that Churchill went to. So I tried something which worked when I was learning Spanish last year. I stuck sticky notes up round the house and went from one conference to another in order through the different rooms. My boyfriend Mat really gave me a hard time about this but I don't care – it worked for me.

Seb

I like listening – I learn a lot from this, so I recorded my notes on key issues and played them back to myself. I had fun imitating Churchill's voice, though my dad found the tape and thinks it's funny to keep saying 'We shall fight them on the beaches' to me in his cringing Churchill voice. It's helped me get the key issues clear and it's stopped me getting bored with revision.

Getting started. . .

Two types of questions

There are two questions to prepare for. **Part (a) questions** need a comparison of what the sources say about a given issue and also a comparison of their 'provenance'. You need to make sure that you cover as many aspects as possible about provenance – i.e. the nature, origin and purpose of the source and its value. You have to link provenance and content. This will help you to make a really thoughtful and considered judgement as to which source may be the better evidence for a particular event or issue. Don't introduce this suddenly at the end but include it in your answer throughout.

So it's a good idea to have a check list in your mind about the sort of thing you might be comparing. Remember that not all sources lend themselves to all the possible comparisons which could be made. Sometimes the date will be the key thing to look for; at others it may be the possible audience that the writer is aiming at.

None of this is new to you, but you have to bear in mind that it's easy under pressure of time to focus on what the source is saying and not give enough attention to the source as evidence.

Comparing sources

When you revise, go back over previous answers and see how many points in the list you covered and if necessary do a better version. In the examination, remember the list and don't forget to compare:

- *When were the sources written?* Is there anything important to say about this? If one source were written, say, in 1940 and another in 1945, is this significant in terms of what might have happened to change the views of the authors? Is there anything significant in the timing of the source – if sources on appeasement in 1938, for instance, are being studied, would it help to know whether they were before or after the Munich agreement?

- **What are they**? This may be obvious, but is the source a speech, or an extract from a diary, or a memoir, or a history book. This will make a big difference to its value as evidence.
- **What is the audience and why was the source produced**? A speech in parliament or in cabinet may well have a very different style and tone to say, a speech delivered in front of a large audience or a speech on radio, addressing the nation.
- **Is the source typical**? This is sometimes the key question. Churchill issued a notorious memo on the use of poison gas in the Normandy landings – is this typical of the man, or was it an untypical idea made at a time when he greatly feared high British and American casualties and wanted to do everything to minimise them? An MP criticises Churchill – is he typical of public opinion?
- **Is the source reliable**? Is this person in a position to know? Is he writing for a particular purpose which might make his view questionable? Remember that unreliable is not the same as useful. It might be very useful to know why a source is exaggerating or distorting an event.
- **How useful is the source as evidence**? Don't forget to assess this and make a judgement about which of the sources could be more useful – they may be equally useful, but you need to discuss their pros and cons.

Some students use the mnemonic **WWWTRU** to sum up the above. However, do be sure that this is not a mechanical process as it does depend on what sorts of source you are looking at as to what aspects of evidence or analysis you consider.

Part (b) questions also need an evaluation of the sources, but in the context of another major task: considering an interpretation. Revision should mean that you have considered the major issues beforehand. It is not a good idea to be thinking how good a wartime Prime Minister Churchill was for the first time in the exam, for instance. The whole revision process should have been built round thinking about major issues.

- For example, did Churchill exaggerate the dangers of communism and social unrest after 1918? Why was he not in office between 1929 and 1939? Was he justified in criticising appeasement? And so on.

Your views on the major issues might have changed over the course, but you should have thought about them well in advance of the examination.

Interpreting sources

Revision of the key issues will help you INTERPRET the sources and identify what each is saying about the key issue. In turn this will help you to GROUP the sources. It is likely some will support the interpretation in the title (let's say, that Churchill was justified in criticising appeasement) and some will support the view that he was not justified. It is much easier to comment on sources if they are grouped.

So if, say, Sources C and E generally take the view that Churchill was right, you have not only to explain what they say, but whether they are justified. To do this you have to look at their nature as evidence AND to use your own knowledge. If you know that public opinion was very much against war because of the losses of 1914–18, then you could say that Churchill was unrealistic in urging a firm stand. If you know that Churchill himself had helped to reduce the armed forces in the 1920s, then you might find it unrealistic of him to criticise the poor state of the armed forces in 1936. It is very unlikely that you will have no knowledge to use, but you must make a conscious effort to bring what you know to bear. Don't give up because you don't know very detailed facts – use what you do know.

Finally, offer a clear judgement on the key issue in the title of the question. It should be an issue you've thought about before. There is no correct answer and the judgement should follow logically from what you've said about the sources.

So to sum up:

- Don't be taken by surprise by the issue in the question – you should be prepared for it by having thought through the key issues in the specification.
- Make sure that the answer is SOURCE-led. Don't write an essay on the issue with a few references to the sources. The main task is to look at what the sources say and evaluate this by considering the nature of the source and your own knowledge.
- Group the sources.
- Offer a clear and logical judgement at the end.

Show you know what the issue is, group the sources, explain their view, evaluate their view (referring to their provenance and using your knowledge) and come to a firm conclusion.

Refresh your memory

Revision check list

Key issue One

How and why did Churchill react to the problems of post-war Britain from 1920 to 1937?

▷ Why did Churchill have fears about the Russian Revolution; strikes and social unrest in Britain, Ireland and the Empire?

▷ Did he exaggerate these fears or were they justified?

▷ How successful was he in promoting policies to meet the fears, for example in the war of Russian intervention and settling the troubles in Ireland?

▷ How successfully did he deal with Britain's financial and economic policies in his period of office as Chancellor of the Exchequer?

▷ What are the arguments for and against his adopting the policy of returning Britain to the Gold Standard in 1925?

▷ How well did Churchill react to the General Strike? Did he make the situation worse? Did he offer moderate and conciliatory measures after the Strike?

▷ Why was he not in office for 10 years after 1929? Was this the result of his misjudgements?

▷ Was his contribution to the abdication crisis helpful to himself or to Edward VIII? What consequences did it have for Churchill politically?

Key issue Two

What were Churchill's views about imperial and foreign policy from 1930 to 1939, and how justified were they?

▷ Were Churchill's views about the role of the Empire outdated?

▷ Why did he oppose more self-government for India and was this view merely racist and out of keeping with the times?

▷ Why did it lead to a clash with his party?

▷ What was the basis of Churchill's fears about Germany from 1933 and how justified were the policies he put forward about rearmament and foreign policy?

▷ Was his view of a Grand Alliance feasible? Were his criticisms of foreign policy realistic?

▷ Did he or Chamberlain have a clearer view of Britain's best interests in dealing with the dictators?

Key issue Three

How far does Churchill deserve his reputation as a great wartime Prime Minister?

▷ Why did Churchill become Prime Minister in 1940?

▷ Was he right to adopt policies towards continuing the war?

▷ How important were his speeches and his style of government in maintaining the war effort?

▷ How well did he manage relations with his generals?

▷ To what extent can his view of wartime strategy be defended?

▷ How justified have criticisms been on Churchill's policy towards the aerial bombardment of Germany?

▷ Did Churchill do enough to plan for post-war reconstruction in Britain?

▷ Why did Churchill lose the election of 1945?

Key issue Four

How successful was the international diplomacy of Churchill during the Second World War?

▷ What were Churchill's aims in foreign policy and what did he see was Britain's imperial role during and after the war?

▷ How well did he manage relations with Roosevelt, Stalin and de Gaulle?

▷ What contribution did he make to the series of international conferences during the war, and how successfully did he promote British interests?

▷ What plans did he have for post-war Europe and to what extent can they be defended?

Skills focus: comparing evidence

(a) Study Sources B and C.

Compare these sources as evidence for opinions among Churchill's fellow Conservatives about Chamberlain's handling of the Munich settlement.

Sources

B **Churchill gives his view of the Munich settlement to the House of Commons.**

No one has been a more resolute and uncompromising struggler for peace than the Prime Minister. Everyone knows that. I will begin by saying what everyone would like to ignore or forget, but what nevertheless must be stated, namely that we have sustained a total and unmitigated defeat. We are in the presence of a disaster of the first magnitude. The system of alliances has been swept away upon which France has relied for her safety. You will find that Czechoslovakia will be engulfed in the Nazi regime. The betrayal of Czechoslovakia will mean that the road down the Danube Valley to the Black Sea, together with the resources of corn and oil, has been opened to Germany. What I find unendurable is the sense of our country falling into the power of Nazi Germany, and our existence becoming dependent on their good will.

Speech, 6 October 1938

C **A Conservative supporter of Chamberlain records his thoughts about Churchill and Chamberlain following the debate in the House of Commons about Munich.**

Is Winston any more than that fat, brilliant, unbalanced, illogical orator?

Winston's contribution today enlivened the House, annoyed the government, but did not weaken the government's excellent case. The Prime Minister was magnificent, making a moving appeal. The House of Commons was with him and he seemed aware of the strength of his support. Even the restless antics of Winston and the opposition within the Conservative party were powerless to stem the Chamberlain tide which swelled and swelled as he spoke. I was almost the first to congratulate the PM and he put out his hand and tapped my arm, beaming with pleasure.

Sir Henry (Chips) Channon MP, *Diary*, 6 October 1938

Examiner's tips

Highlight the issue in the question. The question isn't a general comparison.

▷ Look at what the sources are and when they were written.

▷ Remember to make point by point comparison – don't write too much about any one source.

▷ Make a brief plan to help you isolate the key similarities and differences.

▷ Remember the time you have for this – not more than 20–25 minutes once you've read ALL the passages through. Don't do anything before you've done this – your brain can work on more than one thing at a time and you should let it be digesting all the passages.

▷ Remember that the bulk of the marks are for an evaluation of the two sources as evidence, commenting on their provenance (AO2a). You will also need to demonstrate an understanding of the two sources by comparing their content (what they say on the issue) and, using the provenance, to make a judgement as to their relative value as evidence (A01b)..

There are a few marks (6/30) for communication (writing clearly) and contextual knowledge (what is happening of importance at the time). Both help you to assess the two sources as evidence (AO1a).

Katie's answer

Both these Sources are from Conservative MPs but they have very different views about Chamberlain and the Munich crisis. C is very much in support of Chamberlain while B, even though Churchill does admit that he has struggled for peace, is against what he sees as a 'disaster' brought about by Chamberlain. For C the government has an 'excellent case', but B sees no excellence.

The system of alliance of France has been destroyed and Germany will engulf the Czechs and soon have access to the resources of the Danube valley that will make her a stronger enemy. These points are not considered in C who just sees the enthusiasm of the Conservatives for Chamberlain's peace settlement.

C is more focused on the political aspects, as the House of Commons is described as being 'with him' and a tide of support. This is a narrow focus whereas Churchill is looking beyond politics to the international situation and the strengthening of a possible enemy, Germany.

The tone of B is a lot less personal — he makes it clear he is not attacking Chamberlain personally but praises him. C on the other hand, because this is not a public statement but a diary is very critical of Churchill, calling him fat, unbalanced and illogical and saying he is 'restless'.

There is a lot more personal opinion here than in B which is more statesmanlike. Both are primary sources and both come from a similar time when emotions within the Conservative party and the country are very strong. Both are reliable because they give the views of different people in the Conservative party and both are quite useful for knowing what Conservatives thought.

Examiner says:

This is a good start because Katie has not listed points from each source separately, but has adopted a point by point approach.

Examiner says:

This is a developed explanation which goes back to the text.

Examiner says:

This is quite perceptive – one is indeed more of the reaction of a politician. This might have been developed a bit more.

Examiner says:

It is a good idea to talk about tone, but the comments on provenance aren't very developed here.

Examiner says:

Katie has some good points, but the comments on the differences between the nature of the two sources as evidence need to be developed and the overall judgement isn't very incisive or strong.

Examiner says

Katie has been thinking along the right lines, but could develop more analysis about the provenance and show how context might have affected the two sources – without necessarily inserting factual information for its own sake. The mark scheme will give her credit for using a range of criteria to discuss provenance; it will give credit for the understanding of evidence and for communication and knowledge. She is on her way to a good answer, so let's see an improved version.

Examiner says:

This has kept the good point by point comparison, but has extended the analysis of typicality.

Katie's improved answer

Both these Sources are from Conservative MPs but they have very different views about Chamberlain and the Munich crisis. C is very much in support of Chamberlain while B, even though Churchill does admit that he has struggled for peace, is against what he sees as a 'disaster' brought about by Chamberlain. For C the government has an 'excellent case', but B sees no excellence. The system of alliance of France has been destroyed and Germany will engulf the Czechs and soon have access to the resources of the Danube valley that will make her a stronger enemy. These points are not considered in C, who just sees the enthusiasm of the Conservatives for Chamberlain's peace settlement. Churchill had considerable experience in government and had made a deep study of international affairs prior to the Second World War. He had also been a consistent critic of the government over the threat of Germany and rearmament since 1933. His criticisms are typical of his views, but not typical of Conservative views generally. Public opinion and the very strong regard that Chamberlain was held in by most of the party make Channon's view more typical. Churchill was seen as 'restless' by many and his criticisms of Munich seen as unrealistic, particularly since he himself had run down arms spending in the 1920s.

C is more focused on the political aspects, as the House of Commons is described as being 'with him' and a tide of support. This is a narrow focus whereas Churchill is looking beyond politics to the international situation and the strengthening of a possible enemy, Germany. Again this is typical. Churchill and his small group of supporters were outside the mainstream of Conservative thought that is much more represented by Channon.

The tone of B is a lot less personal — he makes it clear he is not attacking Chamberlain personally but praises him. C on the other hand, because this is not a public statement but a diary is very critical of Churchill, calling him fat, unbalanced and illogical and saying he is 'restless'. There is a lot more personal opinion here than in B which is more statesmanlike. Churchill may be making sure that gets a sympathetic hearing by praising Chamberlain, and indeed, he did want to come back to office, so he is careful not to go too far. This is a speech in the Commons and reasoned argument is important. His real view of Chamberlain was rather less balanced. Channon does not have to 'watch his words' as it is a diary. There is no reason to doubt that these were genuine feelings of emotion towards Chamberlain. There were bitter memories of World War I and fears of terrible air attacks, so when he expresses admiration, he was expressing what many felt. Churchill was more prepared to face war and having seen it first hand, less reluctant to face it as an option. Unlike Churchill he is not trying to persuade the government to another course of action or appealing indirectly to the country or even the world at large.

Examiner says:

This extends the analysis of the nature of the sources and the context in which they were produced.

Both are primary sources from politicians and both come from a similar time when emotions within the Conservative party and the country are very strong. Britain had faced the real threat of war before Munich and there was a huge relief that it had been avoided. However, it was more apparent to many that Munich had been peace at a high moral price, so Channon's very pro-Chamberlain stance did not remain typical of Conservative opinion. It is very much of its particular time in the aftermath of Munich.

Churchill's speech is also made at a time of high emotion, though he was more shamed and disappointed that Britain had seemed to subordinate itself to Germany. Both are reliable because they give the views of different people in the Conservative party and both are quite useful for knowing what Conservatives thought. Both sources give immediate Conservative reactions in the wake of a severe crisis. C may be more typical of Conservative views, as Churchill was seen as very much of an outsider; but B is useful for explaining later reservations about Chamberlain's policies. When it was clear that Munich had failed, then Churchill's powerful rhetoric became more important than Channon's somewhat superficial and toadying approach as revealed in his diary. To answer the question fully there would need to be a rather wider range of Conservative opinion. C seems to be firmly in the Chamberlain camp, to the point of uncritical support. Churchill in B however represents a minority of maverick opposition Tories, like Duff Cooper. In the middle were many who had reservations about Chamberlain's confidence in his ability to deal with the dictators and his rash assertion of 'peace for our time' but saw Churchill as too extreme.

Examiner says:

Katie has developed her comments on the context of the sources here.

Examiner says:

There is rather more judgement about relative usefulness here and a good consideration of what else might be needed for completeness.

In terms of the Assessment Objectives

AO1a – Katie's second answer is soundly expressed and shows contextual knowledge. It would gain Level 1 marks (communication and contextual knowledge and terms).

AO1b – her comparison of the content of the sources is sound and an effective judgement is provided, gaining a Level 1 mark.

AO2a –Katie's understanding of how to consider evidence is good. The comparison of provenance includes the nature of the sources; their purpose; their date; their typicality; their completeness and especially their utility. This is a Level 1 mark.

Note: It is not necessary to know about 'Chips' Channon – the key point is that this is a diary opposed to a speech and how typical both are in the context of the time.

(b) Study all the sources

Use your own knowledge to assess how far the sources support the interpretation that Churchill's criticisms of Munich were unjustified.

Sources

A The King expresses his support of Chamberlain's policy at Munich.

I am sending this letter by my Lord Chamberlain to ask you to come directly to Buckingham Palace so I can express to you personally my heartfelt congratulations on the success of your visit to Munich. In the meantime this letter brings the warmest of welcomes to one who by his patience and determination, has earned the gratitude of his fellow countrymen throughout the Empire.

George VI, *letter*, October 1938

B Churchill gives his view of the Munich settlement to the House of Commons.

No one has been a more resolute and uncompromising struggler for peace than the Prime Minister. Everyone knows that. I will begin by saying what everyone would like to ignore or forget, but what nevertheless must be stated, namely that we have sustained a total and unmitigated defeat. We are in the presence of a disaster of the first magnitude. The system of alliances has been swept away upon which France has relied for her safety. You will find that Czechoslovakia will be engulfed in the Nazi regime. The betrayal of Czechoslovakia will mean that the road down the Danube Valley to the Black Sea, together with the resources of corn and oil, has been opened to Germany. What I find unendurable is the sense of our country falling into the power of Nazi Germany, and our existence becoming dependent on their good will.

Speech, 6 October 1938

C A Conservative supporter of Chamberlain records his thoughts about Churchill and Chamberlain following the debate in the House of Commons about Munich.

Is Winston any more than that fat, brilliant, unbalanced, illogical orator?

Winston's contribution today enlivened the House, annoyed the government, but did not weaken the government's excellent case. The Prime Minister was magnificent, making a moving appeal. The House of Commons was with him and he seemed aware of the strength of his support. Even the restless antics of Winston and the opposition within the Conservative party were powerless to stem the Chamberlain tide which swelled and swelled as he spoke. I was almost the first to congratulate the PM and he put out his hand and tapped my arm, beaming with pleasure.

Sir Henry (Chips) Channon MP, *Diary*, 6 October 1938

D The Secretary of the Committee of Imperial Defence, who was later to become Churchill's wartime Chief of Staff, expresses his view of Munich.

It seems to me that from a purely military point of view it would have paid us to go to war in 1938. German preparations were incomplete. Munich lost us the great Skoda arms works in Czechoslovakia. On the other hand, given the hysterical reception given to Chamberlain on his return from Munich, it seems doubtful whether if we had fought at Munich, we should have fought as a united nation. South Africa would have remained neutral and Canada would not have rallied to us. On balance, the advantages which we derived from the surrender at Munich outweighed the disadvantages.

Lord Ismay, *Memoirs*, 1960

E A modern historian is critical of Churchill.

Those in power in the 1930s had to balance the threats from Hitler and Mussolini, and they could not forget Japan or rely on the French; and there was little money to rearm. As Churchill was not in the government he did not have to make hard decisions. In his memoirs he skips over the period from 1924-29 when he did make decisions to cut spending on the armed forces. India and the Abdication nearly destroyed him – but Hitler remade his political career.

Reynolds, David (2004) *In Command of History*

1   Group these sources and look carefully at the brief description – this will give you a starting point.

2   Make sure you really deal with the debate here and come to a clear view of it by the end.

3   Make sure you use ALL the sources.

4   There is little point in commenting on the origin and purpose of E in the same way as you need to do in A–D but you can be critical of what it says.

5   Don't worry if you feel you don't have enough specialist knowledge – say you don't know anything about the Skoda arms works – this doesn't matter, but try to use the contextual knowledge you do have and apply it to the sources. You might question whether D is guessing for instance about South Africa and Canada and whether the rearmament really was advanced enough for Britain to go to war. You might question, given the problems faced when Britain did go to war in 1939, whether this view is right. You might know quite a bit to comment on the views in E, but don't worry if you can't comment on everything.

Baz's answer

Source A says that the King thought that Chamberlain's policy was right. It refers to his patience and determination and to the gratitude of the nation. This might show that Churchill was unjustified in criticising Chamberlain because so many important people thought that appeasement was right. Without public opinion it would not have been possible to go to war, so Churchill was being unrealistic.

Source B says that policy was not justified because despite Chamberlain's struggle for peace, Britain had suffered a defeat. Not only had the French system of alliances been lost, but Germany would probably take over Czechoslovakia and gain the Danube valley. Germany's greater resources would make Britain dependent on her, so appeasement would have bad results and so criticisms were justified.

Source C is more like Source A because it clearly thinks appeasement is right and that Churchill's criticisms are not justified. For Channon, Churchill is just an orator and unbalanced and illogical. So Chamberlain must be logical. He had made a moving appeal and the House of Commons, like the King in A, was behind Chamberlain. Far from being justified, Churchill's criticisms are seen as 'restless antics'. With the MPs in support of him, Chamberlain must have been right.

Source D says that Churchill was justified. This generally argues that we should have gone to war in 1938 because Germany was not ready and if we had fought we should

Examiner says:

It's not a good idea to start by taking the first source and then running through them in the order they appear in the exam paper. Grouping the sources gives you more chance to discuss their views.

Examiner says:

It's a good idea to compare and cross-reference, but not enough is made of the similarity.

have had the Czechs and their arms. However, he also says that from another point of view we were right not to go to war because public opinion and the Empire were not ready, so he thinks that Churchill was partly right and some criticisms were justified.

Source E says that Chamberlain had to consider threats from all three dictator powers and there was not enough money to rearm — partly because of Churchill himself and his earlier policies. It was all very well for Churchill to make criticisms, but he was not in government. There is a suggestion that Churchill was just using the threat of Germany because he had failed earlier, so his criticisms were not really justified.

There were many reasons for appeasement in the 1930s as Britain had lost many men in the First World War. Britain had to worry about her empire and had no allies, as the USA was neutral and Russia was busy with purges. France was not reliable. Chamberlain knew that Britain did not have enough planes and he was realistic. Churchill, as Source E says, was not in the government so did not know as much about the real situation. The generals had told Chamberlain that Britain could not fight all its enemies at once and Churchill could not know this. His speech in B is not realistic and is a speech in the House of Commons. Sources C and A link up and show that there was a lot of support for appeasement.

Some of these sources, like D and E, can look back with hinsight but others are more from the time. Overall some say that criticisms were justified but from my own knowledge I know that there were many problems in the 1930s and Chamberlain did what he thought was right.

Examiner says:

The sources are explained carefully and links to the question are clear, but there is little evaluation. The formula 'Source...says' can easily lead to description.

Examiner says:

There is some knowledge here and it is applied to the interpretation, but not to the sources. There is a little cross-reference, and the evaluation of the sources is not strong.

Examiner says:

hindsight, please

The overall judgement isn't very developed.

Examiner says

Baz has considered the interpretation and understands what the sources are saying. He also has some knowledge and has thought about the issue. He could do better with what he's brought to the question by focusing on the issue, grouping the sources, using his knowledge more effectively and offering more in the way of evaluation. Let's look at his second attempt.

Baz's improved answer

Churchill's criticisms of Munich can be seen to be justified by hindsight as Britain went to war in 1939 and Chamberlain did not gain peace by making concessions to Hitler. However, as these sources show, it was not so clear at the time that Chamberlain was wrong. Sources A and C show very strong support for appeasement in the country. Only Source B by Churchill himself offers such strong criticism. The later sources, which do have the ability to look back and see what happened after Munich, do not wholeheartedly support Churchill. D agrees with A and C that public opinion was not ready and E argues that Britain could not have risked war because of the threats it faced.

Public opinion was very important and Churchill did not seem to consider it enough when making criticisms. Source A shows that the King was very much in favour of Chamberlain. It refers to his patience and determination and to the gratitude of the nation. This might show that Churchill was unjustified in criticising Chamberlain because so many important people thought that appeasement was right. Without public opinion it would not have been possible to go to war, so Churchill was being unrealistic. This is backed up by Source C because it clearly thinks appeasement is right and that Churchill's criticisms are not justified. For Channon, Churchill is just an orator and unbalanced and illogical. So Chamberlain must be logical. He had made a moving appeal and the House of Commons, like the King in A was behind Chamberlain. Far from being justified, Churchill's criticisms are seen as 'restless antics'. With the MPs in support of him, Chamberlain must have been right. However these sources are from a narrow section of the public – the royal family and a Conservative MP who would not necessarily have been in touch with public opinion. There were demonstrations against Munich and even some people in the establishment, like Duff Cooper, did not agree with such flagrant appeasement. Also, there was a natural mood of relief as war had been prevented. Many thought that Britain would be bombed heavily and millions would be killed in the first week of war, so these sources are not necessarily typical of what people really thought throughout the country.

Source B is of course clear in justifying criticisms of Chamberlain saying that policy was not justified because despite Chamberlain's struggle for peace, Britain had suffered a defeat. Not only had the French system of alliances been lost, but Germany would probably take over Czechoslovakia and gain the Danube valley. Germany's greater resources would make Britain dependent on her, so appeasement would have bad results and so criticisms were justified. Churchill was making a speech to the Commons so would have to support his argument and was right when he said that Czechoslovakia would fall

Examiner says:

This starts in a more considered way than the previous answer and groups the sources. This takes more time to plan but gives a more controlled answer that focuses more on the interpretation.

Examiner says:

This uses some own knowledge and refers to the typicality of these sources. There is sense of the evidence being assessed.

Examiner says:

This brings in some knowledge about Churchill and his reliability and is rather more critical than in Baz's first version. But there is nothing here that is really detailed knowledge. He is using what he knows and applying it to the source.

to Germany. However, that was only a 'guess' in October 1938 and Churchill had not been proved right in many other matters. Source E refers to his lack of judgement over India and the Abdication. There were other examples where he had shown poor judgement, such as Gallipoli, so it is not surprising that many saw his criticisms as unjustified. Britain was not prepared for war militarily and Churchill's hope that somehow the League or other powers in Europe would join a Grand Alliance was not realistic. His arguments in B seem a lot about Britain's pride – not wanting to be dependent on Germany, rather than the real situation.

In Source D a general argues that we should have gone to war in 1938 because Germany was not ready and if we had fought we should have had the Czechs and their arms. However he also says that from another point of view we were right not to go to war because public opinion and the Empire were not ready, so he thinks that Churchill was partly right and some criticisms were justified. This seems to argue that Churchill was right and that in military terms we should have gone to war, but this is doubtful as E says that Britain had to face Germany, Japan and Italy in any possible war. E also says that Churchill himself was to blame for the poor military situation. From my own knowledge, this is true as Churchill used the Ten Year Rule in the 1920s to justify cuts in arms spending and was criticised by the leading generals and admirals. Chamberlain was rearming in 1938, but Britain did not yet have the vital Spitfires that it would develop by 1939-40. Also this source is by a military adviser and is looking back so might not have wanted to suggest that the military were just unprepared. He is more inclined to blame public opinion and the Empire. Churchill did not always consider the importance of the Dominions actually agreeing to the need for war. They came in in 1939 because it had been clear that everything had been done to keep peace by Chamberlain.

Source E says that Chamberlain had to consider threats from all three dictator powers and there was not enough money to rearm – partly because of Churchill himself and his earlier policies. It was all very well for Churchill to make criticisms, but he was not in government. There is a suggestion that Churchill was just using the threat of Germany because he had failed earlier, so his criticisms were not really justified. It was very difficult for Chamberlain, given Britain's economic weaknesses and the rundown of arms to pursue a policy that might have led to a war with three major powers. He had to consider the possible threat by Japan to our Far East colonies and from Italy to the Suez Canal. Churchill did not seem to mention this in his speech and just focused on Germany. However, the source suggests that Churchill was not justified because he was just making use of the threat from Germany to regain his political position which he had lost since 1929 over issues like India and the Abdication. This seems unfair. Churchill was a patriot who had a real concern for the Empire and he always showed a